My
Gorilla
Journey

My
Gorilla
Journey

*Living with the orphans
of the rainforest*

Helen Attwater

Photography by
Mark Attwater

SIDGWICK & JACKSON

First published 1999 by Sidgwick & Jackson

an imprint of Macmillan Publishers Ltd
25 Eccleston Place, London SW1W 9NF
Basingstoke and Oxford

Associated companies throughout the world

ISBN 0 283 06336 X

9 8 7 6 5 4 3 2 1

A CIP catalogue record for this book is available from
the British Library.

Typeset by SetSystems Ltd, Saffron Walden, Essex
Printed and bound in Great Britain by
Mackays of Chatham plc, Chatham, Kent

For Mark,
who opened the door to an
extraordinary world

You thought yourself bewitched and cut off forever from everything you had once known – somewhere – faraway – in another existence
Joseph Conrad, *Heart of Darkness*

Contents

Foreword

Helen Attwater's account of Congo is spot on. The first few pages pulled me in, and I could not stop myself – I read it overnight in one sitting.

This is so much more than a story of the attempt to save orphaned gorillas: it is a stunning political, social and ecological commentary. Helen has deep feeling for the animals and their plight, but the parallel story of the hopeless human situation in Congo is equally well told.

It is not always a happy tale, but it is a compelling one. It took me back to Congo in a flash, and it has left me in the same state of shaken emotion that I experienced when I was there. I did not meet Helen at that time myself – she arrived after Redmond O'Hanlon and I had set off for the north. I did however know Mark Attwater, and was immediately taken with his kindness and humanity. I kept my head down on return to Brazzaville, to try to avoid exactly the kind of events about which Helen writes.

When speaking of the work of Dian Fossey and Jane Goodall, Helen speculates that women may bring particular and special skills to the study of apes. Helen's own expertise in her observations and writing about gorillas, as well as her descriptions of the people who surround them, goes a long way to demonstrate this.

The humane courage of the Attwaters is set against a Congo backdrop of disease, death and flying bullets. Many of us have convictions; the difference here is that they rolled

up their sleeves, stuck out their necks, and acted on their
beliefs.

LARY SHAFFER
Professor of Psychology
State University of New York,
Plattsburgh, USA

Acknowledgements

My heartfelt thanks to: Andrew Crofts for his professional help in re-organizing my original manuscript, my agent Robert Kirby of Peters, Fraser and Dunlop for his faith in the book and Gordon Scott Wise, my editor at Sidgwick & Jackson, who was brave enough to take the book on and whose enthusiasm made all the difference. Also many thanks to Lary Shaffer for writing the foreword and to Redmond O'Hanlon for putting his celebrity stamp on my manuscript.

I take this opportunity to thank my parents and my sister Sue for their patience and advice.

There are many people in the Congo to whom I am indebted. Some appear in the story and some do not. To name but a few, Stephen Blake, Dr Flore Bettini, Peter and Jane Chandley (the former British Ambassador and his wife), Walt and Diane Hughey, Mr and Mrs William Ramsey (the former American Ambassador and his wife), Richard and Katrina Allhusen, Don and Thérèse Webster, Dr Ernie Davies, Dr J. Michael Fay, Dr Suehisa Kuroda, Dr Conrad Aveling and Matthew Hatchwell whose support kept us going in difficult times. And, of course, Albertine, Jean, Catherine, Paul, Nkodia, Juislain and all the other Congolese staff at the orphanage without whom there would have been no story to tell. Thanks also to NDinga Assitou, Raphael Tsila, Marc Ampion and Monsieur Amina of the Congolese Government Wildlife Department for their valuable support and a very special thank you to Aliette Jamart and Yvette Leroy.

Finally, I must thank John Aspinall for giving Mark and me the opportunity and the means to turn a dream into a reality.

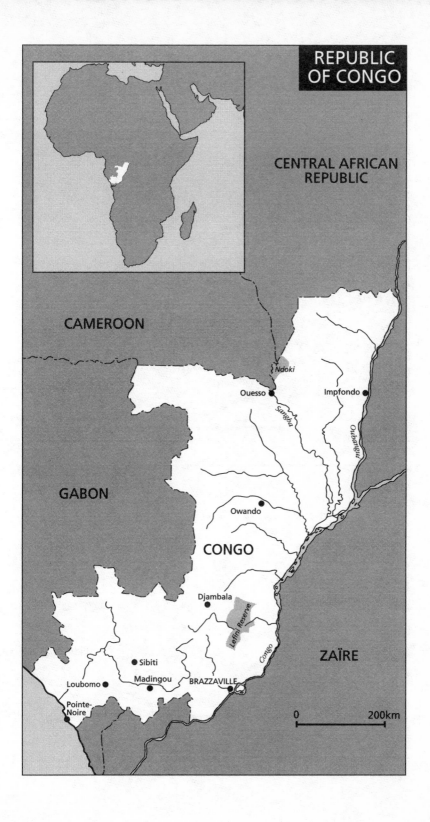

REPUBLIC OF CONGO

CENTRAL AFRICAN REPUBLIC

CAMEROON

GABON

Ndoki

Ouesso

Impfondo

Sangha

Oubangui

Owando

CONGO

Djambala

Lefini Reserve

Sibiti

Congo

ZAÏRE

Loubomo

Madingou

BRAZZAVILLE

Pointe-Noire

0   200km

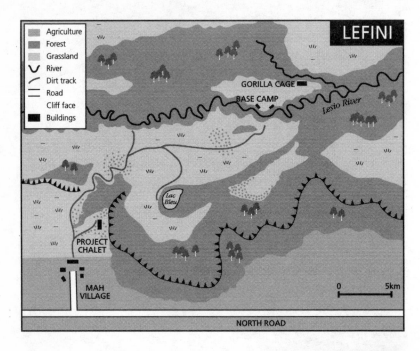

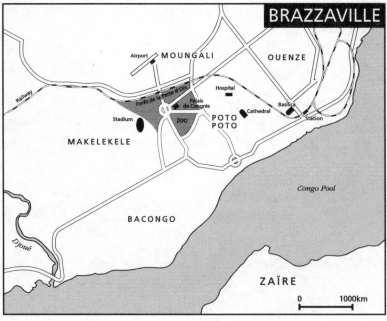

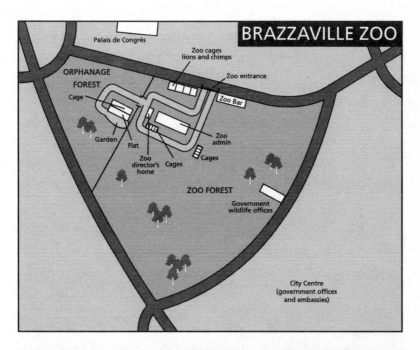

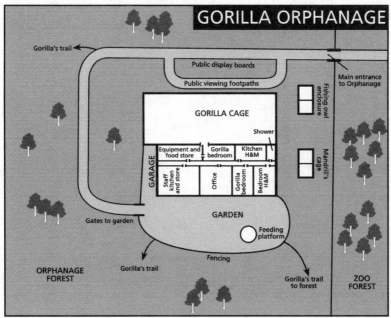

Chapter One

Dawn in a New World

I was woken by white sunlight streaming in through the small bedroom window, making me squint as I sat up in bed. Mark had already gone. I could hear voices outside the flat, men talking loudly in rapid, guttural tones. Then I heard Mark's irritable voice briefly before the other man responded in French.

'Oui, Chef, oui Chef, je travaille,' he insisted.

My mouth was dry and my vision slightly blurred. Mark had warned me that I should be careful to drink plenty of water or dehydration would set in fast. After the long flight and half the night spent chatting I was already feeling the effects. The humid air clung to my skin as I heaved my weary body out of bed and staggered down the corridor to the kitchen where I downed several glasses of water. My vision immediately started to clear and I felt more energetic. I shouted out to Mark that I was up and went into the bathroom to shower away the dirt and sweat of the past twenty-four hours.

Most of the passengers fled the plane in Lagos, leaving only a handful of intrepid travellers to go all the way to Brazzaville. I looked anxiously around the almost empty plane, trying to work out what had brought my fellow travellers here. There were some white faces, expatriates, with interests in the oil and timber industries, I guessed, but the rest looked either like Congolese students returning from France, or Congolese businessmen coming home from doing deals with their former colonial masters. Dotted amongst the old hands were a few like myself, setting out on unknown adventures to one of the last untamed areas of the globe. We were in search of Joseph Conrad's dark and brooding *Heart of Darkness*, buoyed up by a romantic vision of the mysterious forests of Central Africa. No doubt the old hands watched us knowingly, aware that the reality awaiting us would prove too harsh for most of us to handle. They would know that some us would flee home in a matter of only days.

The plane took off again from Lagos with its lightened load. I gazed, trance-like, through the window over the apparently infinite miles of uniform dark green stretching below in every direction as far as the eye could see. Below this blanket of green lay a world teeming with animal, plant and insect life. This land was one of the last black holes on the maps of the world's explorers, a melting pot of primitive life and disease. It was also the home of the western lowland gorilla. I felt small, awed and far from home.

By the time we landed a few hours later, night had fallen like a stifling blanket. The humid, cloying air wrapped itself around us as we piled onto the hot, wet tarmac. Within seconds our faces were beaded with sweat. We hauled our densely packed hand luggage towards the stark lines of a small dilapidated concrete building. If it weren't for the heat, we could have been approaching a border post in Eastern Europe somewhere, but this structure served as the international airport terminal for the Congo.

Airport officials in sweat-stained khaki uniforms toted Kalashnikov machine guns and shouted angrily at us as we stumbled into the passport control section. I wondered if the intimation was that we should pass over some currency to ease our path forward, but I knew nothing of the ways of this country. It was all a frightening, confusing and unfamiliar jumble of noise and aggression.

Inside the building heat had intensified further. The militia, their faces studiously officious, herded us into a tight knot, barking orders. Over their shoulders I saw a plump middle-aged white woman bustling towards us, her beady eyes staring intently at me through thick, black-rimmed glasses. Her greying hair was pulled severely back into a tight bun and she looked a match for any of these half-trained soldiers.

'Helen!' Her voice carried clearly over the raucous babble of Lingala, the local tongue. I realized with relief that this was the Madame Yvette Leroy I had heard about, the 'Maman Gorille' of Brazzaville.

She shook my hand hastily, apparently anxious to get the formalities over as quickly as possible, the sooner to escape to some sort of sanity. 'I recognize you from a photograph Mark showed me. Give me your documents!'

She snatched my passport and vaccination papers from me and disappeared, leaving me feeling even more naked and abandoned. But she soon reappeared, shoved the papers back into my hand and pushed me towards the exit. I tried to thank her, but my words were lost in the chaos of people fighting their way through the narrow wooden door which led to the relative sanctuary of the foyer outside.

Another noisy crowd, this time of waiting friends, relatives and taxi drivers, was corralled behind a barrier. There I spotted Mark. We managed to reach one another, both awkward to be reunited after such a long time apart. My instinctive response was to touch him, but I felt suddenly shy and he seemed to be feeling the same. I was also shocked by his appearance. His gaunt face and sallow complexion showed the effects of malaria and overwork, and he had lost a lot of weight since I had seen him a few months earlier.

Mark took my luggage and led the way towards the doors, pursued by a bunch of young boys struggling to wrest the bags from his grip. Despite protesting that he didn't need their help, they hung on, turning a short walk into a gruelling tug-of-war.

We picked our way over to a green Suzuki jeep and headed off into the night. As we rattled down the wide avenue that would take us the short distance to the zoo, I noticed that beneath the street lights sat students, intently reading textbooks. 'They have no electric light at home,' Mark explained.

On either side of the avenue were dilapidated villas, their former colonial glory long since eaten away by termites and overwhelmed by the rich green vegetation that pushed into every nook and cranny, forcing the bricks apart. Behind these, shanty-town Brazzaville sprawled as far as the eye could see, a mish-mash of tin-roofed shacks and muddy streets. We turned off the avenue, leaving the street lights behind. The moonlight made strange, foreboding shapes of the trees on either side of the approach to the zoo. We drew up by a pair of iron gates, opposite a huge, looming grey edifice.

'That's the Palais de Congrès', said Mark, 'our neighbour. Whenever a prominent member of the government deigns to turn up in parliament there the zoo gets overrun by militia.' I stared up at the stark, Marxist lines of the huge building. 'It was built by the Chinese,' he explained, 'after the Congo was given its independence in 1961.'

He hooted the jeep's horn loudly and a short, thin figure crept cautiously out of the shadows. His military uniform had seen better days and he dragged a machine gun casually behind him. His eyes glared wide and white in the moonlight as he tried to make out who was waking him. When he recognized Mark he gave a smile of relief and opened the heavy gates of the zoo to let us pass, staring at me with unashamed curiosity.

Inside the compound the darkness became sinister, tall trees rising like statues either side of the mud track. We crashed over ridges and splashed through puddles of rainwater two feet deep. Over the sound of the jeep's engine I could hear frogs burping as they luxuriated in the heavy rain which had just fallen, and insects grated and chattered. I inhaled the sickly, putrid odour of vegetation fermenting in the damp heat. The air was heavy and suffocating. When I touched my skin I found it coated in a fine film of sweat.

Mark finally swept to a halt in front of a scene which looked, in the headlights, like a vast, boggy building site. 'Here we are,' he said cheerfully, jumping down with a splash and lifting out my cases. I followed him towards a doorway, feeling my feet sinking into the mud. I glimpsed a shadowy figure sitting nearby in the darkness. As my eyes focused to the moonlight, I saw the figure struggle to his feet from the wheelbarrow he had been resting in. Suddenly I was confronted with an old, gaunt face, eyes luminous white and gappy teeth, blackened by years of chewing kola nuts, spread in a wide grin. We stared at each other in silence.

'This is Alphonse Ngangueri,' Mark said, 'the night guard.' He changed to halting French. 'This is Madame Marc, Alphonse. She has come to visit us for a few weeks.'

Alphonse seemed pleased by this news and stuck out his hand, clasping mine and muttering enthusiastic but unintelligible greetings. We made our way in. I thought the flat bare and unwelcoming. It was designed around one long corridor with a row of precisely equal-sized, box-like rooms on each side, a design which I soon realized allowed no air to circulate and only intensified the heat. Rooms on one side were supposed to be Mark's kitchen, office, bedroom and sitting room. The identical rooms on the other side were for the staff store room, medical room – and gorilla bedrooms.

Once inside and alone Mark and I talked until the early hours, becoming re-acquainted and comfortable with one another as he spilled out his plans and dreams. Since the age of six Mark had dreamed of coming to the most mysterious and inhospitable part of Africa, the Congo Basin, to work with gorillas. Growing up in Kent, near to John Aspinall's zoo, Howletts, he had been inspired by the gorillas he had watched as a child. The Attwater household had lived with a stream of animal visitors from ferrets and snakes to birds of prey, some of which Mark released into the wilds of the surrounding hilly countryside. His long-suffering mother frequently received phone calls from teachers informing her that Mark had disappeared yet again, wandering off to spend hours roaming the woodlands, enthralled by his kestrel and buzzard in flight, and alert to every minute sign of life in nature's intricately woven world. Inevitably he had ended up leaving school as soon as possible to work as a junior keeper at Howletts.

We had met about a year before at the Royal Festival Hall in London, where we both had worked. I had needed a break from nursing and the famous concert hall made an interesting contrast to hospital life. Mark had left zoo-keeping for a while to work backstage at the Hall whilst trying to find work that would take him out to Africa. We were immediately inseparable. Then he was offered the job of setting up an orphanage for gorillas in the Congo.

I was only going to be in Brazzaville for a few weeks, long enough to decide whether I felt able to give up my life in London once and for all, leaving my family and friends and buying a one-way ticket back to Brazzaville. After the months apart, we had much to talk about and catch up on. His enthusiasm was infectious and we both felt buoyed up on an absurd wave of optimism, certain that together we could succeed against the odds. I hardly noticed how tired I was until my head hit the pillow that night and I fell immediately into a deep sleep.

Chapter Two

The Zoo

I dressed and made my way out into the garden where two men were working, one with a hoe and the other with a wheelbarrow.

The man with the hoe whose voice I had heard from the bedroom was a short, wiry man called Joachim Nkodia, who bristled with energy. His sullen side-kick, Joseph Malonga, stood some distance away, his long, thin body bent double over a wheelbarrow full of top soil which he was dumping on the lawn for Nkodia to rake over. This, along with Alphonse the night guard, was the sum total of the orphanage's staff.

As I emerged into the sunlight Nkodia paused in his work and his large mouth spread into a broad, rascally grin. He put down his hoe and made his way towards me with his hand outstretched. 'Bonjour, Madame Marc,' he said, as he clasped my hand in his, coy but enthusiastic. He beckoned Joseph over and introduced us. Joseph shook my hand gingerly and lowered his gaze to the ground, apparently unfamiliar and slightly uncomfortable with white women and unsure what he should say.

'Morning!' Mark appeared round the corner. 'Fancy a guided tour?'

The orphanage, located within the grounds of Brazzaville Zoo, was funded by John Aspinall, the British gambler and millionaire who had become famous for channelling the profits of his gaming operations into wildlife projects, mainly based at Howletts Zoo in Kent and at his nearby estate, Port Lympne. With his unrivalled reputation for the successful breeding of rare animal species in captivity, and his gambler's instinct, he was perhaps the only person who would have had the confidence, funds and commitment to animals, to back such an off-the-wall project.

Madame Yvette Leroy had been responsible for bringing the plight of orphan gorillas to Aspinall's attention. Arriving alone in Brazzaville in the late 1970s, recently divorced with grown-up children who had left home, she had set about creating a business to support herself. Initially she ran a restaurant, then provided a provisioning service to expatriate employees of the timber and oil companies based on the coast and in the interior. It was this link that led to her taking in an orphan gorilla, who she named Djala. As Djala grew and became increasingly un-manageable in Yvette's small town villa, she feared that one day he would be taken from her and sent to the zoo or given as a 'presidential gift' to a neighbouring head of state. Desperate, she wrote to John Aspinall and pleaded with him to apply for an importation permit from the British government. In the mean-time, she would persuade the Congolese government to issue export permits to release Djala.

Djala travelled to Howletts Zoo, but by then three more orphans had arrived at Yvette's villa who also needed long-term homes. The situation repeated itself, but this time controversy surrounded the issue of exporting these wild-born apes from Africa. The tabloid press roused public support for the plight of the three orphans, but the conservation establishment argued that, whatever the circumstances, international laws put in place to protect wild-born apes from unscrupulous animal dealers should not be ignored.

Eventually Aspinall and the Congolese government came up with a long-term solution to the problem – the creation of a gorilla orphanage within the grounds of Brazzaville Zoo. Although too late for the three orphans in question, it would prevent the situation recurring by providing a refuge for any further orphan gorillas that might turn up. The 'Congo Three', as the press had named them, travelled to Howletts to join Djala, and plans for the Brazzaville Gorilla Orphanage began.

Aspinall agreed to put up the necessary funds. He invited Mark to run the project, whose burning commitment to animals and experience as a zoo-keeper at Howletts some years earlier made him ideal for the task.

A practical solution to the problem of securing a safe long-term future for orphaned gorillas within the Congo, which would also benefit gorilla conservation on a broader scale, needed to be found. Mark was convinced that the best way forward was for the project to try to prepare the rescued orphans for reintroduction back into the wild once they were mature enough to fend for themselves. As far as he was concerned, exporting them to zoos was not an option. His goal was to reinforce gorilla protection in the wild as well as guaranteeing the well-being of individual animals in his care.

The original structure Aspinall had commissioned for the orphanage had been a complete disaster. The gorilla enclosure consisted of a barren stretch of earth walled in by a high barrier of eucalyptus logs, nailed together vertically to form an impenetrable wall, giving the occupants no view out and the breeze no way in. The heat was intense and no shade was available to escape it. Beyond the wooden barrier was a high mound of earth intended as a public viewing platform, ignoring the fact that no animal, or human for that matter, is ever comfortable being spied on from above with no available refuge from prying eyes. The mound had been created by laboriously moving earth by the barrowful from the garden in front of the flat, leaving a deep bowl which was now filled with stagnant water and provided an ideal breeding ground for mosquitoes.

The manager's flat was equally disastrous. As things stood the staff were expected to share Mark's kitchen to prepare bottles and food for the gorillas, and to shower in Mark's bathroom. Directly adjoining the flat was the gorilla enclosure. The ill-thought-out design of the complex meant that all the animals' soiled bedding material and left-over food had to be carted through the flat to reach the rubbish dump outside. The design of the present facility was so impractical and hazardous that Mark had refused to take on any gorillas until it was completely rebuilt.

Orphan gorillas who had arrived during the course of the year were being temporarily housed with Madame Leroy, a short distance from the orphanage. Aspinall was due to come from England to decide whether or not to allocate the funds necessary to transform the present facility into a workable proposition that could offer orphan gorillas a safe home.

In addition to the construction of the orphanage, Mark also needed to set up an active legal confiscation system with the Congolese Government Wildlife Department. The appropriate laws were already in place, but so far they had not been applied with any conviction. Not only was gorilla poaching a long-standing problem in Central Africa, but so were the orphans created as poachers killed adult female gorillas for meat, their infants taken alive in the hope they could be sold to expatriates in the towns or on timber concessions in the forest interior. Unwittingly, expatriates buying these tragic orphans, who were bundled into sacks like trussed-up chickens and touted around Brazzaville, merely endorsed the illegal trade in infant apes, encouraging the poachers to go in search of more animals to turn into orphans and hard currency. Some expatriates were fully aware of the poachers' means of procuring baby gorillas, but chose to ignore this in order to provide their children with entertaining pets in the boarding school holidays. If poachers learned that they would face prosecution for trading in infant gorillas and the animals were confiscated without payment, Mark believed we might eventually break the vicious cycle.

'Do you want to see the zoo?' Mark asked after we had looked round the orphanage. 'It's pretty bad, I warn you.'

The zoo had been created by the French in colonial times as a holding station for wild animals trapped for export to zoos worldwide. It was now owned and managed by the Congolese State who possessed neither the funds nor the expertise to provide even the most basic care for the captive animals who had to look on the grim concrete-block crates as their permanent homes and lived out their miserable lives in the dark, decaying, damp prison cells until they died of starvation or sadness. Their corpses were thrown carelessly into a far corner of the zoo, the smell of their rotting carcasses putrid in the humid air. New animals were brought in from time to time and hurled into the cages to rot along with the fabric of the buildings.

'Apparently at least twelve infant orphan gorillas have died alone and abandoned in here over the last year,' Mark said as we passed row upon row of gloomy cages, stretching all the way to the entrance. The white sun beat down on the unshaded areas of the zoo, making the animals squint painfully as they approached the bars to see who was there, but the precious rays could penetrate no further into the dark, damp interior of their cages.

As we passed one small cube of dirty cracked concrete with thick steel bars on one side, I saw an ancient, hairless, out-stretched arm, its palm facing upwards, fingers opened in a gesture of pleading. As I neared the cage I spotted an old brass plaque. The barely legible words informed us that this was Gregoire and the date beside his name was 1944. Peering into the gloom I could make out the hairless, emaciated figure of an old chimpanzee. He grimaced in fear, his few remaining teeth black with decay. He moved his outstretched hand again and, sensing that he was no threat, I placed my hand in his. Another arm shot out from the bars to enfold my hand completely, clasped between his two. Satisfied that I was not going to pull my hand away, he proceeded to clap gently against my hand, his face contorting in tentative delight at this precious social contact.

Releasing my hand he rushed to the opposite end of the barred wall, stretching out one hand again in an unmistakable invitation to play, inviting me to run to the other end and put my hand in his again. This harmless repetitive game continued for some time until I finally started to tire and, feeling guilty and reluctant to leave, I moved on, leaving him to resume his solitary contemplations in the bare cell that had been his home for forty-five years.

In years to come the Jane Goodall Institute did its best to improve the lot of these chimpanzees. Although initially renowned for her research into wild chimpanzee behaviour, Jane Goodall had in recent years turned her attention – and the press coverage that came with it – to the plight of orphaned chimpanzees in Africa, as well as to the welfare of those used for medical research worldwide. She was to set up an orphan chimp sanctuary just outside the coastal town of Pointe Noire and some of the Brazzaville Zoo chimps were able to leave their miserable prison.

In the next cube a considerably younger male chimpanzee hurled himself around his cage in a terrifying threat display, bouncing off the concrete walls and screaming with blood-curdling intensity. This frustrated adult male in particular caused the sanctuary many problems. On one occasion he had plucked an infant chimpanzee by its feet from its keeper's back as they passed by outside the cage, squeezing the tiny chimp back through the bars until its poor head popped grotesquely away from its body.

I quickened my pace past his cage and on down the line of solitary monkeys and mandrills to the lions who paced from side to side in their tiny quarters.

'There was a leopard here recently,' Mark told me. 'They used to collect his urine and sell it for medicinal purposes. One day his keeper accidentally raised the steel partition that separated the leopard from the lions and they tore him to pieces in a starved feeding frenzy.' I shuddered.

At every stop Mark seemed to have another story of gruesome accidents and careless cruelty, his face set in an expression of resigned disgust. We passed antelopes and red-river hogs, jackals, mongooses and birds of prey, all in equally depressing conditions. Only the crocodiles seemed peaceful as they lay, immobile and sinister, immersed in the shallow water of a small concrete pool. The plaintive cries of fishing eagles pierced the heavy air and fourou flies bit persistently at my ankles, leaving tell-tale red pin-pricks of blood where they had feasted. These later swelled into white welts which itched for days on end, waking me in the night as I scratched myself raw and in desperation immersed my hot feet and ankles in a bucket of cold water to ease the pain.

As one of the red-river hogs snuffled noisily alongside us in his pen Mark stooped and, pushing his arm through the wire, scratched his flank. The pig lay down, rolling onto his back in ecstasy, inviting Mark to tickle his exposed belly.

I had grown up with the usual domestic pets such as dogs, cats, guinea pigs and hamsters. Like many, I lost that particular childhood easy intimacy with animals, choosing a career and a lifestyle in London that buried those instincts well and truly. I felt lucky to be given a second chance through Mark.

In the past the French colonial powers had done nothing to encourage an awareness of wildlife conservation in the Congolese people. Even now, it seemed at times that the French actually lobbied against wildlife conservation efforts in the Congo, regarding those who worked in the field with patronizing amusement or, if one appeared to be achieving some degree of success, outright hostility.

There were few staff visible in the grounds of the zoo. Mark explained that most of them only ever turned up to inspect the vicious steel snares they had laid in the zoo forest to trap the one lucky sitatunga antelope that had escaped his pen some years earlier.

Consisting of about forty acres of officially protected forest, called the 'Forêt de la Patte d'Oie' (Goose's Foot Forest), the zoo was the last vestige of the lush vegetation that had once covered Brazzaville. It was now a shady oasis amidst the dry, dusty shanty-town, which sprawled in all directions. The remnants of the wire netting fencing intended to keep the public out were no obstacle to those using the grounds as a short-cut, a public toilet or a source of free firewood.

The few staff who did turn up regularly would spend their time idling in the dingy offices annexed to the zoo, gossiping and sleeping the hot hours of the day away. None of them would dream of resigning from their government posts which assured them a monthly salary. They lived in the hope that they might be relocated to an air-conditioned office somewhere in the city. They were ashamed of their jobs. The occupation of zoo-keeper was the lowest on the pecking order, so they resented their charges and were loath to cater to even their most basic needs, such as providing drinking water and clean cages. They viewed their duties with disgust and the animals as vermin.

Even the zoo director's post was a political one, its only

attraction being the large wooden house on stilts within the grounds of the zoo and the possibility of trading illegally in wild animals.

We made our way back through the zoo towards the orphanage in thoughtful silence. At least in this part of the zoo, on land given to the orphanage, we could ensure better conditions for our charges. The only possible solution for Brazzaville Zoo was closure. As we came into the garden I spotted a particularly colourful bird perched on a branch of one of the tall trees on the borders of the forest.

'Nkodia,' I called, 'do you know the name of that bird?'

'Oh yes Madame,' he replied enthusiastically, 'it is a bird of the forest.'

I pressed him for a little more detail, but it was obvious that everything he saw was either a 'beast of the forest' or a 'bird of the forest'. He must have seen my disappointment as he soon shuffled back to his work, embarrassed.

That afternoon we drove the short distance to Madame Leroy's villa, which lay in one of the poorer areas of town. As we pushed open the rusty iron gate to her front garden we heard voices from the room she used as an office for her business. Her voice could be heard clearly, drowning out the man's deeper voice. Three gorillas, aged between one and two years, played on the tiled veranda outside the office. As they paused, breaking off from boisterous play to raise their heads and look at us, we wondered whether to return at a more convenient moment. A Congolese man dressed in the uniform of the National electricity company, then backed out of the office, pursued by Yvette, who continued to hurl abuse at him. A tiny gorilla clung to her back, cringing as she chased the man past us out of the gate.

Finally noticing our presence, she greeted us and launched into a rant about corruption and the size of her electricity bill.

Then suddenly her mood changed as the gorillas rushed forward, arms outstretched. She bent down, the youngest infant still clinging to the back of her dress, and gathered them in her arms, cooing gently.

'Voilà mes bébés,' she announced proudly.

Playing with the gorillas in her back garden later that afternoon, I looked up and glimpsed Yvette peering through the net curtains at us, her expression anxious. I had an uneasy feeling that there was going to be trouble between us before long. Despite, and perhaps because of, our mutual concern for these animals, there was to be an uneasiness in our relationship. I learnt that as a single woman in Brazzaville life had been far from easy for her and she had perfected the habit of screaming at people to get things done, effectively disguising her shyness. She was generally defensive and suspicious of people and her defensiveness extended to her concern for her 'bébés'. Although she had pushed Howletts to send someone out to help and to set up the orphanage, when we finally arrived she had mixed feelings. She realized that she could not provide the environment these rapidly growing gorillas needed, and she was not prepared to give up her business to run the orphanage. But it was obvious that the actual process of letting go of what had been a major part of her life for several years was going to be very painful. Despite both our good intentions, this transition was unlikely to go smoothly.

We were to witness a variety of 'acts', all of which disguised the real person beneath, who remained a complete mystery. She did not appear to have any close friends. She only ventured out socially to attend diplomatic dinners, during which she was expected to hold forth about the plight of orphan gorillas and live up to her reputation as the eccentric 'gorilla lady' of Brazzaville, or to travel the short distance to the airport where she played a very efficient role as facilitator, assuring oil and timber company employees safe conduct through customs and onto internal flights to Pointe Noire and the interior.

I had been instantly fascinated by the gorillas. I already knew that my mind was made up. I would return to Brazzaville as soon as I could leave my job in London.

The sun faded to an orange glow at around five o'clock that evening and a damp darkness swiftly descended. Arriving back at the flat we realized we had eaten nothing all day. Gripped by a sudden hunger, we cooked up a massive bowl of mashed potato and corned beef hash, gorging ourselves before retiring to bed.

Chapter Three

Meeting Max

The days of my short visit passed quickly as a succession of electricians and plumbers, friendly but mostly incompetent, came and went, leaving greater devastation than when they arrived.

Aspinall flew in from England to see for himself why Mark was threatening to resign over the state of the orphanage structure. The moment he saw the gorilla enclosure he agreed that it was completely unsuitable and declared that we should start again from scratch. 'Let's build a fifty-foot high pagoda,' he pronounced with a flourish, entranced by his own extravagant vision, 'so the gorillas have a bird's eye view of the city.' His excitement was infectious. When his imagination was engaged, money became no object. We had been worried that he might pull out, cutting his losses, but he surprised us by putting forward further funds for what would have seemed to someone with less commitment a project unlikely to succeed.

It was a typical Aspinall gesture, outrageously generous but impractical when we couldn't even find workmen capable of repairing the system we already had. After much discussion they arrived at a more practical solution and Mark began to feel more optimistic.

Taking advantage of Aspinall's visit I suggested my services as a potential employee on the project. My training as a nurse and my ability to speak French were obvious advantages. To my surprise and delight he welcomed my suggestion and I became an official member of the orphanage team.

It seemed no time at all before I was back at Maya Maya airport, bidding Mark a tearful farewell as I headed back to London to sort out my affairs in order to return to the Congo. The heat which had been so oppressive now felt comfortable and comforting, a constant womb-like wet warmth. I dreaded my return to a cold, wintry London. In my impatience to get back to Brazzaville, I scarcely paused to think. I had little idea just how profoundly my life was about to change.

I now had to work out my notice at the Royal Festival Hall in London. My colleagues were stunned by the speed and certainty of my decision to leave and felt personally involved and excited for me, having witnessed the early days of my relationship with Mark.

Back in England, without Mark, the certainty I had felt whilst in Brazzaville faded as I contemplated the potential disease threats ahead. I had suffered serious illness as a child which left me with the impression that 'things happened' to me. There were fourteen vaccinations recommended for the Congo, including yellow fever, polio, tuberculosis, meningitis, rabies, hepatitis and typhoid, and I was well aware that there were an infinite number of infectious and parasitic diseases I might encounter for which no vaccine was available. Returning from his first brief visit to Brazzaville two years before in 1987, Mark had been admitted to hospital in London with amoebic dysentery. This did nothing to inspire my confidence. Most of the time, however, I felt sure that these were all risks worth taking, that it was a challenge I wanted to accept.

Two weeks before I was due to return to Brazzaville Mark

phoned in a highly excited state to tell me that he had his first ape resident at the orphanage.

'He's not a gorilla,' he admitted, 'he's a pygmy chimpanzee, a bonobo. I confiscated him from a Zairian trader. I've called him Max.' As the conversation continued, his voice became muffled. 'He's sitting on my knee now, grooming my arm and sticking his fingers in my mouth,' he explained.

I shared his excitement, but had I realized just how great an impact Max would have on our lives I might have been a little more circumspect.

Returning to Brazzaville on the morning of 5 June 1989 the temperature was cooler than I remembered. The dry season had just begun with its grey skies and cool but still soggy air.

'Everyone gets sick in the dry season,' the locals kept saying, which seemed illogical but proved to be true. Colds and bronchitis were a persistent problem with both staff and animals, and amoebic dysentery was more common when there was less rainwater to wash things clean. Malaria, it seemed, was the only affliction which remained a constant through both dry and rainy seasons.

On the way back from the airport Mark tried to prepare me for my first encounter with Max. I was so excited to see Mark again I barely paid any attention to his diplomatic warning. Max was waiting for us outside the flat with Alphonse. On spotting Mark the small, dark, leggy figure emitted a squeal of joy and leapt off the bench into his arms, his face contorted in a grimace of delight, his eyes searching Mark's for reassurance. He then looked warily across at me, turning back to Mark as if to say: 'Well, who's this then? I hope she's not going to be a problem.'

As I struggled with my luggage Mark attempted to put the tiny three-kilogram bundle down so that he could help me. Max clung on with astonishing strength. When he finally realized that Mark meant business, he hurled himself to the ground, clasped his head in his hands and screamed in terror, peeking through his fingers occasionally to check what effect his tantrum was having on Mark.

When he saw this tactic wasn't working, he leapt to his feet and clung desperately to Mark's leg where he remained glued for the next half an hour, apparently terrified that Mark might abandon him to my unfamiliar company. Over the following few hours, as he watched me unpack, Max evidently accepted that I was there to stay and he had better do something to ingratiate himself. He sidled up to me on the sofa, grinning questioningly, his dark brown, gentle almond-shaped eyes gazing penetratingly into mine in search of a sign of friendship. He moved across to me cautiously, reaching up to my hair, examining it with nimble fingers, pursing his lips with concentration as he gently groomed me. I started to groom him back, returning his generous gesture, and we were soon firm friends, so firm that when I went to the bedroom that evening to sleep off the effects of the long flight, I realized that Max intended to stay right by my side throughout the night.

It was impossible not to love Max and respond to his affectionate and demanding nature, but once the novelty of the situation had worn off a little I found myself starting to resent the way he monopolized our time and attention. For Mark, even taking a shower became a complicated affair. Max would perch on the side of the wash-basin whilst Mark cleaned his teeth, remaining silent in exchange for a taste of toothpaste. He would then sit on the edge of the shower basin as Mark showered, squeaking anxiously at first and then in delight when drops of water spat out in his direction. Any attempts to shut Max out of the shower at this delicate stage of his confidence building would result in a panic tantrum. He would hurl himself dramatically to the floor, curl into a tight ball and scream loudly until Mark responded.

As Mark went about his daily business in the orphanage Max would cling to his leg, spindly arms gripping tight as he sat on Mark's foot, mimicking the mode of transport he would have adopted with his natural mother in the wild.

After our first night together I naively suggested that it might be an idea to get Max accustomed to sleeping in a box near the bed rather than actually in the bed.

'I don't think that will work,' Mark said diplomatically, trying to break the news gently to me. He was right. Max bluntly refused to remain in the box and screamed continuously until we gave in and allowed him back on the bed. I felt tired, frustrated and irritable at times. I had to keep reminding myself that Max needed to be forgiven his attacks of insecurity, panic and bewilderment. This was only natural after months of captivity and abuse prior to his arrival at the orphanage.

If Mark wasn't available Max was willing to attach himself to my leg instead. I once made the mistake of trying to prise him off and leave him with Alphonse for a few minutes one evening. As I struggled to detach him his little hands gripped tighter and tighter, his sharp finger nails ripping into the flesh of my calf. In the face of such strength and determination I gave up.

As a result Max came everywhere with us. Our one attempt to leave him alone in the bedroom while we ran errands in town resulted in our returning to a scene of complete devastation, the curtains and their rail ripped from the wall and my hard suitcase shredded, its stuffing pulled out through a hole in the plastic sealing which he had managed to drill with his sharp little teeth.

One evening Madame Leroy agreed to baby-sit for us. As we returned from town later that evening Max heard our jeep approaching, freed himself by sinking his teeth into her finger, leapt from her arms, ran out of the house, down the garden, through the gate and into the car before we had even come to a halt. Madame Leroy declined to have him back and so from then on we were more or less stuck with him twenty-four hours a day.

Around 15,000 bonobos live a precarious existence in isolated pockets of forest in Central Zaire. Like gorillas they are still hunted illegally for their meat and the pet trade. They also suffer from the political instabilities that beset that particular region. The bonobo is believed to be man's closest relative amongst the great apes and will probably be the first to become extinct in its natural habitat.

Despite superficially resembling the common chimpanzee, the bonobo is smaller and more athletic, with long rangy limbs and a smaller head in comparison to its body size. Bonobo behaviour, however, is very different. Not underpinned by the patriarchal framework that characterizes common chimp society, bonobo society is based on a fluid dominance hierarchy unique amongst primates, with sexual activity used as a sort of social bonding 'glue'. Max would bring sex into everything. At an early age he took to trapping moths and cockroaches and pushing the squirming insects down his nappies, delighting in the stimulation that resulted. He also found new and interesting uses for Coca-Cola bottles, positioning himself strategically above the rim of the bottle before rubbing himself into a sexual frenzy in and out of the narrow bottle neck, frequently shocking unprepared visitors. Even particularly tasty food or a scolding could bring on a frenzy of sexual rubbing.

The appeal of bonobos as house pets was unfortunately obvious. It had led to a lively trade in Kinshasa, which would sometimes spill over the river into sleepier Brazzaville when times were hard in Zaire and expatriate clients were thin on the ground.

In his first few weeks at the orphanage Max had been introverted and panic-stricken, constantly seeking reassurance and approval, refusing to accept either milk or water from a feeding bottle. When there was a danger he might dehydrate, Mark wrapped him tightly in a towel, immobilizing him as he struggled defiantly, and squirted milk into his mouth through a plastic syringe. Once Max realized the milk tasted good he gave in and accepted it. On being released from the towel he hugged Mark effusively to assure himself that Mark was not angry with him. We continued this bizarre routine, but he grew to believe it was normal and then took some persuading to feed from a bottle or cup.

Once weaned onto solids he would fixate on one sort of fruit after another, eating nothing but bananas for days on end before changing to something new. He started to put on weight and unleash his natural chimp curiosity. It was as if he had passed through the mourning period for his mother and was ready to trust and accept us as his adoptive parents.

Just as his curiosity was growing, so were his powers of speed, agility and memory. Nothing in the house was safe. One of us had to distract his attention while the other hid things like our anti-malarial tablets. As with toddlers, the forbidden was always the most attractive. He would remember where they were hidden and find them days later, the moment he was left unsupervised. Child-proof lids were no match for his sharp little teeth and several times he nearly poisoned himself with our medicines. On one occasion he managed to unbolt a drawer in which I had hidden my anti-malarial tablets and, had I not been alerted by his excited squeaking, he would have swallowed the entire contents of the bottle. As it was I rushed to the bedroom and found him with his cheeks bulging, crammed with tablets, his eyes wide with guilt and fright at being caught red-handed. A battle ensued and I finally managed to extract about twenty tablets from his mouth, amidst much screaming and panic.

On another occasion he consumed the entire contents of a bottle of cough medicine he had stolen from one of the staff. His distended belly was as tight as a drum, his eyes rolled, and he looked demented. He was soon feverish and, panicking, we tried to make him vomit up as much of the medicine as possible. We fed him a vile mixture of salt water and swung him round by his arms in a desperate attempt to make him sick. He squealed loudly, bewildered, but absolutely refused to vomit and eventually we all gave up exhausted. He had such a hang-over the next day we assumed that he had learned his lesson, but a couple of weeks later he re-offended, breaking into the medicine stock in the clinical room and consuming an entire bottle of syrupy Flagyl antibiotic suspension. His mischief did however prove useful on this occasion, by demonstrating that Flagyl was a safe drug to use as a treatment for infant apes.

Private time for Mark and I continued to be a problem. We had finally managed to persuade Max to sleep on a towel on the floor just outside our bedroom door after a few weeks, but he could still hear our voices and would hoot and chatter whenever we spoke, drowning out any chances of peaceful intimate conversation.

Wild bonobos are notoriously lazy in the mornings and Max was no exception. Every morning he was a mess. We would step over his sleeping form on our way to the kitchen, bidding him a good morning. He would eventually raise his head reluctantly, rubbing his eyes, stretching his long arms languorously over his head and tousling his long hair, making himself look even more dishevelled. Stretching his legs and curling his toes, he would sleepily watch us make our way to the kitchen and collapse back to sleep for another quarter of an hour before coming in search of his morning drink. His laziness made us feel better on the mornings when we didn't feel like getting up either — however bad we felt, Max always looked worse.

Occasionally, on the long evenings, when darkness fell with predictable swiftness, we would get a short break when Max would sit in the garage outside and chat to Alphonse, who appeared to appreciate the company.

Max soon discovered that he could always create a drama by removing his nappies. On several occasions, whilst I lay ill in bed, he would keep me company lying by my side, grooming me and inviting me to play. It was not until he got bored and climbed off the bed that I would see the wet patch he left on the sheets. Infant apes also, I discovered, had an inconvenient habit of responding to stress with a dramatic explosion of liquid diarrhoea. I soon learnt that it was pointless wearing anything vaguely feminine that couldn't withstand a good scrubbing.

Max was adept at imitation and could do a very good facsimile of the chores that needed doing around the house almost perfectly, only letting himself down at the last minute with a show of impatience or loss of concentration. He taught himself to dig holes with Nkodia's spade and to write, after a fashion, with Mark's pen. He enjoyed wearing our shoes and socks, although he never quite mastered the art of tying laces. He brushed his hair and washed towels in a bucket in exactly the same way he had seen Nkodia do, even wringing the water out of them, but spoilt the effect by racing round the garden, dragging them through the mud. This intelligence was all the more remarkable as we had deliberately never encouraged any form of inappropriate or unnatural imitation.

Thinking we were now out of the woods as far as Max's medical problems went, we started to relax our vigilance. We realized this had been premature when his condition started to deteriorate rapidly a few days after catching a cold from Nkodia. To start with, his activity levels were unchanged by the sniffling, sneezing and coughing, but one morning we woke to find him unusually withdrawn and quiet, his breathing raspy and laboured.

Trying not to panic, Mark carried him through to the kitchen where I listened to his chest with a stethoscope. As I placed the cold metal on his hot chest he raised his eyes questioningly, searching my own for reassurance. Wearily he held out his hand towards the unfamiliar instrument and I helped him examine it. Satisfied that it was no threat, he submitted to the rest of the examination. I was shocked as I listened to the crispy wheezing of his lungs: if we did not start him on a course of antibiotics immediately he would soon be in serious trouble. Lacking even the strength to drink from his feeding bottle, we encouraged him to take sips from a plastic cup, pausing between each one as he struggled for breath. We had no problem getting him to take his first dose of penicillin and he even attempted a token squeak of appreciation as the sweet syrup slipped down his throat.

A couple of days later he showed little improvement and the infection gave no sign of clearing. By now he was exhausted, wheezing and confused. His spirits flagged and he became more introverted and miserable by the hour. After a particularly bad night lying on Mark's pillow as Mark listened to his laboured breathing, fearing every few minutes that he had taken his last breath and holding him at intervals on his knees, gently tapping his back to help clear his congested lungs, we decided to give him some ventolin, like an asthmatic child.

Having watched him progress from being a withdrawn, panic-ridden bundle of nerves to a larger than life character, it was terrible to see how rapidly he had deteriorated. It was clear that in our work with these fragile infant apes we would need to keep a vigilant eye on them at all times as their health and mental condition could decline frighteningly quickly with little apparent warning. This time, however, the treatment worked and he gradually regained his strength and spirit. Within a week he was fully recovered and had resumed his pestilential activities, indulged by us more than usual in our relief at such a narrow escape. The only legacy that remained was a snotty nose that Max dealt with by proudly placing his index finger over one nostril whilst blowing with all his strength to expel the sticky mucus from the other.

Max was back in action and by the time the first infant gorilla arrived at the orphanage he had everything and everyone under control.

An official of the Congolese Government Wildlife department once informed me excitedly that chimpanzees were being illegally exported to Russia. I asked him why he thought that was.

'It's probably for use as domestic slaves,' he replied, with a completely straight face.

It seemed more likely to me that anyone taking on a chimpanzee would find themselves becoming the slave.

Chapter Four

Brazzaville in the Rain

Named after its colonial founder, Count Pierre Savorgnan de Brazza, Brazzaville was a town like no other. It had long-since lost its small importance as the capital of French Equatorial Africa and de Gaulle's base for Free France during the Second World War. The ground that had been stripped bare to create the city was alternately baked dry and dusty by the relentless sun, or transformed within minutes into a gluey, sinking, treacherous bog during the rainy season. The thin strips of tarmac which served as roads heaved with battered old trucks belching smoke and rusting cars that crawled a few inches above the road surface, their suspension long gone. The hot, parched streets were alive with the activity of market traders noisily advertising their wares and groups of people gathering on street corners to gossip and debate. Women cooked on the sidewalks over charcoal stoves while young men and boys played football with anything that came to hand.

In one area of town wide avenues laid by the French remained, lined with columns of tall old trees and a few surviving colonial-style houses whose patios might, in former times, have seen tea being served by domestic servants in white livery rather than rowdy groups of ragged youths playing table football. Every square inch of space was crammed with broken bric-à-brac, making it impossible to tell where precious family possessions ended and the garbage-filled gutters began.

Everywhere you looked there were signs that nature was fighting to reclaim what was rightfully hers. Even in the city centre lush green vegetation broke through on every untended corner, rioting over walls and breaking through cracks in the tarmac, its green tendrils sprawling, growing almost visibly.

The architecture from the post-colonial communist era looked as if it had come straight from the outskirts of some grim Eastern European city, naked of decoration, constructed along stark, soulless lines. The 'city centre' was tiny, consisting mostly of government buildings, with one supermarket charging inflated prices for imported goods and several banks, only one of which functioned. Around this small nucleus sprawled endless shanty-town, 'les quartiers', narrow streets crammed with breeze-block shacks which housed entire families under corrugated tin roofs. These were the areas most of our local staff would come from.

This grid-work of devastation seemed to go on for ever, a mish-mash of businesses advertising elaborate afro hair-styling and stalls selling cans of sardines, single cigarettes and chewing gum. Young boys pushed barrows containing iced drinks while others hauled 'pousse-pousse' chariots whose old bicycle wheels strained under precarious piles of household furniture, mat-tresses, or sheets of corrugated iron. Women swayed sensuously along the sidewalks, balancing heavy loads skilfully on their heads. They wore strips of brightly coloured fabric, 'panne', dyed in dazzling fuschia pinks, yellows, greens and blues, wrapped around their waists with matching tops, while the men mostly lounged around gossiping in jeans and T-shirts. The wealthier citizens wore more traditional forms of dress such as the bou-bou, a long, elaborately embroidered collar-less tunic with matching trousers and pointed leather slippers. The women's hair was woven into elaborate patterns of plaits worn either close to the skull or stiffened with wax into points which radiated out from their heads in all directions.

Occasionally children or cheeky teenagers would cry out 'Mondele' (white person) and point unashamedly, but the atmosphere was friendly. I was surprised by how comfortable I felt amongst these people who were full of contradictions, excitable at times, somnolent and fatalistic at others, alternately dramatic and voluble or sullen and morose.

In the months prior to my arrival in Brazzaville I had read André Gide's diary, *Travels in the Congo*, written in 1925. His words now came to life. Nothing, it seemed, had changed:

> At first I was delighted with everything; the novelty of the climate, of the light, of the vegetation, of the perfumes, of the birds' song, and of my own self in the midst of all this was so great that I could find nothing to say from excess of astonishment. I did not know what to call things. I admired without distinction . . . I was in a state of intoxication . . . The town, which is enormously distended, owes its whole charm to the climate and to its position along the river shore.

In the centre of the town, the corniche, a recently laid road that bordered the Congo river, afforded a clear view of the skyscrapers of Kinshasa, the capital of Zaire, on the opposite bank. I felt no desire to cross the water. Sleepy Brazzaville with its green banks, only broken occasionally by two or three buildings, had a lazy charm I had found nowhere else.

The tallest building in Brazzaville, built as a deliberate challenge to Kinshasa, was a shimmering glass-walled tower financed by Elf Congo as a 'gift' to the country. It rose skyward as far as the eye could see, but stood mostly empty now, apart from a few government offices. It had been designed under the naive assumption that air-conditioning would be available at all times. It never was and the building had long since become an airless, stifling oven.

Stopping the car one morning on the corniche, we climbed out. The river rushed past at our feet, swollen to capacity by the rains north of the equator, its waters glistening, throwing back the sunlight, threatening to break its banks and sweep both cities away like flotsam. The water formed swirling patterns in places where the strong undercurrent pulled and floating islands of vegetation passed by on their way from the remote rainforests of the north, heading towards the rapids just south of Brazzaville where they would be pulped in the frothing, spitting waters. In the distance, through the haze of heat, I could make out the slim figure of a man punting his silent pirogue across the river to Kinshasa.

'We could visit the famous Brazzaville Rapids,' Mark suggested, inspired by the sight of the river. 'There's a bar overlooking the water where we can have a cold drink before heading back.'

I could hear the water long before I saw it as it cascaded violently over the massive rocky boulders, heaving and foaming and leaping into the air before subsiding to a murmur further downstream. As we sat, mesmerized by this living, breathing, swirling wonder of nature, I tried to imagine how the first explorers must have felt as they set out on foot in this immense, raw wilderness before the discovery of antibiotics, knowing that exhaustion and disease would almost certainly fell them in their tracks. A bunch of chattering children arrived at the river's edge, stripped off their clothes and bathed in the shallow water, lathering themselves with soap, screeching with pleasure as they splashed one another.

As we made our way back to the jeep a small boy stood expectantly beside our now gleaming car that still bubbled with soap suds. We paid him one hundred Congolese francs and he ran off delighted.

By the time we reached the orphanage it was the hottest part of the day. The sun beat down mercilessly. Nkodia and Joseph lay spread-eagled in the garage, snoring loudly. We let ourselves into the flat to do the same.

That evening we sat in the garden talking with Nkodia, the only light coming from the moon and the sparks of fireflies. These chats were to become a regular evening event that helped us explore and understand each other's different cultures. In the years to come we would rely on Nkodia's wisdom as the orphanage staff swelled to sixteen and it became hard to keep up with the problems that arose between them.

One of the subjects we explored early on in these conversations was sorcery. On several occasions Nkodia had explained to us that he needed an advance on his salary to pay off his 'uncle', the family mafia figure who ran a small-scale protection racket. The power of this 'uncle' figure was accepted without question in Congolese society. Not necessarily a blood relative at all, the 'uncle' of the family was highly influential and imbued with witchcraft powers that he used mostly to his own advantage. If Nkodia did not pay up, his uncle would put a bad fetiche (spell) on him or his children. Nothing we could say, with all our western logic, could persuade him otherwise. We were impotent in the face of such strongly ingrained beliefs.

Local people who started earning a reasonable salary by working for a 'white' project immediately became a target for local mafia extortion and the more unscrupulous members of their extended families. In most households they were the sole earners and they seldom saw any personal gain from their labours: any money they took home was sucked into a bottomless pit of needs, with every intimate and distant relative turning up on their doorstep as soon as news of their good fortune got round. We learnt that if we wished to give a gift to an employee it was wiser to buy them something rather than give cash. We had recently given Nkodia an advance to purchase a water pump, but the money had evaporated, some used to bail out a relative, some to pay off his uncle and the rest stolen by his brother. The pump remained a distant dream.

We realized as we listened to our local staff that most aid projects had left behind a trail of disillusion and disappointment, and all new projects were understandably treated with either suspicion or contempt. A lot of projects were funded by large aid organizations who had budgets to spend and did not particularly care whether their efforts succeeded. We hoped that we would not prove to be another disappointment.

One afternoon the sky suddenly darkened, black and ominous, and the still air seemed to hold its breath in anticipation. A frenzied wind whipped up from nowhere, throwing the great trees to and fro like rag dolls, making their trunks creak and groan. Then all was still, the air close and silent before the rain arrived in a deafening roar. Explosions of white light ripped across the darkness, forking down to earth as a drum roll of thunder shook the ground. As the black sky rolled past and the earth shook I felt the savagery of the country and my thoughts turned to the gorillas. I tried to imagine, as the rain crashed down on the tin roof, wild gorillas in the forests of the far north, crouching Buddha-like, their infants nestled close into their bulk for shelter as the water dripped from their thick pelts of dark hair and the elements raged around them.

When the rains began it seemed that the whole of Brazzaville ground to a halt. People, just like the gorillas we would come to know, would sit immobile, their arms crossed over their knees, their heads bowed in a torpor. Nkodia and Joseph stayed home, leaving the drenched orphanage silent and deserted, the work untouched.

When Mark insisted that they come to work even when it rained, they seemed surprised. We bought them rain jackets, but this made no difference to their reluctance. Initially they responded to Mark's demands with sullen confusion. When they realized that he only demanded from them what he expected of himself, their attitude changed and they began to take pride in their punctuality. Mark was determined to make them fulfil their own potential and not to make excuses for them as most Europeans did. Even the Congolese themselves, when asked why their country was such a disorganized mess, would reply, parrot-fashion, 'We are a backward country, what do you expect?' and would go on to blame the French or the government. Mark wanted to overcome this negative, resigned state of mind.

Chapter Five

Sid and Rupert

Rupert had been confiscated in the coastal town of Pointe Noire, the second largest urban centre in the Congo some 500 kilometres from Brazzaville, by Madame Aliette Jamart who ran and funded her own orphan chimpanzee sanctuary just outside the town. Occasionally, in pursuit of a poacher with an orphan chimp, she would find that the chimp turned out to be a gorilla. Small, wiry and possessed of terrier-like tenacity, Madame Jamart relished the prospect of a fight.

'Hélène!' she would screech in rapid, lisping French down the phone, barely waiting for my response or drawing breath before launching into the sort of 'rant' against poachers and local wildlife officials for which she was famous. Local government wildlife officials in Pointe Noire dreaded her arrival in their office. They would inevitably give in to her demands to confiscate animals if only to silence her. She was anxious to quickly hand over any baby gorillas she confiscated.

'I must send them up to you soon. Gorillas are too complicated, they always die,' she complained.

Her defiant, feisty manner hid a heart of gold and surprising vulnerability – there was always room in her small town house for more animals, even though the personal funds she sank into

her chimp sanctuary had left her virtually penniless. Like Yvette
Leroy, Aliette Jamart's somewhat eccentric, obstinate behaviour
was probably the result of the alienation she must have felt from
her own community. The French expatriates considered her work
to be of little importance and she struggled constantly with the
wildlife authorities. Both women had for years fought lonely,
exhausting battles to protect their ape charges. Emotionally
driven, they were formidable, determined and prepared to go to
extremes to protect their animals.

Thinking of the tragic figure of Dian Fossey, whose emotions
spiralled out of control towards the end of her life and possibly
even caused her death, I began to wonder whether it was possible
to work with apes and remain rational. It seemed the fiercely
protective emotions they inspired in women were unavoidable.

Jane Goodall and Aliette Jamart, initially planning a joint
chimp sanctuary, had fallen out and gone their separate ways.
Yet again, two people with a common passion for apes had been
unable to work together. Goodall now planned an electric-fenced
enclosure outside Pointe Noire, whilst Jamart still hoped to
house and provision her chimps on an island in the Conqouti
region of South-West Congo.

Although a scientist, Jane Goodall had suffered the disap-
proval of the conservation establishment when, in her early
studies, she gave names to the chimpanzees she studied instead
of using the accepted system of numbers and codes. Academics
claimed that this indicated a degree of emotional involvement
with her study subjects that might interfere with her ability to
observe their behaviour on a strictly objective, scientific level.
She went on to shed significant light on chimpanzee behaviour,
her most famous discovery being of chimpanzee tool-using skills
that indicated even more firmly their closeness to primitive man.

She, and Louis Leakey's other two female protégées (Dian
Fossey who spent 30 years studying mountain gorillas and Biruté

Galdikas whose work with orang-utans continues today), seemed to have confirmed that women were uniquely suited to studying apes. Leakey felt that they were possessed of great patience and their perhaps less threatening physical presence would be less likely to disturb wild apes. His hunch paid off: all three made unique contributions to ape conservation.

The activities of the oil and timber industries in the area surrounding Pointe Noire had resulted in intensive poaching of both gorillas and chimps, as the timber trucks and roads carved through the forest offered easy access for hunters to track timid wildlife. This, coupled with relatively quick access to Brazzaville, made the region ideal for poachers. The Pointe Noire to Brazzaville railway, which had cost the lives of tens of thousands of forced labourers in the 1920s, still functioned, if somewhat erratically. Poachers could travel between the two towns within hours, ensuring that their goods arrived in relatively good health, with better prospects of a sale.

Between them, the timber industry and firearms had long since destroyed what had once been a fair competition for survival between man and gorilla. The local people's 'slash and burn' method of crop growing encouraged the succulent secondary floor-based vegetation favoured by gorillas. In the past, although they were hunted for their meat, because they occasionally raided crops and were considered a 'pest', they were not killed for commercial gain on a scale that is possible today.

Rupert had been luckier than some gorillas. Two days after Aliette Jamart found him, he arrived on our doorstep, our first official gorilla orphan.

Mark named him after the poet Rupert Brooke, partly in jest and partly because this composed little gorilla – with his handsome face and thick pelt of dark brown hair – exuded an extraordinary air of calm. It was probably precisely because of this personality trait that he arrived at the orphanage in relatively good condition. Most orphan gorillas would become hysterical when captured, screaming in fear and biting fiercely in an attempt to escape, which only served to enrage their captors who would then beat them senseless in savage attempts to silence and control them. Rupert's intelligence would have enabled him to work out that it was more sensible to resign himself to his fate, remaining calm and quiet and therefore giving them no reason for further abuse.

Infant apes confiscated in Pointe Noire often arrived at the orphanage in better shape than those confiscated in the capital Brazzaville. Those infants captured in the north of the country usually endured a long journey by boat to Brazzaville after spending weeks or months on the outskirts of the hunters' villages, awaiting transport. All that time they would be secured to wooden stakes by ropes tied tightly round their hips that allowed no escape from the taunts of curious, frightened and tormenting children. They were often close to death by the time they were rescued and frequently died soon after reaching the safety of the orphanage.

Despite his composed façade, Rupert's behaviour over the next few days revealed the traumas of his capture. He had almost certainly witnessed the slaughter of his mother and perhaps other members of his family group who may have tried to come to her rescue. His withdrawn posture and sad, resigned expression with fearful, dull eyes warned us to tread very carefully. He was just about old enough to have understood clearly whatever horrors had befallen his mother and the rest of his family group and he obviously did not want to risk any further unnecessary contact with man.

He fed exclusively on the succulent stems of Marantacae, a staple part of the wild gorilla diet, which we cut for him in the forest. He refused the feeding bottle and preferred to drink water from a bowl either by pursing his lips against the water's surface and sucking or by dipping one hand into the water and licking the drops from the long hair on the back of his hand. He soon felt safe in a nest made of leaves in a wall cupboard in the medical room, high enough from the ground to afford a view of possible danger.

Rupert proved to be a fairly easy introduction for us to the ways of orphan gorillas. As he settled in he grew more trusting and remained extraordinarily gentle, which made playing with him relaxed and less edged with the serious competitiveness of less confident gorillas. Nothing could have prepared us for the next arrival.

Sid originated from the same region of forest in south-western Congo as Rupert, but had obviously not fared as well at the hands of his captors. Opening the box in which he had travelled from Pointe Noire we peered in to see a creature that barely resembled a gorilla at all.

Once out of the box, he cowered at the other side of the room. We guessed he was around two and a half years old, but his emaciated and hairless body made it hard to tell. His skin, red and raw, had started to peel off in layers, and his face was covered by a blotchy fungal growth that gave him a ghostly appearance. On closer inspection we found he was missing a finger. We wondered whether it had been sold for its witchcraft value when the hunter's family had hit upon hard times, or was the result of a snare. He was short and squat, almost deformed, as if his growth had been stunted by incarceration in a cage too small to even allow him to sit up straight. The most shocking thing however was the fear and bewilderment in his dull eyes as they peered pleadingly at us from his hideous face. He expected to be beaten. When violence was not forthcoming he shifted his gaze to the floor. I felt a desperate urge to comfort him, but couldn't think how to approach him without causing more terror. Our hearts sank as he remained crouched and trembling at the opposite end of the room, his terror impenetrable.

I had read a number of descriptions of brutal gorilla hunts, amongst them a particularly gruesome account by Fred Merfield in his book *Gorillas were my Neighbours*, written in the 1950s. The author describes how he watched a female gorilla, pursued by hunters, climb a tree in the heart of the forest, her baby clinging to her back, two vicious spears projecting from her side. In her panic she grew careless, transferred her bulk to a branch not strong enough to support her weight and came crashing to the ground. 'Spears, cutlasses and several shots from the old guns finished her off, but even when she was dead they could not resist the delight of stabbing and slashing at her body.'

He then described the death of an old male silver back gorilla:

> Running around in the undergrowth, as I had seen gorillas do so often before in more happy circumstances, and there were a dozen spears projecting from his chest, back and sides. Making no attempt to retaliate, he was just sitting there, rocking to and fro as more spears were thrust home at close quarters; his mouth wide open, crying shame on his tormentors. The gorilla's anguish was too much for me . . . three or four more spears hit him and then another man, armed with a heavy club, leaned forward and slowly, methodically, began clubbing him to death.

The words spoke for themselves. It was a sobering thought that this terrible trade, as recently as thirty years ago, had supplied gorillas to zoos worldwide and that the older apes we see in zoos today have experienced exactly this sort of capture.

Orphans like Rupert and Sid represented just the tip of the

iceberg for the Kakamoeka district. When Mark heard rumours that a Portuguese timber company based on the Kouillou river were trading illegally in infant apes, he went down to Pointe Noire to investigate, determined to find some incontrovertible evidence that would implicate them. He discovered it was all too easy to 'order' infant gorillas or chimpanzees from the local population, transport them to Pointe Noire in logging trucks disguised as timber goods and load them onto a boat destined for Eastern Europe, where they would fetch a considerable price on the zoo market, if they survived the journey. It only needed money to change hands once for the word to spread like wildfire throughout the surrounding villages, inspiring every villager to go out into the forest and hunt with the specific intention of capturing a live infant.

Magne was a village on the Kouillou river. The saw mill that dominated the village spewed shavings and engine oil directly into the water. Adjacent to the mill was a typical shanty-town, housing the local workers. It was a soulless place. Mark spent a week in the village and discovered both gorilla and chimpanzee orphans housed in makeshift chicken wire cages on the company director's property. They mysteriously disappeared a few days later and could not be traced. He took photographs, taped conversations between himself and the company staff, and returned to Brazzaville in the hope of starting an official government investigation, possibly even a prosecution. He spent hours making transcripts and developed the films before sending them to the Minister responsible for wildlife conservation as well as to external environmental investigation agencies. We were advised, as diplomatically as possible, that if we pursued this investigation any further we might find ourselves on the next plane to Europe. The Minister was a close friend and business associate of the timber company director.

The repercussions of the intensive hunting of apes in the

Kouillou area were devastating. Those gorillas who escaped the guns suffered stress. This increased their susceptibility to disease and social disruption which often caused the complete fracture of family groups, with the inevitable loss of their reproductive potential. Gorillas, as we had already witnessed, were extremely sensitive to stress, a factor which made their already threatened existence in the wild even more precarious.

Sid's insecurity required a very different approach from that of Max. Where Max craved reassurance and company, Sid craved peace and solitude in those first few days at the orphanage. As we approached to change his bedding or leave food he would flinch. I felt ashamed to be a member of the human race at those moments. Unlike Max, he made no demands at all, which was all the more alarming. We were anxious that if he did not soon form a bond of trust with either Mark or myself, he would die of grief. The process of building trust was painfully slow. Initially we entered his room only to leave food and water for him, then we were able to spend short periods of time in his room, simply sitting quietly and submissively, back to back with him to assure him of our non-threatening intentions. As the days passed he came to fear our presence less and his expression changed from one of terror to confusion. On the fourth day we had made progress and were able to sit near him. He even accepted the segments of orange we offered which were his current craving. Newly arrived orphans would often suffer cravings for particular food items. Only when their health began to recover would they start to become more adventurous with their diets.

Eventually we reached the point where he no longer feared physical contact with us. A tentative bond of trust had been forged and we decided it was time for Sid to leave the safe confines of his room. While we appreciated his need for space and privacy to recover and breathe mentally, we also believed that the stimulation of sunlight and a change of scene might provide a necessary distraction from his sad thoughts.

Mark gently took his hand and, trembling, he emerged into the brilliant sunlight, peering cautiously around the garden. They walked together hand in hand, Sid squinting up at the bright sky and craning his stiff neck to see the trees bordering the nearby forest, clinging to Mark's hand in terror. He tired quickly and they sat down together on a log. Mark produced an orange from his pocket and peeled it, sharing the segments between them, Sid gazing trustingly into Mark's eyes, sitting close, gaining comfort from his new-found friendship.

In the following weeks his appetite grew to be insatiable, but he failed to gain the weight we expected. His belly, tight and uncomfortably distended with food, was a sad travesty of the normal soft, pendulous gorilla belly. His legs and arms remained stick-like, barely able to support his massive stomach. Tests revealed a colossal infestation of intestinal parasites, particularly hookworm. While you would expect to find these parasites in moderate quantities in the gut of a wild gorilla, Sid's generally poor state of health had given them a chance to multiply to dangerous levels. They were sucking up every ounce of goodness he ingested, leaving him anaemic and undernourished. We kept repeating the same tests, hoping that eventually a natural balance would return. We were reluctant to try a de-worming treatment for fear that it might cause internal bleeding, diarrhoea and further disturbance to Sid's already fragile digestive system, possibly even killing him.

Several weeks later there was still no improvement. We had no choice but to try to de-worm him since it seemed unlikely he would survive much longer with such a high level of parasites. We delayed treatment as long as possible in the hope that he would trust us enough to allow us to help him if things went wrong. We administered the treatment and waited. Within hours Sid was feverish, his fragile body shivering involuntarily. He lost all interest in food and life in general, and seemed thrown back into the depths of depression, gaining little comfort from our presence.

A few days later the fever subsided and his appetite returned with a vengeance, along with an apparent appreciation of the support he had received from his new family. He now took enormous pleasure in his food, grumbling loudly and contentedly as he sat guarding his stockpile, which he obviously expected to have snatched away at any moment. With the parasites under control he started to gain weight. The sparse tufts of coarse greyish hair were replaced by a thicker, hazelnut brown, healthy coat. The skin on his hands and feet started to peel away like the shedding of a snake and new soft skin appeared underneath.

His bowels, however, remained unpredictable and he was prone to explosions of liquid diarrhoea, probably because his body was not yet ready to deal with the vast quantities of food he now crammed in at every opportunity. This habit proved unpleasant for whoever happened to have him on their lap at the time, and however much one tried to prepare oneself with a protective towel, somehow he always managed to take you by surprise.

In the flat he wore nappies, but it was hard to find a size big enough for a two and a half year old gorilla. Although he now trusted us it still only took the slightest harsh word or gesture to throw his fragile confidence and send him plummeting back to the depths of depression. He would often sit on the sofa with us in the early evening, quietly enjoying our company. Irritated by his nappies, he would soon find his way out of them and piss on the sofa. This would lead to stern words and banishment to his room. We felt guilty as he returned our sharp reprimands with dejected looks, but we needed to stick to strict hygiene rules. Our living space could have become a filthy disease-trap.

It would have been easy to let the animals run completely wild in the flat, but the result would have been total chaos and a serious health risk to both humans and gorillas. As it was we were already vulnerable to every parasite the gorillas carried, particularly when they were ill with diarrhoea and needed intimate contact. At times I felt overwhelmed by my responsibilities and fearful for my own health. As a nurse I was well aware of the risks involved in working with sick apes, so closely related to humans, and more aware than Mark. This was sometimes a bone of contention between us.

Physically Sid and Rupert could not have been more different. Rupert's handsome, rounded face and well-proportioned features almost gave him the appearance of a mountain gorilla. Sid's longer face was ugly but loveable, his small deep-set piggy eyes betraying his vulnerability. Emotionally these two gorillas were also at odds. Rupert's sensible, measured approach to life contrasted with Sid's limited intelligence and tendency to panic, his insecurity often leading him to misinterpret friendly intentions for aggression.

To begin with they feigned typical gorilla indifference to one another, unsure of their ground, but as the weeks passed they formed a brotherly bond. They grew to know one another's areas of vulnerability, at times playing on them and at others using this knowledge to reassure each other. Rupert's self-assurance helped Sid to remain calm and cope with new situations. They seemed to complement one another. As we watched them exploring the garden together we felt rewarded for all the weeks of anxiety and hard work. We began to dream that one day sad, fearful Sid with all his handicaps might be able to roam the forests again as a wild gorilla.

Chapter Six

Redmond and Boha

One afternoon, shortly after the arrival of Sid and Rupert, a scruffy, bearded figure appeared at the orphanage gates. Mystified, I stared as he gesticulated wildly, pointing at a curious-looking bump under his jacket. Reaching into the folds he gently eased out a moving bundle of fur, a tiny infant gorilla who now uncurled himself, gazing first trustingly up at the face above him, then round the orphanage with inquisitive, wide eyes.

Mark finally recognized Redmond O'Hanlon. They had met some months earlier, prior to Redmond's three-month trip into the interior of the mysterious Likoula Swamps, a trip he was later to turn into his best-selling book *Congo Journey*. He had lost a lot of weight since Mark had last seen him, his trousers hanging loosely from his hips. His grey, wavy hair, always unruly, was now long and lank. His eyes betrayed the disturbing experiences of his past few months. I found it hard to equate this bedraggled, exhausted figure with the eccentric, jovial author of *Into the Heart of Borneo*.

Mark beckoned him into the garden where Max set upon him with delight, tugging at his beard and squealing in his face. The tiny gorilla, now more confident of a friendly reception, ventured off Redmond's lap. Struggling with Max, Redmond explained how he had persuaded a villager in the far northern village of Boha to hand over the baby ape, no more than six months old. From that point on, he continued wearily, he had lived day and night with this demanding infant. Despite his protestations, it was obvious that he had become deeply attached to his little companion. We would feel answerable to him should anything happen to the friend he was entrusting to our care.

Having set out in search of the legendary dinosaur of Lac Tele, the Mokele Mbembe, Redmond actually made a more mysterious discovery in the murky depths of a witchcraft world that he struggled to understand. Despite his attempts at humour and his usual, jovial façade, I sensed his rising panic to get out of the Congo to a place of solitude and normality where he could attempt to make some sense of the experiences and emotions that crowded his head. Although I identified with these feelings, I could not allow myself to indulge them as my own journey was only just beginning.

I liked this gentle man who, once back in England, could not forget his little gorilla and even sent money out to Brazzaville to supply him with nappies.

Boha, as we named the little gorilla, had only recently mastered the skill of walking and was still unsteady on his feet, frequently giving up the struggle to revert to crawling around on his belly like a human infant. Although still consuming five bottles of milk formula a day he was now starting to eat solids and usually ended up with more sticky banana pulp plastered on his face than in his mouth. His rounded, soft features and small but perfectly proportioned body, already resembling a miniature silver back with his broad shoulders and dignified stance, brought out all my latent maternal instincts. I watched as he grew in size and confidence with a glowing pride.

His recovery was not dogged with the psychological compli-cations of the older gorillas like Sid, whose understanding of his

experiences was clear and devastating. Boha's universe up to this
point had focused on physical needs like food, warmth and
comfort. Now, as he matured, he explored the only world he
knew, the orphanage. Physically he developed in tune with this
environment, acquiring the essential resistance to diseases he
encountered. He suffered none of the complications that had
plagued Sid's struggle to adapt from the familiar environment
of his forest home and family group to a new and threatening
one.

My pride in the three gorillas was undoubtedly maternal. I
delighted in each new step they took as if they were my own
children. In years to come I could not help but make compari-
sons between the gorilla infants I had known and my friends'
human offspring. Human babies seemed so clumsy and depend-
ent. Infant apes needed strength in their tiny arms in the early
weeks of their lives to cling to their mothers as they moved
about the forest. In similar fashion they clung to our human
arms, backs and legs as we, their adoptive parents, went about
our daily chores. Any attempt to prise them off was met with
screams of panic.

Initially I relished Boha's persistent demands, flattered by his
constant need to remain physically attached to me twenty-four
hours a day. But as time wore on I became increasingly weary
and irritable, and needed to remind myself that his demanding
behaviour was completely normal in ape terms. I experienced
the same guilt, shame and confusion that all mothers do at times
when their nerves are frayed by lack of sleep and they lose their
tempers with their children, causing tears and extending the
cycle of guilt and exasperation.

Sid and Rupert now slept together at night and spent their
days exploring the orphanage grounds. They were cautiously
friendly towards Max, observing his manic chimpanzee antics
with bemusement and an air of quiet superiority. They appreci-

ated his effusively affectionate nature, and his persistent invitations to play kept them occupied when boredom and introspection threatened.

As our responsibilities grew we realized that we were going to need more help. Nkodia and Joseph were fully occupied with maintenance work and preparations for the arrival of the new gorilla cage from England. The daily demands of Max, Sid, Rupert and Boha left precious little time to deal with other administrative and logistical problems that arose.

Albertine Ndokila was in her late twenties with three children of her own when she started work for Madame Leroy, looking after the four orphans who remained in Yvette's care until the orphanage cage arrived. Albertine's solid build and fierce features belied a calm, gentle nature. She also possessed the required authority for maintaining discipline amongst the animals when boredom set in and they engaged in mock power struggles with one another and occasionally Albertine herself. It was obvious she was not comfortable working in the volatile, stressful atmosphere of Madame Leroy's villa and she readily agreed to join us. It was to prove one of the best decisions we made.

As Boha's confidence and co-ordination grew he interacted increasingly with Sid and Rupert. He was now willing to venture short distances away from me to play with them, only stopping to check every now and then that I was still nearby should he need me. The older gorillas were gentle with him, deliberately restraining their superior physical strength and keeping a watchful eye on me, aware that if their play turned rough they risked my wrath. Together they were forming the nucleus of a family group which might help future new arrivals to settle. It would reduce their feelings of isolation and fear, easing them back into normal gorilla society once they were physically fit enough to handle social interactions with the more confident gorillas. The sensitivity with which Sid and Rupert handled Boha reassured us that they would be equally sensitive in their approach to new and vulnerable youngsters.

Boha learnt quickly from his older companions, exploring confidently, carefully observing and copying to the best of his ability everything that Sid and Rupert did. Whilst they sat in the garden eating fruit and vegetation cut from the forest, he would push his face into theirs, asking for a sample and learning through trial and error the required skills for tackling the tough outer skin of many tropical fruits, their pithy interior flesh and the large stones which, if gorged in a frenzy, could obstruct the immature intestines of infants. I sampled most of the fruits myself, curious to understand their attraction, but found them bitter. The latex stuck fast to my teeth and tongue, leaving a persistent, acrid, after-taste. The large stones found in some fruits were easy for inexperienced infant gorillas to choke on. We wondered how wild youngsters avoided this problem and presumed that this knowledge formed part of an education they received from their natural mothers and other family members.

What had begun as a cautious friendship with Yvette Leroy deteriorated as the day of her gorillas' transfer to the orphanage approached. Although in her heart she knew that it was the right thing to do – her villa was hardly the ideal place for these boisterous infants who needed to learn the essential skills of forest life and normal gorilla behaviour, and whose routine at present was dull and unstimulating – Yvette's emotions were in turmoil.

Any suggestions or concerns we voiced about the animals in her care were met with increasing hostility, her judgement becoming more and more clouded by the fear that we were a threat to her position as the local gorilla expert.

Somewhere along the line our tentative willingness to work together to secure a future for the gorillas had become a battleground. She simply could not cope with the impending loss of her 'children'. We certainly did not intend to cut her off from them, but she did not seem able to share them.

Initially wishing to help us, she had agreed to receive our mail at her own private postal box in town, to which only she had the key. As her defensiveness increased she started to resent us 'using' her facilities, forgetting that she had volunteered them. She indulged in petty acts of malice, such as throwing away our private mail from home, and we heard rumours that she was bad-mouthing us to the French expatriate community. This seemed a likely explanation for the suspicion and even outright hostility we encountered on our occasional trips into town.

In September there was an outbreak of amoebic dysentery at Yvette's villa. Being highly suspicious of human medicines, she was reluctant to use the antibiotic Flagyl, as she was certain that its side-effects had been the cause of deaths amongst newly arrived infants in the past. We could sympathize with her fears, but had witnessed the dramatic curative effect of this drug with our own charges and remained convinced that the drug could save them.

As the days passed the four gorillas grew weaker until, desperate, she gave in and agreed to start treating them with the antibiotic. Fearful of the possible side-effects, however, she cut short the treatment once their strength started to pick up. This of course created the serious risk that the parasites would develop resistance to the antibiotic, and the illness become completely untreatable.

Entering her villa on one of our daily visits, we found her dressed entirely in black, her hair scraped severely back from her tear-stained, pale face and covered with a black scarf. She raised her eyes from the floor which she was sweeping in a robotic, distracted manner and paused, venting her grief in a stream of vicious accusations, blaming us for the deaths of two of her gorillas, and banning us from ever crossing her threshold again. We left immediately, not only in sympathy for her grief, but also because it was clear that then was no time for a rational discussion about what had actually happened. We hoped to be able to return later to patch things up, and to take steps to avoid the same tragedy for the two surviving orphans.

However, her course was now set against us as she attempted to involve the government wildlife services in a crusade against us, publicly accusing us of building the orphanage with materials stolen from the town hall. We kept our heads down and continued our work, developing a siege mentality to her persistent underhand tactics. Coupled with the conservation world's reservations as to the value of gorilla reintroduction and its likelihood of success, it made us even more determined to prove that our faith in the gorillas was not misplaced. It almost seemed that adversity spurred us on to make our dream become a reality.

The most common criticism by the conservation establishment of ape reintroduction projects was that they could not justify the funds they spent in terms of the protection of the truly wild ape populations who were endangered by the destruction of their habitat and poaching.

We felt that the orphanage justified itself in terms broader than purely the welfare of its individual gorilla charges. The very act of confiscation was a discouragement to poachers, our presence reinforcing laws that had, until now, rarely been applied. If the reintroduction of our gorillas was successful there would be potential for a gorilla tourism programme, using them as a flagship species and heightening awareness of their status as a protected species nationwide.

We believed that if orphan gorillas were reared from an early age in social groups and equipped with the skills of forest life, they would one day be ready to cope with a return to the wild.

No previous attempts of this kind had been made. Efforts to reintroduce individual, human-reared, gorilla orphans into wild family groups had mostly failed.

It was virgin territory with very little information or experience to draw on. Our success would largely depend on an in-depth understanding of the gorillas and an ability to assess the pace of their progress, providing the appropriate support and protection along the way and not asking too much of them too soon.

With this is mind, we decided one afternoon to take Sid and Rupert for a walk in the forest immediately surrounding the orphanage to see how they would react. This small area of forest housed many species of plant life which would have formed part of their basic diet in the wild. We felt absurdly positive as we observed them. They showed no hesitation in choosing which foods to eat, climbing the trees in search of wild fruits with surprising skill and confidence. They adapted effortlessly, Rupert watching Sid as he lumbered off, grumbling happily in anticipation of reaching the succulent yellow fruits he had spotted high in the trees. The improvement in their general health, from the addition to their diet of more natural gorilla foods and from the tranquillity of the forest itself, was soon obvious. We realized how essential it was for new arrivals to get out into the forest as soon as possible to re-establish healthy digestive systems, peace of mind and the continuation of a forest education which had been interrupted at capture.

The only problem was that this patch of forest was completely open to the public via the main airport road. People would enter in search of firewood or wild fruit. They would set snares and defecate in the undergrowth. The risk of our gorillas coming into contact with human diseases was significant, but the undoubted benefits outweighed this risk. We hoped that a planned vaccination programme for all infants arriving at the orphanage would at least offer some protection from diseases like polio and tuberculosis. If reintroduction was to be a realistic goal they must learn the required skills. This forest offered them the ideal training ground. Despite the vendettas apparently in train against us, we returned to the orphanage after that first day in the forest with Sid and Rupert feeling hopelessly optimistic for the gorillas' future.

Chapter Seven

A New Home
Arrives

At the end of the year the new holding cage arrived from Kent. It had been built to much the same design as the enclosures at Howletts, a massive steel-grille gymnasium, seven metres high, fifteen metres wide and thirteen metres long. Madame Leroy and the Congolese Wildlife Department had been very keen that we should have the sort of moated enclosure popular with American zoos, one which would give the false impression of space and liberty, but is designed more for the viewing public than the ape occupants. A moated enclosure could not offer the three-dimensional space and gymnasium equipment so essential for our gorillas if they were to develop the required musculature and climbing skills to survive in the wild. While apparently less 'politically correct', the cage we preferred bore a closer resemblance to the gorillas' natural habitat. Aware of their reputation for neglecting the animals in Brazzaville Zoo, the Congolese government seized on the snob value and aesthetic appeal of a moated enclosure, and we had to fight hard to get what we wanted. Aspinall backed us over this issue and wrote a personal letter to the Wildlife Department stating his intention to pull out if his wishes were questioned. This had the desired effect.

The need for the cage had become urgent. While we could

just about manage to house Rupert, Sid, Boha and Max at night
in the existing facilities, we had nowhere to house newcomers. If
our experiences of the past few months were anything to go by,
we would be confiscating more orphans on a regular basis. The
new cage would not only need to provide a suitable temporary
holding facility for orphans intended for reintroduction, but also
a permanent home for those who never made the transition back
to the wild. One of the gorillas still in Yvette's care, awaiting
the arrival of the cage, was five-year-old Magne. Sadly, it seemed
that he might be one of those unlikely to survive in the wild.

For the past year Yvette had been forced to confine Magne to
a small cage in her back garden. Deprived of gorilla company
and any outlet for his growing energy, he had already begun to
display neurotic behaviour and would rock back and forth as he
sat holding the bars of his cage, watching the younger gorillas
rush around the garden, letting off steam. Exposure to Sid and
Rupert might help him develop more appropriate, natural
gorilla, behaviour but it seemed more likely he would end up
spending his days in the cage whilst the others progressed to a
wild future.

The cage travelled in kit-form by boat from England to the
West Coast of Africa, docking at Pointe Noire. As we awaited
its arrival, we prepared by laying the concrete foundations.
When it did finally arrive at Pointe Noire, it spent a month in
customs, during which time a mountain of paperwork needed to
be completed and a number of bribes distributed before the
three containers of steelwork were allowed to continue their
journey by rail up to Brazzaville.

The cage was probably the first to be constructed under the
active supervision of its future inmates. As the workmen sweated
profusely, labouring under the merciless glare of the sun, Max
swung happily from the pulleys being used to lever the huge
steel grill squares that comprised the cage walls, leaving his

footprints in newly mixed cement, while the gorillas circled curiously at a distance before ambling over to investigate.

We now needed to remove the massive mound of earth that had been built round the original enclosure, a tedious task made less laborious and time-consuming when we were offered access to the Brazzaville Town Hall trucks.

Don Webster, a British expatriate who worked for the town hall, became our local guardian angel. Now in his fifties he had come to the Congo as a young man working for a road-building company. When the contract ended he stayed on, becoming embroiled in local life. He soon had a Congolese wife and three children. He tackled the frustrations of life in Central Africa with all the famed stoicism of the British working class. Although he and his wife, Thérèse, were initially puzzled by what we were hoping to achieve, Don was pleased to see new faces from England and became a vital source of support and logistical help when even the smallest problem seemed to take days to solve. The Congolese authorities and police were quick to seize on naive new arrivals to the country. There were not that many white faces around it so it was easy for them to spot new targets for extortion and intimidation.

Don was pleased to find the extra work since his town hall wages barely covered the cost of food for his family and the medicines he needed for his poor health. He would arrive early each morning, knock loudly on the flat door and shout, 'Where's my cup of tea?' We would then share a pot of tea whilst Max, Sid, Rupert and Boha ran wild around us, praying that Albertine would show up soon so that we could get on with overseeing the building work or running errands in town. If she didn't show up we would be grounded for the day.

The sheer quantity of food we bought made us very popular figures in the local market. The moment we pulled up in the jeep we would find ourselves surrounded by market 'mamas' elbowing one another and noisily declaring the price and superior quality of their merchandise. These disputes frequently escalated into apparently violent outbursts which would subside as quickly as they erupted. The market stalls were crammed together beneath a hot tin roof, the sickly smell of warm fish and meat and the raucous din of the market sellers competing with one another to attract potential clients, all made it a place we did not linger in. During the rains the market would become a mudbath. In the dry season dust covered everything. It was tempting to grab the first thing we were offered in order to escape the noise and intense heat.

There were often three generations of a family crammed behind each stall, wizened old grandmothers barking orders as their grandchildren chased in and out of their legs giggling and fighting with one another. Tempers simmered and erupted in brief abusive outbursts in the hot overcrowded space. These people were not used to the luxury of space and privacy I had taken for granted all my life.

After weeks of bartering with different mamas we discovered Marie-Blanche. A vast, effusive woman, she prided herself on providing the highest quality at the best prices, and soon secured our exclusive custom.

Sid and Rupert were the first to put the cage to the test. The design and strength of the structure had borne in mind not only its occupants' strength but also their ingenuity and tenacity when confronted with unwelcome restrictions. Fairly confident that there were no weak areas we coaxed them in for the night. As they explored the cage and the large quantity of succulent leaves we had installed as bedding, we left, locking the doors behind us and retiring to the flat with Max. Max needed our human company in the evenings. We provided a stimulating change from the gorillas he spent his days with, whom he found at times slow-witted and dull.

In the early hours of the morning I became vaguely aware of clanging noises outside. I assumed that Alphonse was tidying the garage with more than usual enthusiasm before he left. When we did finally emerge from the flat we found Rupert and Sid waiting expectantly outside the front door for their morning milk drinks. Woken by the unfamiliar sounds of dawn in the forest surrounding the cage, they had set to work together to find a way out of the irritating contraption, prising apart one of the joints which held the squares of steel grille together to make just enough room for two small gorillas to squeeze through. Had Max been part of the escape team they would probably have been out within a matter of minutes, his ingenuity and Sid's brute strength making a formidable combination. We spent the day tightening all the bolts.

One morning a well-dressed French woman appeared at the orphanage in a state of distress. 'I was in the town centre this morning,' she explained, 'and I was approached by a man who asked me if I would like to buy a baby gorilla. He then held his hold-all open towards me,' she continued breathlessly, 'there was something alive inside. I didn't want to encourage him so I walked away and came straight to you. Can't you confiscate the baby?'

Thanking her for the information we made straight for the wildlife offices and found two agents to come in search of the gorilla with us. We were not able to enforce Congolese law ourselves and enforcement was always more effective when it came from the Congolese themselves. If we had carried out confiscations alone, the poachers would have assumed that we intended to sell the gorillas on and pocket the proceeds, and that we were paying government officials to keep quiet. Occasionally we managed to persuade poachers to visit the orphanage following a confiscation to see the gorillas when they had been nursed back to health, in an attempt to prove our honest intentions. Their first reaction was to assume we were mad, but once they had spent some time talking to us and, more importantly, to the local staff, they began to understand our aims. In one or two cases we actually had poachers returning to the orphanage asking for jobs.

With our two reluctant and confused Congolese colleagues crammed in the back of the jeep we began to cruise the streets in search of 'the man with the gorilla'. We soon spotted him loitering outside the supermarket, trying to interest shoppers in the contents of his hold-all. Screeching to a halt we climbed out of the jeep. Mark and I hung back, allowing the two wildlife agents in their green uniforms to do the talking. The man spotted them too late to make an escape, then proceeded to try and bluff his way self-righteously out of the situation.

The agents explained firmly that he was breaking the law and confirmed that there was an infant gorilla in his bag. They handed the bag to Mark and escorted the irate man back to the jeep. We dropped them all off at the wildlife offices and made our way back to the orphanage with our latest charge.

We waited until we reached the peace and quiet of our flat before unzipping the filthy, sodden bag. Peeling back the flap we saw a tiny emaciated figure, not more than a few months old, lying motionless at the base. She did not even dare to raise her head as light penetrated the bag, remaining huddled at the bottom, her body rigid with fear.

Mark placed his arms gently around the small bundle of matted fur. She responded with a pathetic warning cough. He placed her on a towel on the tiled floor and she curled into a ball, refusing to acknowledge our presence.

We waited patiently and quietly until she raised her head and scornful eyes came to rest on our faces. There was no flicker of curiosity in those eyes. All hope had long ago been beaten out of her. She was dangerously dehydrated and unless we managed to get some fluids into her she would be dead within hours. Although reluctant to rush her, we didn't have much time. We decided to leave her with a bowl of water and some juicy morsels of fruit, hoping that once alone she would drink voluntarily. But when we returned a little while later she had touched nothing and remained stubbornly curled into a tight ball. We were now forced to give her fluids, using a syringe as we had done initially with Max. We wondered whether it would be kinder just to let her die in peace rather than cause further terror in our attempts to save her life. Our experience with Sid, however, was still fresh in our minds and we decided that we must try to save her, unlikely as we were to succeed. Like many of the orphans we were to come across in the following years she had retreated into herself, refusing to acknowledge the world and welcoming death.

As we approached to wrap her in a towel she grimaced in fear, baring anaemic white gums. She offered no resistance to our attempts to feed her, only watching us with dull resigned eyes and the occasional flicker of defiant loathing as we slowly succeeded in persuading her to swallow small amounts of re-hydration salts.

Relieved to have got some fluid into her but worried by her lack of protest, we released her from the towel. She immediately started vomiting up the precious fluid. Vile, yellow-green sticky vomit the consistency of bile now coated the matted fur on her chest. There seemed no point trying to give her anything further. An anti-sickness injection had little effect on the violent retching that shook her tiny body which was now deathly cold and clammy. All we could do was wrap her in a blanket and hold her as death approached. Our human presence was unwelcome. There was no solace or comfort we could offer. It was too late to make amends for the wrong she had suffered at human hands.

She died a few hours later. It often seemed as if adrenaline alone kept these orphans alive during their capture. When they reached the safety of the orphanage and started to relax their defences they simply died.

Madame Leroy had often told us of baby gorillas she had rescued that had 'died of a broken heart' soon after their arrival at her house. We had thought this explanation unlikely until we witnessed it for ourselves. Gorillas were evidently capable of profound feelings of loss, depression and melancholy.

Exotic animal collectors who provided stock to zoos worldwide at the turn of the century complained that baby gorillas died within days or weeks of capture. Explorer and collector, Paul du Chaillu, in his book *Gorilla Country* written in 1906, wrote of a baby gorilla: 'To the last he continued utterly untameable'. 'Inconsolable' would have been a more accurate word to use. This infant had been chained by the neck and could hardly have been expected to be anything other than 'untameable' under such conditions.

The gorilla's physically intimidating appearance belies his emotional fragility and peaceful nature. Indeed he uses his impressive physical bulk to warn off danger in order to avoid direct physical confrontation. When surprised in the camouflage of dense forest these timid creatures will display their strength with bluff confidence in a series of escalating vocalizations and gestures involving coughs, barks, screams and the destruction of any branches to hand. The gorilla's placid nature may have been appropriate when gorillas reigned unchallenged in the rainforest but now they found themselves ill-equipped psychologically to cope with a changing, threatening world.

Chapter Eight

Kidnapping Nigel

Gorillas weren't the only wild animals on sale in Brazzaville. Between the supermarket and the Central Bar, a popular meeting place for expatriates, there was always a cluster of traders selling monkeys, birds of prey and parrots. They soon recognized our jeep and became more discreet in their illegal trading activities. After several raids and confiscations by the wildlife authorities, they gave up trading illegal goods and concentrated on legal livestock. Mark's relationship with them was honest and humorous, and because of this no grudge was held against us personally. In fact these same traders knew the infant ape trading network well and would sometimes provide valuable information when we were trying to locate orphan gorillas in town.

The government wildlife agents, initially reluctant and perplexed to be involved in these confiscations, soon developed a pride in their work, even starting to take their own initiatives to clamp down on trading in town and at the airport, where animals were crated up and sent out on Aeroflot and Ethiopian Airlines flights. Having initially encouraged them to do this, we soon found that we were being asked to house all sorts of other animal species which they had confiscated on their raids. The parrots we could eventually release, the chimps we passed on to

Aliette Jamart. The monkeys, however, posed a more complex problem because several species confiscated were of Zairian origin, not found in the Congo, and therefore could not be released. Sadly, they often ended up in the zoo simply because we did not have the space or the funds to house them at the orphanage.

It was quite usual for expatriates to buy parrots from these street traders, thus ensuring that the trade flourished and that wild flocks continued to be depleted. Pierre was an African Grey Parrot given to us by one of the American Embassy guards when his period of duty in Brazzaville was up. Pierre adapted quickly to life at the orphanage. He was already familiar with people and the gorillas were just hairy humans to him. With the uncanny skill of vocal imitation that parrots are famous for, Pierre had soon perfected Max's squeals of excitement and our irate responses.

'Max! Max!' he would screech in the early mornings, followed by a variety of other impressions. It became impossible at times to tell who was who.

Although the gorillas now fed on the natural vegetation in the forest surrounding the orphanage, they still needed supplements to ensure a balanced diet. Late every afternoon, as the sun glowed orange on its descent, we would sit with them whilst they tucked into an assortment of fruit and vegetables bought from the local market. They would politely gather round the large plastic bowl, delicately plucking out their favourite items, rarely fighting amongst themselves, although occasionally breaking out into the odd tussle with Max.

Pierre would perch precariously on the side of the bowl, struggling to keep his balance and enjoying the sociable, easy company of the gorillas. They showed no resentment towards him or any of the other animals that arrived at the orphanage.

Mark and I could not help thinking that it was a pity that man was not as accepting of other species.

Max was less tolerant. When the zoo director's domestic pig wandered into the grounds, as he often did, Max would take great pleasure in giving chase. Undaunted by the intruder's enormous bulk he thundered along behind the terrified pig, his hair bristling, his hands and feet pounding deliberately loudly on the hard, dry earth. I often used to come across the pig when walking through the zoo. He would bury himself in the dirt to sleep, bursting dramatically from the ground when woken by my approaching footsteps and fleeing down the path in front of me. One day the pig simply disappeared so I guess he didn't always manage to outrun his pursuers and ended up on the Sunday menu at the director's house.

Max was always quick to defend his territory. If he heard Nkodia arguing with some offending member of the public in front of the gorilla cage, he would add his voice to the fray, screaming abuse at the object of Nkodia's wrath.

Towards the end of the year my sister, Sue, travelled out to Brazzaville for a visit. Whilst I was delighted to see a familiar face from home I was worried by the responsibility I felt for Sue in this extreme environment. Sue fell instantly in love with Sid and the feelings were more than reciprocated. Sid recognized in her a gentle, caring friend with an apparently infinite supply of patience. He spent every moment he could with her, gazing lovingly into her eyes and searching desperately for her whenever she disappeared from sight. Within a week, however, Sue had fallen horribly ill, more than likely infected by Sid or one of the others. I felt completely responsible as she lay on the bed, feverish, pale and weak. She was dehydrating at a terrifying rate as spasms of vomiting and diarrhoea gripped her body. She became mentally confused and stuporous as Sid fretted in the grounds outside.

Despite my experiences with tropical diseases I was very worried. I tried to maintain a show of confidence when she looked at me with fearful eyes and asked whether she was going to die. I thought she might have malaria, the symptoms of which could be so diverse that diagnosis was often difficult without access to accurate blood tests. I was desperate to get a professional medical opinion.

I drove into town in search of help and eventually found a French doctor on duty in the main university hospital. He promised to come to the orphanage as soon as he had finished work. A few hours later we heard the sound of an approaching motorbike and soon the doctor wafted into the flat in a cloud of after-shave.

'Acute gastro-enteritis,' he announced after examining her and handed me a prescription which I then rushed into town to find. That night I sat beside her, trying to help her keep down small sips of water and by the morning she seemed calmer and less feverish. The illness vanished almost as quickly as it had arrived, leaving Sue weak, drained and confined to bed. Deserting her bedside for a moment to fetch some water, I left the door ajar and Sid spotted her. It was the end of several days of frantic searching and, seizing his chance, he bolted into the room, landing enthusiastically on the bed with a heavy thud, hurling himself into her arms and pissing joyfully on the sheets. This effusive reunion touched Sue and seemed to speed her recovery, allowing her to spend her last few days with Sid before leaving Brazzaville tired but euphoric from her experiences. Sid, sadly, just had to learn to forget her, but at least this had been another positive experience with humans.

One morning, after fighting our way through the market mamas and lugging huge quantities of fruit and vegetables into the jeep in the blazing sun, Mark and I stopped off at the Central Bar to quench our thirsts. As usual the expatriates in the bar were surrounded by street traders. Although these traders could be annoyingly persistent they usually knew when to back off, unlike their equivalents across the river in Kinshasa who we heard would often resort to violence if their wares were rejected. The Brazzaville traders did not believe in the 'hard-sell' and mostly just shrugged lazily when no interest was shown in their goods. Brazzaville was an altogether sleepier, more easy-going place, which in many ways made it even more frustrating when you wanted to get things done. After a couple of half-hearted attempts to sell their wares the traders would wander back to the street corner to smoke cigarettes and indulge in intense debate with one another.

This particular morning a young man from out of town appeared at the bar amongst the regular traders, dragging a noosed infant mandrill along behind him. Every now and then he would stop and point to the sad creature and suggest a price to the mostly disinterested or disgusted occupants of the bar.

When he reached our table we engaged him in conversation, suggesting that he would find it impossible to sell his bedraggled monkey and expressing concern for his costs in feeding it.

'Why don't you give the creature to the zoo?' we suggested.

'Someone,' he insisted, 'will buy my monkey,' refusing to believe our gloomy predictions.

The regular street traders had all gathered on the other side of the street to watch what would happen next, unwilling to inform this outsider that we worked with the government wildlife department. I could see Mark's anger simmering as he watched the continued suffering of the mandrill.

The man realized we were not going to buy and moved on to other drinkers who pushed him away impatiently. After a few more minutes loitering around the bar he moved off down the street with his poor captive struggling to keep up on his spindly legs. At that moment Mark's temper erupted and he leapt to his feet, signalling me to get into the jeep. I was hardly into my seat before we were screeching down the street in full pursuit, Mark's face a mask of grim determination.

He pulled up beside the trader. 'Can I have a closer look at the monkey?' he asked.

The man gave a sly smile, assuming that Mark had just been showing uninterest at the bar earlier as a bargaining tactic. He passed the mandrill through the car window to Mark who threw it, screaming, onto the back seat and stamped on the accelerator. The wheels spun as he shouted at me to close the window.

Neither of us was in any doubt that this unconventional method of confiscation would lead to trouble with the authorities.

We rattled through town with the mandrill shrieking indignantly in the back, shitting and pissing everywhere as he leapt about in panic. What we hadn't realized was that the whole scene had been witnessed by an under-cover member of the State Security Services who, seeing a perfect opportunity to hassle a foreigner and hopefully extract some cash, jumped on his state supplied motorbike, revved the engine noisily and set off in pursuit, visible a few moments later in our rear view mirror in a cloud of dust.

Realizing that we were now in trouble we drove straight to the Wildlife Services office, with the motorbike on our tail, to see NDinga Assitou, the Director. Always dressed impeccably and taking an obvious pride in his appearance, NDinga's aquiline features expressed a sharp intelligence. He could be a formidable ally. He had spent several years as a student at Moscow University, studying politics, and had returned home with a white Russian wife, a status symbol in Brazzaville that suggested that he possessed money or intellectual superiority. He must have found his native country an infertile ground for the hopes and ideals he carried home. Although wildlife conservation was not his chosen profession he was quick at interpreting the pertinent laws of wildlife protection and could easily verbally outmanoeuvre poachers. He relished the challenge these confiscations presented.

Leaving the mandrill to calm down in the empty jeep, we ran in, with our pursuer hot on our heels, to explain to NDinga, as best we could, what had happened while the indignant State Security agent screamed accusations against us. NDinga knew enough of Mark already to realize that when it came to cruelty to animals his anger could be awesome. He took the agent, who towered above him, aside and explained with enormous assurance and authority that the trader had broken the law in full view of the expatriate community, thereby making a mockery of the Congolese wildlife authorities, and that he should back Mark's action, however unconventional. The agent's face fell, deflated, his early pomposity subsiding to mumbled apologies. He beat a hasty retreat.

'Don't think that is the end of the matter,' NDinga warned when we thanked him. 'He has been humiliated and when he gets back to his office his colleagues will wind him up to seek revenge on both of us.'

Three days later we received a police summons. The trader was complaining that we had injured him as we drove off with his mandrill.

We spent the next three days sweating at the police station while Nigel the mandrill, as we named him, settled into the orphanage, unable to believe his luck. The police authorities were unfamiliar with the laws concerning certain protected species of wildlife and they assumed that the plaintiff had rightful cause for complaint.

NDinga prepared our case with his usual attention to detail, arriving promptly at the massive, colonial-style police station with an impressive dossier tucked under his arm. We were grateful to have him there. Our weariness with the daily business of keeping things going felt overwhelming as we sat beneath ceilings which the damp had stripped of paint many years before, on rotten wooden benches half eaten by termites. Frightened faces lined every corridor we were escorted down: rows of offenders awaiting news of their fates. Many of them were Zairois immigrants, rounded up by the police as they traded their goods on the streets near the beach and beaten brutally for their assumed sins. The police insisted that anyone from across the river was either a thief or a prostitute.

For three days NDinga worked like a dramatist while we sat and sweated, grateful for whatever breeze made it into the building. In a fever of excitement, he worked skilfully, extracting information that implicated the trader. By admitting inadvertently that he had eaten Nigel's mother several weeks before – 'during the hunting season' he assured the police officer – the trader drove the final nail into his own coffin.

'There is no hunting season for mandrills,' NDinga pointed out triumphantly, 'they are a protected species. This man is admitting to committing an offence under Congolese law.' The case was immediately closed and we hurried out of the sinister building, heading for a cold beer at the Central Bar where the whole drama had started.

Chapter Nine

Sickness and
Witch Doctors

Max insisted on travelling everywhere with us and this included trips in the jeep. Most of the time he was a good passenger, although occasionally an attack of high spirits would strike him at the wrong moment, like when he decided to leap up behind Mark while he was driving and playfully clasp his hands over Mark's eyes, causing him to swerve violently before managing to prise Max off. On the day that we were stopped by the police and asked to show our papers, however, he was sitting quite quietly on my lap, contentedly watching the world go by.

It was always tricky dealing with the police. They enjoyed exercising their petty powers to inconvenience and unsettle people. This time was no exception as they leafed slowly through our passports and driving licences, searching for possible pretexts to exact a fine or extort a bribe or simply to cause trouble. When they asked for our car papers our hearts sank.

We knew that there was a potential problem here. Although our predecessor at the orphanage had purchased the project jeep with Howletts funds, he had omitted to register it with a private number plate. Instead it bore a state registration number which meant that the state could 'requisition' it at any time on the grounds that it was needed by someone more important than

ourselves for some government event or other. Our hearts sank
even further as the officer's sullen face assumed a look of smug
satisfaction.

'This is a state vehicle,' he declared, 'I am going to seize it.'

Climbing into the back seat he barked directions to the police
station. There was no point arguing. We remained calm and did
as he said. Once there he ordered us out of the vehicle with all
our belongings and refused to consider any of the paperwork
which proved that the jeep had been purchased with private
funds. As Mark and the police officer argued furiously Max
became agitated and started to whoop excitedly, anxious to
defend us against our aggressor but attracting undesirable attention. Worried that Max might get himself requisitioned as well,
I took him off to a quieter part of the station until Mark gave
up arguing and we left for the long walk home.

Our daily lives were now made more difficult without access
to a vehicle. We went to NDinga for help. He wrote to the
police authorities demanding the return of the project vehicle,
pointing out diplomatically that the orphanage was a joint
project between the Congolese government and the British, and
as such a gesture of co-operation might be appreciated. The
police were sufficiently impressed by his letter to put out a
notice to all their officers instructing them to look out for a
green Suzuki jeep belonging to the gorilla project at the Zoo.
Since a number of people had told us that they had seen the
vehicle bombing around town with a high ranking police officer
at the wheel, this appeal had no effect at all and we continued
to trudge on in the heat.

Having watched us struggle to and from town on foot for
several weeks, Madame Leroy casually suggested that we might
use the influence of one of her partners' husbands who was an
ex-government minister and still exerted some power. In town
some days later our jeep hurtled past us, driven by the police

commandant. We leapt into the nearest available taxi and ordered the surprised driver to 'follow that jeep'.

We wound several times round the streets of the city before ending up back at the police station where we intercepted the commandant as he leapt out of the jeep. Mark explained as politely as possible that we were the owners of the vehicle and mentioned the name of Madame Leroy's contact. The commandant's attitude changed and, looking uncomfortable, he handed over the keys. Startled by the ease with which he had given in we approached the jeep cautiously, expecting to find the interior trashed. To our amazement it was spotless, far cleaner than it had ever been while we carted animals around in it. The commandant had obviously taken pride in his newly acquired vehicle.

These sorts of setbacks and harassments were daily events which gradually ground down our resistance. At the same time our health was constantly under attack from malaria and amoebic dysentery. The symptoms of malaria varied in individuals. In some it would creep up insidiously in the form of an apparently inexplicable lethargy which would then erupt into a fever. In others it attacked brutally, with no warning, causing anything from vomiting to headaches, diarrhoea, chills, fever, aching limbs and heartburn. Sometimes all these symptoms would descend at once.

The risk of delaying treatment for the most common and deadly form of malaria endemic in the region, the Falciparum parasite, was grave, and so most of us presumed we had malaria whenever there was any doubt, and took either quinine or Halfen. Malaria caused more deaths in the Congo than Aids.

For several days prior to developing my first malarial fever I felt profoundly tired, dragging the leaden weight of my body around the orphanage and experiencing an overwhelming desire to lie down and sleep. My limbs ached and each breath required an enormous effort. Feeling cold one afternoon, despite the humid heat, I lay down on the bed, unable to move. Wrapped in blankets I fell asleep until awoken some hours later by a terrible nausea. I retched convulsively and when there was nothing left to bring up I started to vomit small particles of fresh blood. My head throbbed, my eyeballs ached, every nerve was alive with a searing pain that threatened to rip my head apart.

Mark injected me with an anti-sickness drug and drove into town for some quinine. I fell back asleep and when I awoke again a few hours later the fever had passed and I felt extraordinarily calm, almost euphoric as I luxuriated in the absence of pain.

From then on I became trapped in a vicious cycle of attacks, becoming feverish and taking to my bed about every two months. As soon as the fever passed I would be hard at work again until exhaustion laid me low once more. There was no opportunity for us to pace ourselves under the demands of the animals. We were constantly exposed to the parasites carried by the gorillas and constantly under emotional as well as physical stress. It was hardly surprising that my body kept failing me. Within the first two years I suffered from nearly all the diseases which afflicted the gorillas, leaving me well equipped to spot their symptoms and to sympathize with their suffering. At times I felt overwhelmed by exhaustion and my mood swung unpredictably between euphoria and despair. I survived on will-power alone.

At night Mark and I would collapse into bed and within minutes sink into a deep sleep, oblivious to everything. One such night, Alphonse banged on our window, shouting something about, 'les mondeles vont brûler' (the whites are going to burn). His panic grew more insistent, his voice louder, dragging me back towards consciousness as I realized that his protestations were not part of my turbulent dreams. Raising myself wearily from the bed I attempted to wake Mark, to no avail. Opening the bedroom door I inhaled a lungful of smoke; the terrible stench of burning rubber hung in the thick air and looking down the long corridor I saw clouds of black smoke. I was awake now. Max, sensing my panic, leapt up at me, clinging onto my naked back, his finger nails tearing at the fragile skin of my chest as he tried to wrap his arms tighter around me. I shouted at Mark who was still sleeping soundly and fought to free myself from Max's painful embrace, making him cling on even harder.

Finally I managed to penetrate Mark's slumber with my frantic screams and we made our way through the smoke with our hands over our faces while Max spluttered noisily on my back.

Alphonse leapt ecstatically up and down as he saw us emerge from the flat, shouting in a confused jumble of French and Lingala. As our heads cleared of sleep we realized what had happened. Every evening we would boil the baby bottles in an effort to keep them reasonably clean. In our exhaustion that night we had forgotten to take them off the cooker when we went to bed. The fumes would take hours to disperse and until they did there was no way we could go back into the flat, so all three of us settled down on the lawn outside and within minutes we were fast asleep under the clear night sky. We'd long since given up the protection of mosquiteo nets, early casualties of sharing a home with gorillas and Max, so sleeping in the open posed no great new threat.

In the morning we ventured back inside, gagging on the smell of charred rubber and gazing in horror at the blackened kitchen which looked more like the inside of a chimney. Outside we could hear Alphonse excitedly reliving the night's events, as he described to Nkodia and Albertine how he had saved our lives, his wildly dramatic reconstruction of the heroic rescue leaving them convulsed with laughter.

We knew we had been lucky with our staff. From the outset we had explained to them that we couldn't work well if we were constantly having to look over our shoulders and lock our possessions away, so anyone found guilty of theft would have to be sacked without discussion. We explained that we were all responsible for the orphanage funds and equipment because it was the success of the project that assured our continued salaries, expatriate and local alike. Joseph and Nkodia had open access to the flat and until now this had not created any problems.

Then one day I realized that money I had been hiding discreetly in one of my cupboards had gone missing. To begin with I thought perhaps it was just my memory which was at fault, but larger and larger sums began to disappear as the weeks passed. Certain now that the money was being stolen, Mark and I sat down with all the staff and explained the situation. Joseph remained silent, his face a blank, while Nkodia seemed angry and embarrassed.

'Whoever has done this has betrayed your trust as well as ours,' we said. We explained privately to Nkodia that until the thief was found even he was, unfortunately, under suspicion. Later that day we saw him and Joseph in heated debate in a far corner of the orphanage. Nkodia shouted as Joseph cowered, but there was nothing we could do without proof.

For the next few days the staff muttered and argued amongst themselves. Eventually they came to us and asked if they could consult a witch doctor, who would solve the mystery by 'traditional means'. We told them to go ahead, unsure what this traditional means might be.

The next day they went together to the local market to find the feticheur, sure that he would reveal the identity of the thief. He told them to take turns to lie face down on a piece of rope. If the rope remained straight the person was innocent, but if it kinked they were guilty. The thief would give himself away as

▷ With a young Mabafi.

▽ Mabafi in her basket.

△ Orphaned gorilla and chimpanzee, held illegally at a Portuguese-owned timber concession in the Southern Congo . . .

◁ . . . and a gorilla skull trophy, or fetiche, in a Northern Congolese village.

▽ A young group at the orphanage, 1990. A newcomer with Titi, Bilinga and Mbinda.

△ Kola's group in the orphanage forest, 1990. From left to right: Kola, Titi, Bilinga and Nzambi.

△ Kola.

▷ A young Nzambi in 1990.

△ Max, the bonobo, with his cat.

◁ Blixa playing in the office

▷ Max, playing on the orphanage slide.

▽ At home with Mabafi.

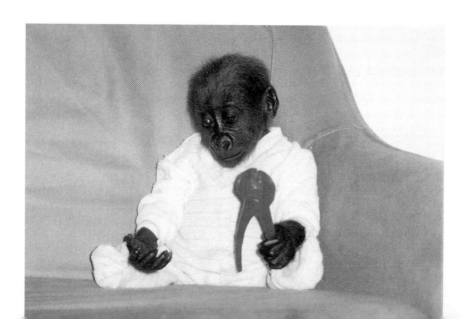

◁ Boko, Catherine and me in the orphanage forest.

▷ Boko, in the orphanage forest, 1991.

▽ Dinga on the slide.

▷ Taking on responsibility.
Kola and his group
(from left to right, Kola,
Boko, Nzambi), under
Albertine's watchful eye.

▽ Mboukou, newly-arrived
in Brazzaville.

△ Boko playing up to a visiting
journalist in the orphanage garden.

▽ An anxious Titi.

he shook with fear. As they took turns to lie on the piece of rope Joseph broke down and confessed. The witch doctor was paid and the staff returned in silence, angry with Joseph and feeling that he deserved to lose his job.

Joseph entered the orphanage, his head bowed in shame. He had lost the respect of his colleagues and, because he had already frittered the money away on ludicrously flamboyant new clothes and alcohol, had no choice but to return to his village. We all felt angry and frustrated that he had let himself down, but we could not give in to these feelings without risking upsetting the delicate balance of discipline and trust which kept the orphanage a happy place. We certainly didn't want to call the police who would happily have beaten Joseph to a pulp if paid and so we asked Nkodia to escort him from the grounds, telling him never to return. We heard, some months later, that on his return home Joseph's wife packed her bags and left, taking the children with her. This news saddened us but we tried to put the unpleasant interlude behind us and move on.

Howletts were surprised to find a witch doctor's fee listed in the weekly expenses.

Chapter Ten

Bereavement and the Arrival of Kola

Early one morning we were woken by a loud knock on the door. Dragging ourselves from bed we opened up to find a scruffy military guard grinning at us on the doorstep. 'I need water,' he announced. 'Give me a cigarette,' he demanded.

Taken aback we stepped outside to discuss the matter and saw thirty machine-gun toting soldiers setting up tents just outside the orphanage garden.

By mid-morning a further two battalions of soldiers had camped out in and around the zoo. Two silent guards sat perched on either gatepost of the main entrance, their guns cocked at some imagined threat on the road approaching the parliament building.

Inside the Houses of Parliament a conference was taking place which would result in the predictable, triumphant affirmation of President Denis Sassou-Ngeusso's leadership of the country. The discovery of oil and the profits that followed had allowed the President several years of relative political and economic stability, but funds were now low and the rumblings of dissent were gathering strength. When the volcano erupted it would affect us all.

Sassou's handsome face, regal and serious, was prominently

displayed on the wall of every government and business office in town. The photo portraits showed him wearing the same standard Marxist green military uniform as the soldiers camped out in the zoo – although his official wife was always dressed in the latest European haute couture, financed by an income from her own charity, Congo Assistance, which very publicly donated cheap wheelchairs to carefully selected handicapped people once a year.

The military stayed with us for ten days, banging on the door at all hours asking for water, cigarettes and beer. To begin with they were amazed by Albertine and Nkodia's easy, affectionate relationship with the gorillas. Their only previous experience of gorillas had come from participating in hunting parties in their home villages or buying the parts of dead gorillas which were sold in the local fetiche market for their medicinal and magical properties. After many days watching us work they were even able to distinguish one gorilla from another, and insisted on calling Rupert 'Denis' after their President. By the end of the week their attitude had visibly changed towards the animals as happened with anyone who had prolonged contact with them.

We exchanged easy, humorous banter with the soldiers and from their sentry posts they would cheerily shout 'Bonjour Monsieur et Madame Gorille', waving as we passed. The Commandant flatteringly offered to become my second husband. When I declined his offer he seemed puzzled, incredulous that I thought one husband or lover was enough, particularly when the second could be Congolese.

One afternoon the soldiers were ordered to smarten up for an inspection as the actual day of the celebrations arrived. Since none of them possessed more than one uniform they spent the evening crouched round small camp fires in nothing but their underpants as their rigorously scrubbed uniforms dried on the surrounding trees.

When they left we found we actually missed their jovial banter. Whenever we came across one of them in town they would make their way over to us and enquire after the gorillas, even coming to our assistance if required.

After years of Marxist paranoia the country was beginning to open up to western influences and other conservation professionals were starting to set up projects in co-operation with Sassou's government. The first of these to find their way to the orphanage was Dr Suehisa Kuroda, an eminent Japanese primatologist, most of whose research had been on bonobos in Zaire. He now headed a team of researchers from Kyoto University, based in a makeshift camp in the vast, swampy Ndoki forest in northern Congo. The team lived on a stock of strictly rationed canned sardines, dried fish and manioc which they had brought up from Brazzaville at the start of their journey. Each day they would trek into the forest in search of the wild gorilla groups who thrived in the dense, flooded forest far from man. But their efforts were for the most part thwarted by the impenetrable vegetation which provided cover from hunters as well as researchers. In their determination to cause as little disturbance as possible to the forest sanctuary they invaded, they lived in conditions that only Japanese stoicism would endure, even sleeping in their wellington boots for months on end.

Dr Kuroda had a handsome, Mongol, warrior-like face at odds with his shy, intense manner. He was surprisingly positive about our gorillas' future and we talked long into the night with him, hungry for the professional knowledge which he could give us.

'We have experienced very few direct encounters with gorillas,' he explained with a shrug. 'Mostly just fleeting glimpses of them. So most of our intended research into their group sizes, feeding and movement patterns through the forest are based on their tracks, dung collection and night nests.'

One member of the team, a Japanese research student, had been named the 'pygmy' by the locals. Being six foot four inches tall, travelling through the low-hanging vegetation was particularly hard, but he remained in the forest interior for a whole year determined to complete his research, not even taking a break in the nearest town, Ouesso. We had met him at the team's headquarters in Brazzaville at the start of his trip, sitting cross-legged on the floor surrounded by stocks of food supplies intended to last him the entire twelve months. When he finally emerged from the forest, he was a little thinner but physically and psychologically intact and even more passionate about the natural world than ever.

J. Michael Fay was an American botanist who had spent most of his adult life in Central Africa. His latest crusade was to have the Ndoki forest declared a national park in order to protect it from the ever hungry timber industry. Although he openly admitted that when he first heard about the orphanage he had been sceptical, he became quickly convinced of its potential as he watched our gorillas' progress in the forest surrounding the orphanage.

The encouragement of experts like these was good for our morale. We felt that our colleagues back at Howletts saw the Congo project as one of Aspinall's gambles that was unlikely to pay off. They were happy to let us get on with our work without interference but funds were frequently late in arriving, forcing us to supplement the budget with personal money or borrow from other expatriates. Often the delays were the fault of the Congolese banking system. Incoming funds would be received by the bank and then lent out to local businessmen – the interest accrued from this money-lending lining the bank directors' pockets – before finally being released to us. After the recent expenditure on the cage and building work we understood Aspinall's reluctance to pour yet more money into such a risky venture. As a result, we were unwilling to ask for the help and facilities which would have enabled us to work more efficiently and with less danger to our own health. We hoped that if we could prove to the Foundation that we were making a success of the project we could then ask for the facilities we desperately needed.

Sid and Rupert were thriving, their health stable and progress rapid. They spent most of their daylight hours in the forest, their confidence growing as they became competent climbers, testing unfamiliar branches to see whether they would support their body weight, aware that dead branches might send them plummeting to the ground, and moving skilfully from tree to tree.

They learned from bitter experience. In his early explorations of the forest Rupert became trapped up a tree. Having transferred from a neighbouring tree, using an overhanging branch as a link, the branch swung back, leaving him stranded and unable to descend the thick tree trunk to ground level. Realizing his mistake he started screaming for help which arrived in the form of Mark with a ladder. Having climbed level with Rupert, Mark spent the next half an hour persuading him to calm down, let go his desperate hold of the trunk and transfer to Mark's back. When he eventually reached the ground Rupert rushed into the undergrowth in search of Sid and finding him, clung tightly to his confused looking friend for comfort.

Sid, with his two years' experience of life in the wild prior to capture, was able to teach us a lot. We watched him tackling termite mounds, smashing them with one blow of his giant fist, grabbing handfuls of termites and cramming them hastily into his mouth in a fever of gluttony, apparently unbothered by the ants that crawled over his face and hands, biting fiercely. He would then flee from the nest, scratching and giggling as he patted his body with flailing hands in a futile attempt to rid himself of the angry termites which had embedded themselves in his thick hair. Intrigued, Rupert soon followed suit.

The weaver ant, which nests in leaves, weaving the ends together into a neat parcel, was a particular favourite and they would swallow both leaves and ants in one delicious mouthful.

Much as we would have liked to spend all day in the forest with the gorillas there were many other things demanding our attention. We had to rely for much of our information on the gorillas' progress on Albertine, who they now happily regarded as a substitute mother. We considered recruiting students to observe and note the gorillas' behaviour in the forest, but decided that too many new people roaming the orphanage would upset timid newly arrived orphans and increase the risk of their contracting human diseases with possibly fatal results. We often made ourselves unpopular by refusing access to visitors or film crews for fear of causing stress and infection to the gorillas. We tried to explain diplomatically why visitors might present a danger to the animals, but our behaviour was still perceived by many as obstructive and rude. We were amazed by the way many people believed they had a right to see the gorillas, as if they existed purely for human entertainment. If they were ultimately to survive in the wild they needed to retain a certain amount of distrust of man.

The latest new arrival was given the name Kola, after the region of South-West Congo in which he was captured. By giving new arrivals names which identified their region of origin we gained an overall picture of the incidence of gorilla hunting throughout the Congo. Kola was a pitiful sight, terrified, flinching at the threat of our approach, his childish, high-pitched screams of panic unsettling the other gorillas and confusing Max, who would rush protectively to his side and fling his arms around Kola in a surge of sympathy for this terrified infant.

We had to work hard to distract Kola in order to get a close look at his wounds. One toe lay limp, obviously painful when he attempted to walk. His hips were rubbed red and raw from the tight cords used by his captor to secure him to a wooden stake. The deep wounds needed regular applications of antibiotic powder to keep them dry and prevent infection. By now we had learnt that it was wise to avoid giving oral antibiotics if possible since they often provoked a vicious cycle of intestinal problems that could prove fatal.

After a few days Kola started to settle, his fits of screaming panic less frequent and intense as he realized no one at the orphanage intended to harm him. He started to give in to our gentle attempts to win him over and sat for short periods on my lap, although the scars of his recent experiences still surfaced every now and then. Just when I imagined he was relaxed enough to respond to gentle play, or tried to shift my position beneath him, he would panic and sink his teeth into my leg with no warning whatsoever. Desperate for comfort, but not yet entirely trusting, these sudden fits of terror seemed to erupt without obvious cause. The sight of a child would send him into a state of impenetrable panic, suggesting that he had been taunted by children in the hunter's village.

To help build his confidence we let him join us on our bed during our afternoon siestas, a time when we were quiet and relaxed ourselves and not distracted by other demands. For the first few afternoons he remained stubbornly withdrawn and uncommunicative, not in the least relaxed, but eventually he started to uncurl his tense little body. Instead of sitting with his back stubbornly to us in a gesture of rejection, he turned to face us, sitting back relaxed and then lying belly down at our feet. At times I would catch his eyelids growing heavy with the effort of being constantly alert and he would finally give in to sleep until we disturbed him by going back to work. On one such afternoon I nudged Mark and pointed at Kola who appeared to be trying to snuggle up to my foot, but he then sank his teeth into my ankle.

We were worried to find that Boha was losing weight. Repeated stool tests offered no explanation and we wondered if his health problems were linked in some way to the umbilical hernia we had noticed on his arrival. As the weeks passed he became increasingly lethargic and disinterested in life. When he fell victim to a severe attack of amoebic dysentery he had few reserves to combat it. The antibiotics which should have cured the dysentery had no effect, simply making him nauseous and reluctant to drink the fluids necessary for his survival.

Christmas came, although celebrations were officially prohibited in this Marxist state, and on Boxing Day he seemed to pick up a little, making some token attempts to play. We felt more hopeful, but early in the morning of New Year's Day we found him lying lifeless in his overnight basket.

I was unprepared for the emptiness, grief and guilt that followed Boha's dying. The death of newly arrived orphans was always sad, but the loss of an individual who had fully occupied my daily existence for so many months was devastating. I tried to pull myself together, telling myself that Mark and the other gorillas needed me, but being with Sid and Rupert seemed to make me even more aware of my loss. They too felt his absence, hooting occasionally for him and searching the flat. In the years to come we would witness the devastating effect that the death of a member of a gorilla group has on the family and suffer with them the fatal, tragic consequences.

As the days passed my grief remained embedded and immovable. I comforted myself with the thought that Mark and I would soon be leaving for a break in England and would hopefully return to Brazzaville to start afresh, the painful memories behind us.

As we entered the plane, its clean, orderly interior contrasting with the chaos, noise and heat of the airport, I shivered. The dry cold air conditioning was a shock after the comforting, humid warmth outside. This tidy, sterile environment was my first feel of Europe and my stomach knotted.

The plane rose steeply and levelled out just below cloud level. As we turned I looked down over the vast expanse of shimmering water that was Stanley Pool and the high-rise buildings of Kinshasa beyond. We cruised over the hilly savannah north of the airport, leaving the shanty-town sprawl of Brazzaville behind, and tears of confusion pricked my eyes.

Chapter Eleven

Strangers in Our
Own Land

In our absence the orphanage was being managed by Steve
Blake, a Howletts keeper in whom Mark had every confidence.
They had worked briefly together with the gorillas in Kent some
years earlier and had developed a close but competitive, macho
relationship. Steve had always made it clear that he was so
desperate to come out to the Congo he would even do it on a
voluntary basis. His chance had now come and he arrived in
Brazzaville full of infectious enthusiasm for the task ahead.

Short, slim and fit, Steve had once trained as a jockey. He had
an impish face and his reputation for black humour preceded
him. Mark and I often laughed at the antics of the gorillas, even
at desperate times, but never as much as when Steve was around.
His 'Pythonesque' sense of humour struck a chord with both
ourselves and the local staff. His humour and self-deprecation,
however, disguised an ambitious nature and seriously passionate
interest in wildlife protection.

Soon after his arrival Steve was sitting outside the flat,
chatting to some visitors with his chair pushed up against the
metal security grille which covered the outer side of the kitchen
window. Sid was playing contentedly above him, climbing the
grille and hanging from it, dangling one leg in front of Steve in

the hope of initiating a game of chase. Suddenly Steve's head was showered in a stream of yellow diarrhoea. His response was unrepeatable as he shot off his chair. I spotted Nkodia trying to suppress a giggle, anxious not to offend his newly arrived boss. He needn't have worried. Steve was thankfully devoid of the usual expatriate sense of self-importance.

Steve's short stature made him an ideal playmate for boisterous young gorillas like Sid, his lower centre of gravity making it hard for them to topple him as they playfully crashed around. Being tall and slim I found that I was often knocked flat on my face as Sid barged past me, grabbing my leg as I fell and triumphantly dragging me around the forest. My evident displeasure and reluctance to play when he used such underhand tactics soon put a stop to this irritating habit, but he would still seize upon unsuspecting strangers in order to test his growing strength.

The gorillas seemed at times to enjoy poking harmless fun at human physical weakness, a habit which sometimes proved dangerous. Forgetting that we had long necks not protected as theirs were by muscular shoulders, they would swing down from overhead branches, crashing into our heads and risking snapping our necks in two. They needed to learn that this was a potentially dangerous game to play with their human companions.

Although I desperately wanted to see England and my family again, even in the harsh cold European winter, I felt anxious about leaving Brazzaville and the gorillas. For months I had kept my head down and my emotions in check. Now that I was about to be confronted by all that had once been familiar I worried how I would react. I feared my brief trip home might upset the delicate emotional equilibrium I had managed to maintain these past months. I was afraid that the inevitable questions I would be asked about life in the Congo would open up a can of worms which I saw little point in disturbing.

As I clambered into a taxi at Heathrow airport the driver

looked back at me with a bemused expression. I realized I had
given him directions in French. As we headed for my sister's
house in Wimbledon I stared out at the clean pavements, their
concrete slabs perfectly aligned, at the neat buildings which
lined the streets and the pedestrians who moved purposefully
with their heads down in the cold air, intent on reaching their
destinations, no time to stop and pass the time of day. I shivered
in my light clothing.

The first thing I noticed back in the warmth of my sister's
house was the carpet and the warm colours, a stark contrast to
the bleak concrete floors and minimal furnishings of the flat we
had left behind in Brazzaville sixteen hours earlier. That night I
delighted in the cool air and the silence of a night devoid of a
constant background buzz of mosquitoes.

But the feeling of alienation did not pass. I could not let go
and share my recent experiences with my family. I remained
impossibly and stubbornly uncommunicative. I could not begin
to explain how life had been in Brazzaville for the past year.
Despite my protestations of enthusiasm for our unusual lifestyle,
it must have been obvious from the gaunt contours of my face
and recent weight loss that life was far from easy.

I wandered around the local supermarket entranced and
indecisive at the vast choice of food on offer. Having loaded my
trolley and made my way to the check-out I was amazed by how
low the bill was compared to the exorbitant supermarket prices
in Brazzaville. Away from our monotonous diet and the constant
sensation of nausea from the intense heat and anti-malarial drugs,
we both started to put on weight.

I often attempted to conjure up an image of the gorillas in
my mind, but nothing would appear. Life in England was so
different that I found it impossible to imagine our life in
Brazzaville. Back in the Congo I had the same difficulty imagining England.

The second week of our stay Mark retired to bed complaining of exhaustion. He was soon feverish and shivering, pulling the blankets up round his neck with trembling hands and complaining of feeling frozen despite the central heating. Realizing that it was malaria he agreed to start a course of the Halfen tablets we had packed for the trip home. Paracetamol usually brought the fever down but this time it seemed to have no effect. As the clock ticked and he continued to sweat and shake I decided to call a doctor.

The local GP, excited to come across his first case of malaria in Wimbledon, called an ambulance. Mark was rushed to St George's Hospital in Tooting where they whisked him off to an isolation room in the infectious diseases ward. The nursing staff wore gloves, gowns and masks as they performed their duties, fearful of catching some horrible ape disease, and left in haste. Tests confirmed Falciparum malaria and they started Mark on quinine, discharging him a couple of days later still exhausted and suffering the unpleasant side-effects of the treatment. For the next week he remained house-bound, feeling weak, nauseated and with a constant ringing in his ears which left him partially deaf. The fever returned every evening but with less force each time, and eventually he felt well enough to enjoy our last few days in England.

He phoned Howletts to ask for an extra week's leave, explaining that he had been ill with malaria and assuring them that Steve had everything in hand in Brazzaville, but, unimpressed, the management insisted that we return to the orphanage on the arranged date. Mark was angry but too tired to argue, so we flew back as planned, not feeling as if we had had much of a break at all.

*

Arriving back in Brazzaville we decided to celebrate Steve's departure with a visit to the Ramdam, one of the town's night spots. The club was small, airless and hot, full of seedy, middle-aged Frenchmen whose wives had returned home for the school holidays, and pert young Congolese prostitutes. As the men swaggered drunkenly around the dance floor, their beer bellies jiggling grotesquely, the predatory young girls watched, trying to spot a likely client. Most were in their early teens but dressed to accentuate their precociously womanly shapes. They would dance with one another, their fierce features accentuated by brilliant slashes of fuchsia lipstick and electric blue eye shadow, swaying and undulating under the throbbing stroboscopic lights, rubbing their bodies erotically against one another and glancing slyly in the direction of men at the bar to gauge their reaction. Some young men, driven to these clubs by boredom and loneliness, would inevitably fall victim to temptation, but the dangers were great. Many of the girls carried a 'cadeau empoisonné'. They were HIV positive.

The girls were hostile towards white women like myself invading their territory. They would push past me to brazenly make a pass at Mark. At regular intervals fights would break out amongst them, particularly on leaner nights when competition for business was intense. Wigs would fly and the dancers would move back to watch the floor show. Eventually someone would pull the protagonists apart and they would retreat to opposite ends of the dance floor, glowering at one another, spitting in impotent rage and itching to lunge back into the fray.

The expatriate community was small and close-knit in the worst sense. A web of jealousies, fed by boredom, resulted in some of the most malicious gossip imaginable. Everyone felt it their business to judge everything that everyone else did. Many of them were people who had fled failed marriages or failed businesses back home and they vented their bitterness on the Congolese and on any new arrivals. We avoided trouble by keeping ourselves very much to ourselves.

After a night at the Ramdam Club most people staggered home and fell comatose into bed. Mark and I, however, would return to the flat in the early hours of the morning to be met by a wide-awake and excitable Max who assumed it was time to get up when all we wanted to do was collapse into bed for a few hours before the busy morning routine of nappy-changing, bottles and the attentions of young gorillas fully refreshed by a good night's sleep. By the time we had appeased Max and calmed him down we would be stone cold sober and dreading the arrival of six o'clock. England seemed a long way away. It was back to business as usual.

Steve had done well with Kola, who was now more settled and confident. However, we still could not leave Kola with Albertine as he remained stubbornly fearful of the Congolese. We knew we were going to have to force him at some stage to overcome this fear, however cruel it might seem. He needed to find out that Albertine would always be as gentle and trust-worthy as ourselves. As Kola trusted Max implicitly we felt he might tolerate Albertine's company if Max was around. Initially wary of Albertine he eventually realized she wouldn't harm him. An important relationship that would ground him in future difficult times began.

Max knew exactly how and when to provide the necessary reassurance Kola required. He would also at times deliberately exploit this, withholding his support and sitting back to watch as Kola panicked, giving himself the opportunity to then come to the rescue and dramatically fling his arms around him. Later, when more new orphans arrived and the numbers of Kola's group swelled, Max took advantage of the slower-witted gorillas to play one character off against another, causing them to fight amongst themselves for his attentions and affections.

Having secured Kola's trust, Albertine led him and Max further afield to explore the forest, giving Mark and I some welcome breathing space from Max. Albertine was already showing a rare skill in her observations and ability to anticipate the needs of her charges. She thrived on her responsibilities and took great pride in the animals' achievements.

When Bilinga, a one-year-old female gorilla, arrived, she provided the perfect partner for Kola. She had a placid, playful nature that belied an iron will and a fearsome temper. When Bilinga was annoyed, no one stood in her way. But most of the time she was easy-going, relaxing company, something Kola needed. Max's manipulative behaviour, the result of boredom with his gorilla playmates, had begun to prove confusing for Kola. As Bilinga and Kola became acquainted, Max felt pushed out. Kola did his best to perform a delicate social juggling act, attempting to fulfil his loyalties to Max as well as Bilinga. This early development of complex social skills would serve him well. As more new orphans arrived and joined the group, he would be called on as leader to deal with delicate social conflicts that arose in the hierarchy of the group in times of stress. His skills would win the unwavering loyalty and confidence of his group members. We watched his development with surprise and admiration.

Chapter Twelve

A Growing Family

It was becoming obvious that with six demanding ape infants to care for, an increasing amount of tedious paperwork to get through and continuing construction work to oversee, we needed to recruit more local staff. We had been extraordinarily lucky with Albertine and finding anyone to match her skills was not going to be easy.

Catherine Missilou's father had worked for years in Brazzaville Zoo and had asked us on numerous occasions to consider employing his daughter, assuring us that she was willing and well educated. To his delight we finally asked him to bring her along to the orphanage for an informal interview. We were immediately impressed by Catherine's relaxed, easy manner and intelligence. We offered her a job on the spot. After a few days of anxious rough-play with the gorillas she settled into her work, showing a particular interest in the nursing and medical side. She learnt quickly and I soon grew to trust her judgement. Her quick intelligence complemented Albertine's more intuitive skills and they made a good team, relieving us of a great deal of work and worry.

With the cage fully operational, tried and tested by Sid and Rupert, we were now able to transfer five-year-old Magne to the orphanage from his tiny cage in Yvette's back garden. Jean Bafinga, a young man employed by Madame Leroy since the arrival of Djala some six years before, had worked with Magne since his arrival and developed a close relationship with him. A broodingly handsome youth who occasionally used his charms with great effect, Jean approached us and asked for a job, informing us in no uncertain terms that if we didn't agree to employ him his life would be over. All he wanted was to work with the gorillas. He seemed an obvious choice but we were wary of employing a member of Madame Leroy's long-term staff for fear that they would feel their loyalties split. Jean was aware of the conflicts between us but had wisely kept a low profile and not taken sides. He owed Madame Leroy a great deal for giving him a job in the first place. To her credit she agreed to let him come to us with Magne.

Jean came from a poor family and was, much to his embarrassment, illiterate. However, his skills, particularly with the older gorillas, more than made up for his lack of formal education. The only potential problem with his work was an overly disciplinarian, controlling attitude which might end up with the gorillas putting him firmly in his place once full grown. Although some discipline was necessary at times, a successful relationship with the gorillas was more enduring when based on a mutual healthy respect. Achieving this balance was something that Mark was particularly skilled at: he seemed to have an intuitive understanding of the gorillas.

Jean was a complex character, whose displays of machismo hid a sensitive nature and surprising vulnerability. When Madame Leroy's first gorilla orphan, Djala, had travelled to Howletts Zoo from Brazzaville, Jean had accompanied him. He therefore had a little more insight into our lives back home than the other staff. He had, however, hated the bitter cold of our winter and had nothing positive to say about England. Although capable of dedicated hard work, at times he suffered attacks of deep depression when he would sit for hours in the cage with his head in his hands, staring into space, and no amount of encouragement from ourselves or the gorillas could lift his spirits.

At times we would lose patience with these paralysing moods which affected the people and the animals around him, but when he was 'up' his support and enthusiasm more than made up for the bad days.

The last to join the gorilla team was Paul MBongo, a conservative man who took his role of family man very seriously. At times he could indulge in irritating, pompous, self-righteous behaviour which wound up the other staff, but mostly he worked well, providing the logistical help we needed. He was scrupulously honest and we were happy to entrust him with orphanage funds. He took over the driving to and from town to buy food supplies for the gorillas. Our days were becoming increasingly frantic and none of the other staff could drive. Nkodia had protested that he was sure he could learn, but having seen the way he handled the strimmer we had our doubts. Paul had been working nights at a local bakery in his previous job and had valuable contacts in the markets who could supply cheap goods to the orphanage and cut our running costs.

As expatriate staff came and went over the years, Albertine, Catherine, Jean, Paul and Nkodia would provide the continuity which the gorillas desperately needed.

Yvette insisted on accompanying Magne to settle him into his new cage. Having given him a small dose of Valium, we crated Magne up and set off for the orphanage. Once the crate was safely inside the cage we opened the door and he emerged timidly to explore his new environment. His caution was soon swept aside in a wave of excitement as he thundered enthusiastically about his new home, swinging from the ropes, hurling around the old car tyres we had put in the cage for his amusement, barging past Madame Leroy and knocking her flat into the mud.

Satisfied that Magne was suffering no apparent trauma over the move she decided it was time to leave and sidled towards the door, at which moment Magne realized her intentions and focused his attentions on preventing her from leaving. At first he tried to coax her to stay, pulling her back with long gentle arms, but impatience and insecurity soon took over and his efforts became more forceful. At this point Jean came to the rescue, entered the cage and distracted Magne, allowing Madame Leroy to make a hasty exit, her thin cotton dress shredded, her hair a matted mess and her glasses snapped in two. We soon discovered that trying to get out of the cage after a play session with Magne would always trigger this sort of panic.

Sid and Rupert took enormous pleasure in strutting stiff-legged around their half of the cage, safe in the knowledge that they were physically separated from their much larger and more powerful new neighbour by a very solid steel grille partition. They took turns in assuming the dominant gorilla stance, feet and hands planted wide apart, arms and legs held rigid, their lips pulled in tight and pursed, a menacing sight. They would remain frozen in this state for a few seconds, then abruptly break their stance to charge towards the steel partition, bracing themselves just seconds before the final boom of impact with the steel dividing partition. Magne responded in exactly the same excited fashion.

After a few days of this display, which was completely natural for a gorilla when confronted with a potentially threatening new situation, they settled down to less frenzied behaviour, even touching one another through the thick steel bars and grunting their friendly intentions. At this point we cranked up the partition to see what would happen and waited outside the cage, ready to intervene if necessary.

Magne advanced first. Curiosity getting the better of his anxiety, he approached Sid and Rupert who stood nervously side by side presenting a united front. They then displayed, strutting at a distance from one another, the only contact between them made as they brushed flanks whilst barging past each other. Expecting this we waited for the displays to subside, but Magne failed to realize that his unrestrained superior strength and size was frightening the smaller gorillas whom he hoped to befriend. Bewildered by their frightened and rejecting response to his advances, Magne's excitement turned sour and his clumsy attempt at play caused Rupert to scream with terror, bringing an equally frightened Sid thundering to the rescue. Together they bit and coughed angrily at Magne, screaming, their lips pulled back in a grimace of fear, forcing Magne back to his side of the cage where he sat, breathless with exertion, and stared menacingly at them.

The floor of the cage was now sprayed with the liquid diarrhoea of panic and we pulled the steel dividing partition down to separate them again. We tried again over the next few days, but it became obvious that Magne's years of social isolation at Yvette's house had left him with a considerable social handicap. It looked as if it was going to be impossible to run him with the other gorillas, certainly not in the forest. The one time he did escape his cage, when Jean had failed to check the locks adequately, he rushed out, grabbed the staff's clothes from the washing line nearby and rushed back into the cage, to be found some time later running around excitedly with the legs of Jean's trousers on his huge arms, the seat ripped apart. It was beginning to look as if his only hope lay in an exchange with a young zoo-born gorilla. In a traditional captive zoo setting he would be afforded the time he needed to achieve successful integration into a gorilla group whose future did not depend on learning the skills of the wild. The political complications of arranging an exchange, however ethical, made it an unlikely prospect.

Boko was the youngest orphan we had confiscated to date. Barely three weeks old, she was hairless, toothless and hardly possessed the strength in her tiny hands and feet to grasp onto us. She happily fed on human milk formula, choking in her haste and burping up a great deal of air as she struggled with the artificial rubber nipple almost twice the size of her mouth. She suffered none of the psychological problems of older new arrivals, but she still required constant attention, remaining physically attached to either Mark or myself except for brief periods when she slept soundly, her pink lips moulded around her tiny thumb. Thumb-sucking, it seemed, was not an exclusively human habit.

For the first few nights she slept in our bed, her little black head nestled on the pillow between us, but she woke regularly throughout the night, and would nod her head gently against my shoulder to wake me, grizzling softly, and when I failed to respond screaming loudly in my ear. As she was very particular about the precise temperature of her milk feed I would then have to make my way to the kitchen and wait patiently for the milk to reach exactly the required temperature before she would drink thirstily, dribbling milk over both of us.

After a couple of exhausting nights we decided this routine was not compatible with hard work during the day. We tried wrapping her in a blanket in a wicker basket which we placed by the bed, purchasing, at great expense, a bottle-warmer to spare us the trips to the kitchen. Initially she grizzled, unhappy to be physically detached from us, but she soon came to regard the basket as a secure place and would fall asleep almost immediately.

By the time she was five months old she was crawling and eager to catch up with the other gorillas, particularly Kola and Bilinga. Albertine was delighted with this tiny baby who reinforced her status as matriarch of the growing group of gorillas. It seemed completely natural to the animals that Albertine should now have a small baby in her care. Although there were occasional outbursts of sibling jealousy, Kola surprised us by assuming a precociously paternal role, often hoisting Boko onto his back and strutting proudly round the garden, or sitting with one long arm wrapped protectively around her. Boko marvelled at her newly discovered skills of co-ordination and would often place her tiny hands together and clap in sheer delight.

As the size of the group increased Kola and Bilinga assumed a parental role, allowing the youngest members of their group to sleep next to them, ensuring that they had their fair share of food and coming to their rescue when other older and stronger group members tried to take advantage of them.

A number of new gorillas arrived over the next few months. Nzambi was unusually dark-haired, his long, flat-featured face almost black. When he grimaced he revealed a couple of extraordinarily long, pointed canine teeth. Although he made good general progress, wilful tantrums continued to be a problem that resulted in regular beatings by other more mature, sedate members of the group, irritated by his undignified behaviour and ear-splitting screams.

By the time Dinga arrived the group was spending all daylight hours in the forest, only returning to the cage at night. Dinga arrived in the boot of a taxi, his hands and feet tightly tethered, but this self-assured little gorilla was soon strutting with typical gorilla feigned bravado round the orphanage garden. He made rapid progress, was devoted to Kola and took his role of foot soldier in the group very seriously.

Four days later, Titi was found in Brazzaville in the boot of another taxi. His head was crowned by a striking cap of red hair, his defiant expression one of utter disdain, his body pitifully emaciated. Possessed of enormous hands and feet he was clumsy and at times ridiculous as he strutted stiffly in threat display to protect his new-found gorilla family from the approach of any of the humans he despised.

Kola's group now consisted of four males and two females. After initial 'testing' periods, they each established their own roles within the group. Kola and Bilinga presided over the group protectively as parents, Dinga played the role of foot soldier, Titi the thug, Nzambi the charmless eccentric and occasional whipping-boy, and Boko the much-loved and indulged baby. Relationships and tensions between the males of the group were in a state of constant flux as they jostled for position. Despite Kola's exceptional skills as a leader there were times when the constant vigilance required of him to maintain the group's stability would become too much and we were reminded of the fragility of his recently found confidence. We needed to be constantly alert to every nuance of social jostling that went on in the group and occasionally intervene when it became obvious that it was too much for Kola who was, after all, still only a child himself.

At certain times of the year, usually following a heavy rainstorm, clouds of winged termites would appear from holes in the ground. Regarded as a delicacy by local people and apes alike their appearance caused great excitement. Early one morning we looked out of the kitchen window to see the gorillas gathered around Max as he leapt up at a fluttering mass of flying termites on the lawn, grabbing as many of the delicacies as possible and stuffing them into his mouth. Prompted by Max's enthusiasm the gorillas followed suit in their own clumsy manner, hotly pursued by Nigel the mandrill, his newly confiscated friend Vladimir and the orphanage staff, all anxious to claim their share.

Max, perfectly illustrating the bonobo's superior intelligence, then ran off to fetch an empty milk pot, so that he could catch more insects and save them for later. The gorillas watched him for a moment, puzzled, then went back to hurling themselves around after the escaping termites.

Chapter Thirteen

Emergency Evacuation

As we neared the end of 1990, the problem of finding a long-term wild home for our charges began to weigh increasingly heavily on our minds. Mark and I took advantage of a brief lull in our workload to drive the jeep as far northwards as we could get within a day, in the vague hope of reaching the Lefini Reserve.

Composed of a mosaic of lush riverine gallery forests and grassland, this area had been declared a reserve by the French colonial powers in 1951. Its proximity to Brazzaville, however, with relatively easy access via the North Road, had ensured heavy hunting pressure from the French and Congolese alike. As a result, it now housed very little wildlife and the animals and birds that had survived were extremely timid.

On paper it seemed to offer some potential as a site for the reintroduction of our orphanage-reared gorillas. Leaving behind the noise and dust of the tin-roofed suburbs, we felt a palpable relief as we headed towards the rolling green hills that stretched away to the horizon.

After three hours of continuous driving, on a road which fell away to nothing every now and then with no warning, we stopped to rest, our bruised bodies sore from the constant jolting of the jeep as it bounced in and out of the pot-holes.

Stepping away from the road we were soon enveloped by dense scrub forest, the home of hundreds of orb-web spiders who wove their delicate threads amongst the leaves and vines whose twisted tendrils knotted the trees together, sucking the life from them.

I struggled to find my way through the matted undergrowth, panic rising inside me as my feet became entangled and the over-hanging tendrils smothered my face. We finally emerged onto open grassland, finding ourselves at the top of a steep sandstone cliff. A vast valley stretched below us, its slopes clad in lush green, its base a patchwork of grassland and forest. A river meandered lazily across its broad base, its surface shimmering, throwing back the glare of the midday sun. We stood and stared at the vista in silence.

'This must be the southern border of the Lefini Reserve,' Mark said, breaking the silence. 'It used to be a favourite hunting preserve of the French. It's now all but empty. The last sighting of a gorilla in this area was in the 1950s, a solitary silver back who must have wandered into the area in search of food or females. Nothing since.'

We fell silent and reflective again, then both spoke at once. 'This is perfect!'

The valley was devoid of human settlements, the forests below apparently suitable for gorillas. If they proved sufficiently rich in potential food, our gorillas would be able to migrate freely within these forests in search of seasonal fruits and vegetation, their movements limited only by the natural boundaries of the sheer cliffs and the river. In fact, their presence would enrich the forests, contributing to the dispersal of basic plant species as they roamed, foraging and sowing seeds in their dung. The absence of a resident wild ape population in the area avoided any risk that our gorillas, having been in close contact with human diseases easily transmissible to apes, might endanger their survival. The local Bateke people would, hopefully, have broken with the tradition of hunting apes. With the employment opportunities such a project could offer, we hoped to win over the local people and enthuse them with our eventual aim of starting a gorilla tourism programme in the Lefini. The reintroduced gorillas would already be habituated to man and already vaccinated against potentially fatal diseases carried by human visitors, a problem of some significance for the mountain gorilla tourism programmes in Rwanda and Zaire. Our minds whirred with the possibilities ahead, of a day when the gorilla would become a national flagship species, a prized possession.

When we joined the project, the prevailing idea had been to house the gorillas on an island somewhere in the Congo, but we now advised that this solution would result in overcrowding, food shortages and the destruction of a delicate island ecosystem not designed to cope with a population of apes. The beauty of the Lefini lay in its sprawling, dense forests, which covered an area large enough to support several generations of orphanage-reared gorillas. Territory and an adequate food supply would not be a problem.

It seemed ideal, but detailed botanical studies of the forests and socio-economic studies of the surrounding villages would need to be completed before we could be sure that this dream could become a reality. As we bumped our way back to Brazzaville, we felt optimistic, convinced that we had glimpsed a realistic future home for our gorillas. We promised ourselves that we would speak to NDinga, the wildlife director, as soon as possible.

Meanwhile, back in the present, matters were escalating out of control as a steady stream of new orphans arrived on our doorstep. One of these new arrivals was a particular challenge. Confiscated in Pointe Noire, Bimba arrived in Brazzaville a couple of days later with a letter from Aliette Jamart that detailed her exasperation with this obtuse little gorilla, who had refused all attempts to befriend her. She hoped, she said, that we would have greater success than she had.

We headed for the airport to pick Bimba up. The internal flight from Pointe Noire arrived and we waited, hoping to see someone disembark with a baby gorilla in tow. When the plane had emptied we made our way over to the baggage collection depot and asked a surly woman official whether she knew anything about a gorilla on the flight. At first she looked nonplussed.

'A gorilla?' She spat the words at us.

'Yes, a baby gorilla,' we confirmed.

'Ah!' she exclaimed, relieved to have the answer. 'It'll be in the refrigeration compartment of the plane.'

At this point we gave up and, having again searched the baggage depot, we made our way back to the orphanage. In the confusion, it turned out that Madame Jamart's friend had made her own way to the orphanage and dropped the gorilla off.

Bimba's stubborn resistance to our gentle efforts to approach her reminded us of Titi. Crowned by the same defiant halo of amber-red hair, she was minute, with doll-like hands and feet. This fragile appearance belied a determination that soon became apparent. Her curiously flat little features were set in an expression of arrogant disdain as she watched our efforts to befriend her. She feigned disinterest, only glancing anxiously up at us when she thought we were distracted. As we moved closer she assumed a stiff-legged display posture and emitted a series of distinct, stuttering coughs, a clear warning to us to keep our distance. When she pulled her lips back in a nervous threat grimace, we were surprised to see that her milk teeth were already stained black with tannin, a sure sign that she had been consuming a solid diet in the wild prior to her capture, although we guessed she was only about eight months old.

As the days passed and her resistance remained as determined as ever, we started to despair of ever breaking down her defences to the point where she would actually discover that we intended her no harm. We were spared the necessity of attempting to bottle feed her as she was quite happy to drink from a bowl, dipping one hand in and raising it slowly to her mouth to suck the moisture from the hair on the back of her hand in typical wild gorilla fashion. She hoarded any food she was given, guarding it fiercely until we were out of sight and she could consume it away from prying eyes.

In desperation, we decided to see whether the Congolese staff would have any greater success with her. Albertine volunteered her services. Ignoring Bimba's fierce attempts to repel her, she picked her up and plonked her unceremoniously down on her generous lap, giving her a gentle, but stern, warning slap when she turned her head, mouth wide open, with the intention of sinking her sharp little teeth into Albertine's naked, fleshy arm. Miraculously, this no-nonsense strategy worked and, after a tricky few days during which they tussled to establish a power base and mutual trust, Bimba and Albertine became inseparable. Albertine was soon seen going about her work in the kitchen, preparing the early morning milk drinks, with Bimba snuggled contentedly against her large bosom. Bimba would steal the odd glance at us, a smug expression on her face, from her position of safety as Albertine walked to and fro past the office. This arrangement proved perfect apart from on Albertine's days off, when we took turns to grapple with Bimba's insecure panics and often received vicious wounds for our efforts.

The heavy demands of our ever-increasing family of gorillas had started to affect our personal relationship and our health badly. Increasingly tired, both mentally and physically, Mark and I were left with little time or energy at the end of the day for the personal intimacies so important to any relationship. We vented our frustrations by lashing out at one another.

My health problems seemed more firmly embedded and chronic than Mark's less frequent but no less acute attacks of ill health. Every couple of weeks I would be driven to my bed by either malaria or amoebic dysentery. Each time I would be forced prematurely back to work by the insistent demands of the animals until the next illness struck. Physical stress was exacerbated by my feelings of conflicting loyalty to the animals and to my own deteriorating health. At times I could barely suppress irrational feelings of intense, impotent anger towards the gorillas for having reduced me to a physical wreck, but I ploughed on, most of the time sufficiently buoyed up by the knowledge that at least our work was proving successful.

As the end of the year approached, our stretched facilities and energies seemed overwhelmed. We had no space left to accommodate these new and demanding infants who all required intensive care. We were forced to house them in the flat and before long we were living in a chaotic disease trap, dangerous to both animals and humans alike.

One morning I awoke with an unfamiliar, stabbing pain in my chest. I had been worried for some time about the possible effect on my liver of all the toxic drugs I had taken recently to cure my frequent attacks of malaria and amoebic dysentery. I struggled into my clothes and got through the morning's work. Unwilling to take anything for the pain for fear of further aggravating my liver I worked on until, by lunchtime, it was excruciating. I asked Paul to drive me into town to see the doctor responsible for the French overseas volunteers.

Every bounce and swerve of the jeep made me wince. By the time I reached the doctor's surgery I was in agony. As he tried to examine my rigid abdomen I practically leapt off the couch. Panicked now, he called in a colleague and they muttered urgently together in the adjacent office.

'We think,' they told me at last, 'that you have an amoebic liver abscess. It could be life threatening, but there is no possibility here in Brazzaville of doing the tests you need. You should leave for Europe this evening.'

Back at the orphanage I told Mark the bad news. He paled with shock and immediately launched into a furious rant inspired by frustration, guilt and the dilemma of his conflicting loyalties. He would have to accompany me back home as the airline would refuse to take someone in my state of health on the plane alone. I needed him desperately but felt guilty that the orphanage would be left unsupervised as a result. I was profoundly tired with it all.

We called the staff into the flat and explained the situation. Albertine and Catherine agreed to move in during our absence to do the night feeds for the babies. We did not trust Max in the flat without our constant supervision, fearing he would injure himself or destroy our last few possessions.

'He'll have to start sleeping with Sid and Rupert in the cage,' Mark announced decisively. 'Paul can keep supplies coming in to the orphanage, but he'll need access to cash.'

We knew two British diamond dealers in town, Willy and Brett, who might be able to help, but our telephone, which had taken seven months to arrive, was already out of order, so Paul had to go back into town to find them and bring them back to the orphanage. We put our request to them, promising to reimburse them as soon as we returned, and Willy started to mumble something about regulations regarding money lending.

'Don't be so officious!' Brett snapped. 'Of course we'll help.'

Now charmed by the idea of using diamond money to feed a family of apes, Willy gave in. We breathed a sigh of relief and thanked them both profusely. The British Ambassador, Peter Chandley, and his American wife, Jane, agreed to drive us to the airport. Their recent arrival in Brazzaville had brought valuable moral support to our flagging spirits. Reassuringly normal, generous and refreshingly enthusiastic about the Congo, this couple were familiar figures at the zoo, visiting twice a week without fail to make their own determined effort to feed the animals and improve the quality of their miserable lives.

Their residence, which they had made clear was open to us at any time, had been the scene of a bizarre event the previous week. We had been invited to an evening of Scottish dancing with the visiting celebrity, David Steel, (the ex-leader of the Liberal Party), who had come to Brazzaville to investigate the possibility of using the road to Pointe Noire for a car rally. That evening we left the chaos of the orphanage and made our way to the party. Some time later I found myself attempting to perform a Scottish reel with David, feeling completely dislocated from reality. During the course of the evening we had to inform him that, regrettably, the road to Pointe Noire was completely impassable.

The high spirits of that evening seemed far away as the Chandleys arrived at the orphanage in their Range Rover. As we prepared to leave, night fell. Darkness cloaked the orphanage and warm drops of rain fell from the black sky as Mark coaxed a confused Max into the gorilla cage. Initially reluctant, Max soon forgot his doubts and curiosity took over, much to the dismay of Sid and Rupert who had already prepared their night nests and started to wind down ready for a peaceful night's sleep. Unimpressed by Max's excitable behaviour, Sid looked back at us as if to say, 'why?' and coughed irritably at Max, warning him that he was not in the mood for high spirits.

Rupert, the more tolerant of the two, realizing that protest would have little effect on Max's feverish activities, invited him to share his night nest. We walked away to the sound of his low grunts of pleasure and Max's louder squeals of delight.

Rupert's patience was not to last long, however. As we climbed into the car a few minutes later we heard him making it clear to Max that he now wanted some sleep. Max, affronted by this personal rejection, started to scream loudly and hurl himself around the floor in a tantrum. In bonobo circles such a tantrum would have elicited a 'making up' response (entailing a great deal of hugging, squeaking and genital rubbing), but the gorillas despised such undignified, noisy exhibitions of emotion and distanced themselves from him even further. As we drove away towards the airport Max's screams reverberated in the still night air, haunting me in the days to follow.

The airport was its usual seething chaos. Dramatic family reunions and farewells took place against the background of vociferous disputes between airline officials and passengers about luggage restrictions. Tempers were further frayed by the cloying heat of the small, airless building. Teenage boys pursued passengers as they emerged from the baggage collection depot, hoping to earn a few tips for heaving overloaded suitcases and boxes to waiting cars, while others loitered around the exit, lazy and glowering, demanding money.

The pain and heat combined to make bile rise in my throat as we waited for our tickets to be issued so we could check in. I searched desperately for a seat, my head spinning and my legs threatening to buckle beneath me. Finding one at last I sank down thankfully, cradling my throbbing head in my hands and counting the seconds until boarding was announced and I could leave the infernal place.

Inside the plane we were shown to cramped seats at the rear. The extreme temperature change caused by the dry air conditioning sent me into spasms of involuntary shivering.

As the plane lifted steeply from the tarmac Mark fell into a deep, exhausted sleep. I remained sitting bolt upright for the next nine hours, with tears coursing down my hot cheeks, staring at my watch and trying to will time forward. The air hostesses paraded back and forth, smiling at the other passengers and studiously avoiding my distress.

The following morning at Charles de Gaulle airport in Paris, Mark set off to find a wheelchair for me. We made our way to the transfer desk only to be told by a sullen official that the Paris air-traffic controllers were on strike. We would not be able to continue our journey on to London and the hospital that was expecting me. We knew no one in Paris, so set off to search the airport for medical assistance.

After circling the deserted arrivals lounge several times we spotted a door at the back bearing the sign 'Medical Office'. Finding a bored-looking young doctor behind the door, I pushed my precious note from the doctor in Brazzaville into his hand. 'Emergency air evacuation – suspected amoebic liver abscess' it read, but he stared blankly at it, unimpressed, before looking up at me, being several inches shorter.

'I'm not sending you to any hospital until I have examined you myself and made my own diagnosis,' he declared. I was angry but too tired to argue. Sticking a thermometer into my mouth he ordered me to lie on the couch. Every movement was now excruciating. I sat down, but he insisted I lie, saying that it would be impossible to examine me unless I did as he said. I made a token attempt but immediately curled up again, con-vulsed with pain, explaining politely that I couldn't do as he wished. Stamping his feet, growing red in the face, he refused to co-operate any further and stormed out of the room, slamming the door. So much for European civilization, I thought let alone liberty, equality and fraternity.

A nurse appeared at the door. She apologized profusely for her colleague's behaviour and wheeled me out to a taxi which she directed to the nearby Bichat hospital. The cold dry winter air bit through my flimsy clothing as we left the car for the building. We asked at reception for the casualty department. The nurse behind the desk, full of motherly concern, assumed, as I gripped my painful abdomen, bent double with pain, that I was in labour and sent us off towards the maternity unit.

But we had struck lucky. The infectious diseases unit of this hospital was internationally renowned. It took a wait of several hours before I was seen by a doctor and admitted to a ward where I finally slept, only waking each time a new set of doctors came to take blood or ask questions about my strange occupation in the Congo. I could almost see their minds whirring with the vicarious thrill of danger as they contemplated the multitude of deadly diseases I had probably come into contact with. Satisfied that I was now in safe hands, Mark left to find himself a nearby hotel room.

For ten days they continued their tests and although they disproved the amoebic liver abscess theory, they couldn't come up with any firm diagnosis in its place. They postulated that my poor state of health was probably due to our unhealthy living conditions in Brazzaville, suggesting that if we were to continue our work with the gorillas we should insist on conditions that at least minimized the unavoidable risks. Relieved that they were not entirely negative about the situation, and determined to take their advice, we travelled on to London.

Back in England, Mark made plans to return to Brazzaville, this time with Steve Blake as a permanent member of the orphanage team. It was not easy to say goodbye to him just a few days before Christmas, knowing that I wouldn't see him again until I had recovered the strength and courage to return to the Congo.

John Aspinall insisted that I see a Harley Street specialist who could assess my health and my suitability to return to

Brazzaville. I looked up at the grand old buildings of London's West End, such a stark contrast to the streets of Brazzaville, and wrapped a heavy winter coat tightly round my thin body as I went in search of the right front door.

As the words 'gorillas' and 'Central Africa' left my lips, the spectre of 'Aids' loomed menacingly between myself and the elderly doctor who sat peering at me, half hidden behind his heavy oak desk. As I stepped off the weighing scales he announced that I should have an HIV test.

'I've always been thin,' I protested feebly. 'It's not surprising that I've lost a bit more weight, working so hard in that climate.'

The optimism the French doctors had inspired drained away and I felt anger rise inside me. He took more blood and asked me to return the next day for the results. I left the building wondering what had happened to Aids tests counselling. Perhaps the doctor thought that anyone foolish enough to undertake working with apes in Central Africa did not merit counselling. That night I slept fitfully, disturbed by macabre dreams, waking the next morning feeling emotionally drained.

Later that afternoon I was back in the same dark, depressing room. It was the end of the day's work and the doctor was filing his reports. 'Ah yes,' he looked at me vaguely, 'Aids test, wasn't it?' Unable to find my results amid the disorganized mess of files on his desk he picked up the phone and dialled the number of the laboratory. I listened as he spoke, his disembodied voice drifting in and out of my consciousness. My throat felt dry and blood pounded in my head, obscuring the sound of his words and turning them into an incoherent babble. I watched his expression relax and realized he was speaking to me, telling me that the results were negative. He then proceeded to make it clear that he found my desire to pursue such an occupation incomprehensible and that he could under no circumstances provide a report that advised my return to the Congo. I fled the building, relieved the ordeal was over, and desperate to get home to my family.

On receipt of the specialist's report, the Howletts' management explained that if I wished to return to the Congo I would be required to make a personal, signed statement that made it clear that I did so of my own free will, thereby releasing them of responsibility for any possible repercussions to my health that might result. I felt committed to the work we had begun and wanted to return, so signed a statement willingly.

For the next six weeks, days and nights melted formlessly together as I slept and, shell-shocked, wandered aimlessly around my parents' house. The news from Brazzaville was not good. During our absence a flu epidemic had struck the orphanage and Bimba and three of the other newly arrived orphans had died. The staff had done an excellent job of the daily running of the orphanage but they were not trained to deal with the complex medical problems that arose in new orphans. I blamed myself.

Chapter Fourteen

Kola Learns a Lesson

Within a matter of weeks I regained the courage and strength to return to Brazzaville, the pull of Mark and the gorillas as strong as ever. The very day of my arrival Max fractured both my front teeth in an over-enthusiastic embrace and within a few weeks I was also back in bed with malaria. I did, however, take the doctors' advice, and stayed initially at a friend's house outside the zoo rather than returning to the flat, where conditions remained hazardous for both humans and gorillas. We had no space in which effectively to quarantine new arrivals, and the power and water supplies had become increasingly erratic, leaving us for long periods without a functioning fridge to keep food fresh or water to keep things clean.

However, I had soon re-immersed myself in the gorillas' daily lives, slipping back into the routine of everyday life at the orphanage. We would wake early each morning to give bottle feeds to the younger gorillas before taking Kola's and Sid's groups out to the forest, where they would spend the morning exploring and foraging for food. After spending some time with each group, observing their progress, we would leave Albertine, Catherine and Jean with the gorillas, whilst we tackled the pressing paperwork and made the necessary trips into town to the bank, government wildlife offices or the fruit market.

At midday the gorillas would return from the forest and, after a meal of fruit and vegetables from the local market, they would retire to the cage for a siesta. In mid-afternoon they would return to the forest, bursting from the cage, refreshed after their naps. The serious business of finding food in the forest was interspersed with boisterous play sessions that diffused any tensions and enabled them to develop the social skills required for gorilla family life.

As the afternoon drew to a close, they would start to wind down and relax. Even infants as young as one year old, like little Boko, would, after observing the older gorillas, begin to practise the rudiments of nest-building as the light started to fade. With public access to the forest being a problem, we were forced to bring them back to the safety of the cage for the night, but their daytime routine followed, as closely as possible, the activities of wild gorillas in their natural forest home.

We remained convinced that the answer to a successful reintroduction lay in careful preparation at this stage. The forest surrounding the orphanage provided an almost ideal training ground for them to learn the skills necessary for survival and gorilla group life. It had become obvious that new arrivals should begin their education as soon as they were robust enough mentally and physically to cope with the demands of life in a gorilla group.

Newly arrived or sick orphans remained with Mark, myself or Steve until they were strong and stable enough to cope with introduction to their new adopted family group and, importantly, did not present a disease threat to their prospective family.

At night the younger gorillas still required bottle feeding, but now we were at least able to share the chore with Steve. Now a permanent staff member, Steve slept on a straw mattress in a room which contained all the furniture evacuated from the other rooms now turned over to the gorillas. He shared his sleeping space with Mayoko, a six-week-old female gorilla, but didn't seem bothered by the arrangement. He prided himself on his ability to sleep anywhere under any conditions. Nonetheless, in the early hours of one morning he was dragged to consciousness by a strange and persistent tugging sensation. As he surfaced from deep sleep he found Mayoko hungrily sucking on his chest – and a rat chewing happily on his hair. It became obvious that things were getting out of control, even by Steve's standards.

John Aspinall paid a brief visit at the stifling, humid height of the rainy season, when torrential rain poured from angry black skies every third day, leaving the air heavily saturated with warm moisture. On the day of his arrival in Brazzaville the flat had been without water and electricity for nearly a week. After a brief guided tour of our living accommodation, Aspinall agreed that there was indeed a disease risk, and gave permission for us to look for cheap accommodation as near to the zoo as possible. It was to be another three months before we found a small bungalow nearby that suited our needs.

As Aspinall boarded a plane bound for England, reassured that despite our recent problems 'the dream was on course', Madingo, a two-year-old male orphan, arrived. Older than most newly confiscated orphans, he was fairly independent and spent his first few days crouched timidly in the forest on the outskirts of Kola's group, watching them, feeling curious, anxious and alienated. Because of his size and age both Kola and Titi treated his appearance on their patch with caution, perceiving him as potential threat. Resigning himself to the fact that they would not yet accept him, Madingo set off to explore the forest.

We followed at a distance to ensure that he didn't attempt to leave the relative safety of the small forest and venture across the borders of the zoo to the busy roads outside. Anxious at first, he soon became distracted by the discovery of familiar foliage. His low-pitched grumbling sounds, which signalled his pleasure as he crammed fistfuls of succulent leaves into his mouth, soon attracted Titi's attention. Curious, Titi moved over to observe the experienced newcomer while the rest of the group maintained their distance. After some time spent exploring the nearby undergrowth with Madingo, Titi rejoined the group, leaving Madingo to resume his lonely post at a distance, his posture deliberately unthreatening, his sad eyes anxiously downcast. He longed to be accepted as part of this gorilla family but understood that he would need to be patient and diplomatic in order to overcome the group's cautious nature.

Sitting with Kola's group late one afternoon as the fading sun cast its orange glow over the forest and the gorillas relaxed after a busy day, we realized that Madingo had disappeared. His deliberately low-profile presence and the distractions of Kola's group, now seven in number, had made it easy for him to slip off unnoticed. As darkness cloaked the forest, his instincts had pulled him deeper into the shadowy undergrowth in search of a suitable nesting site for the night. We fanned out into the undergrowth to search for him, calling his name, hoping he had not wandered too far and that he would trust us enough to respond. Fifteen minutes later all light had gone, any shadows now obliterated by black night. We fetched torches and returned. Although aware that the bright torch light might panic an already frightened young gorilla, we had no other choice. But our efforts were rendered hopeless anyway by the clouds of mosquitoes attracted to the torches' white beams of light piercing the darkness. Angry squirrels chattered at the disturbance, but Madingo did not emerge. We felt sure that he was hidden close by, watching us, and, fearful for his safety from the feral dogs that roamed the forest at night, we decided to keep Kola's group out in the forest overnight in the hope that the gorillas' presence would encourage Madingo to return.

Anticipating their usual return to the cage at this time of the evening, the gorillas were at first confused. When they realized Mark and I intended to stay out with them, the tension subsided. Kola took the lead and, pulling the nearby foliage neatly under his feet and kneading it to a matted weave, he started to settle for the night. A few minutes later he abandoned his nest and lay down beside me. With his arms clasped reassuringly around my neck, he was soon asleep. The other gorillas nestled together close by, a cluster of hairy limbs intertwined as they slept away the dark hours and we listened for a faint rustling in the undergrowth that might indicate Madingo's presence close by.

Dawn broke over the forest the next morning and the gorillas woke, surprised to find themselves outside. Stretching their limbs and realizing they were hungry, they ambled back to the orphanage to find Albertine, who was preparing their milk drinks in the kitchen. Madingo had not returned but we did find his night nest nearby and a small pile of dung. He had obviously not strayed that far, but risen early and, hungry, set off into the forest to forage. Fearing for his safety, we offered a reward of seventy pounds to any member of the orphanage or zoo staff who could locate and return him to us safely – the price being high enough to ensure that he was worth more alive than as bushmeat for sale in the local market. For the next three days we spent every spare minute searching for him, managing only to locate his abandoned night nests and his tracks in the nearby forest. Then, on the fourth morning, we finally glimpsed him heading through the sparse undergrowth on the edge of the forest bordering the cage. Jean set off in hot pursuit, soon catching up and hurling his considerable bulk on top of a terrified Madingo. He quickly admitted defeat and returned to the orphanage – looking surprisingly well, but rather unsure of the reception he could expect. Jean received his reward, the cost of which was added to our weekly expenses sheet.

We now kept Madingo under careful surveillance as night approached. Eventually Kola overcame his initial wariness, initiating contact with the newcomer. A cautious relationship began to form between them. Kola had the advantage of being physically larger and stronger, and, more importantly, he had the support of the group. But Madingo had valuable wild experience, and his confidence in the forest would attract the attention and respect of the others, making him the greatest threat for leadership that Kola had so far encountered. Kola recognized this risk but his fair nature obliged him to give Madingo a tentative entry to the group. However, play between these two potential rivals was never completely relaxed, the more serious undercurrents never far from the surface.

In the next few months Madingo, who, it became clear, was obviously very bright and possessed considerable social skills, was careful not to overstep the boundaries of respect while establishing himself within the group. Titi remained fascinated by him, and the two of them often set off together to explore the forest, developing a close friendship. Both were naturally ambitious, and, recognizing this streak in one another, they started to work as a team. Titi realized that his age and size would prevent him from ever becoming leader himself, but calculated that if he supported Madingo in any future bid for leadership he would stand to benefit as the new leader's loyal side-kick. However, he still hedged his bets and played the situation carefully; whenever both Madingo and Kola were present he continued to make his loyalty to Kola clear.

As Madingo strengthened his position within Kola's group, another male, Mbinda, arrived at the orphanage, sent up from Pointe Noire by Aliette Jamart. Although only a year old,

Mbinda was fiercely independent. He was truly a gorilla's gorilla and had little time for humans. His attitude to us was not as extreme at Titi's, but all the same he dismissed us an irrelevance to his life with Kola's group. He loved Kola, hugely admired Titi and Madingo and treated Nzambi with contempt. He soon became a great favourite of the group. He revealed precocious social skills, immediately tuning into the subtle nuances of intergroup relations and the different personality traits of each group member, and used these powers of intuition to smooth his own path. But, unlike Titi (and even Madingo at times), he was never underhand in his behaviour. He had no need to be anyway; he was too young to present a real threat, and plucky enough to stand his ground against bullying by the more aggressive younger males like Nzambi.

As we watched Mbinda's progress we felt instinctively that he would do well. He was a very positive addition to Kola's group, and an obvious candidate for reintroduction.

As the size of this largely male gorilla group grew, the dynamics were unavoidably changing and the strain of responsibility was starting to tell on Kola as he tried to maintain his easy, previously unchallenged, leadership. He recognized the threat presented by the friendship developing between Madingo and Titi, and his rising anxiety began to take a toll on his health. Common cold viruses caught from the orphanage staff had been a persistent problem with newly arrived orphans in the early months of their convalescence. What might seem to us a run-of-the-mill cold could quickly become life-threatening in new arrivals who lacked immunity to human diseases and were poorly equipped nutritionally to cope with any further stress. Successive exposure to colds enabled them to gradually build up some immunity and having acquired this immunity some time ago, we assumed Kola would shrug off the cold that was doing the rounds at the time.

We were shocked by his rapid deterioration. He had soon developed a serious chest infection. By the time we had realized the gravity of the situation and started him on antibiotics Madingo and Titi had already launched a persecution campaign, taking advantage of the power vacuum. Dinga remained close by Kola's side as his leader sat, miserable and inactive, making valiant attempts to defend him from the barging and bullying of Madingo and Titi's joint forces. The younger members of the group observed the developing situation with confused and fearful expressions.

We didn't feel that it would be helpful to separate off the trouble-makers but Mark's presence in the next few days, as an authority figure in support of Kola, ensured that Titi and Madingo backed off, allowing Kola to rest and feed adequately until his strength returned. By now he had become reluctant to drink and crouched, breathless, gasping for air. We found he would accept drinks from a baby's feeding bottle, its childhood associations of comfort and security reassuring him that he was cared for, loved and relieved temporarily of his adult responsibilities.

Kola's strength finally returned. But this brought new problems for the two agitators, as he became markedly more severe in his attitude towards them, reasserting his position as leader with renewed vigour and seriousness. He had learnt his lesson, and from then on ruled with a rod of iron.

Mireille was a new member of staff. Her pretty name was at odds with her huge, masculine, hirsute bulk and clumsy, insensitive manner. Always willing to give people a chance, we observed her progress with the gorillas with increasing despair. Watching her take Mayoko out to the forest one morning, I realized even the gorillas' patience with her had run out. Mireille tugged brutally at Mayoko's arm as Mayoko hung onto a nearby shrub, resisting her. When she finally managed to prise a furious Mayoko off the shrub, and swung her up into her arms, Mayoko sunk her teeth into Mireille's ample chest and made a bid for freedom, landing on the earth below with a thud and scrambling frantically back towards the orphanage. Gathering her up in my arms, I sighed as, undeterred by this rather obvious rejection, Mireille caught up, determined to have another go. I told her, as politely as possible, that perhaps her attempts to win over the gorillas should take a gentler form. She stared dumbly at me, apparently unable to understand what I might be getting at, whilst Mayoko clung stubbornly to me, her head buried firmly in my shirt, refusing to even look at Mireille.

Much to the embarrassment of the other staff, Mireille displayed no shame when recounting how she had often eaten chimpanzee meat at home in a small village in the north. She soon lost interest in the gorillas and began to show considerably more interest in Steve.

Since neither she nor Steve spoke French, she would gaze at him with dumb doe-eyes as he attempted to explain by gestures her responsibilities for the day. Obviously impressed with his paternal skills, she proudly announced that she would one day have his child. As her interest in the horrified Steve assumed obsessive proportions, and her skills around the orphanage continued to remain undeveloped, we realized that we had no choice but to let Mireille go. There was a collective sigh of relief from the rest of the staff, despite the fact that she was Catherine's sister-in-law. Their loyalties to their work and the gorillas overwhelmed the more traditional family loyalties on this occasion.

We had heard on the expatriate grapevine of a French doctor and his wife living in Kabo, a timber concession in the far north of the country, who were caring for an orphan gorilla they had rescued from a trader. Anxious that the gorilla should reach the orphanage as soon as possible, we had sent messages up to them, pointing out, as diplomatically as possible, that we were the only official body in the Congo possessed of the legal right to care for orphan gorillas. Receiving no reply we assumed that the gorilla had died. We were therefore surprised when a young French woman appeared at the orphanage clutching a baby gorilla possessively in her arms. Dressed in baby clothes, the infant gorilla had been an obvious child substitute, filling an emotional void in this woman's isolated life in the interior. We invited her into the garden, where Kola's group had gathered around Albertine for their midday meal before retiring for their siesta. We hoped that if she observed his obvious delight at finding gorilla playmates she would feel happier about leaving her gorilla in our care. Torn between her distress at leaving her 'child' and the realization that she had deprived him of normal gorilla playmates for the past few months, she fled the orphanage in tears, promising to return over the next few days to see how he was progressing. She never returned, presumably having found the separation too traumatic. We called the newcomer Kabo, and he was adopted by Kola and Bilinga.

With the recent arrival of Mbinda and now Kabo, Kola's group numbered nine. We were impressed by the way they defined their own roles within it, each assuming precocious maturity and social skills. We were now torn between our desire to see how this large, apparently successful, group of gorillas would develop, and our fear of disease. Keeping them in smaller groups would have reduced the risk. In a group as large as Kola's, we could easily lose all nine gorillas in one epidemic. By the time we would have become aware of a problem, it would already be too late to control the spread.

Concerned to set up some preventive measures, I wrote to

several vets and organizations involved in vaccination programmes for wild and captive ape populations for information
and advice on protecting the gorillas from preventable infectious
diseases like polio and measles. In response, I received an offer
of funding and expertise from one well-known institution. I
requested Howletts' permission to accept the offer, but my
anxieties didn't seem to be greeted with any urgency. I pushed
them to the back of my mind – not difficult when our every
waking moment was taken up with practical, day-to-day matters.

With the continuing progress of Kola's group reminding us
daily of the urgency of finding a long-term wild home for them,
we had recently embarked on negotiations with the Congolese
government for an agreement to secure the Southern Lefini
Reserve as our reintroduction site. Knowing that contracts of
this sort could take months, if not years, to finalize, we needed
to start immediately, before the gorillas became unmanageable
in the limited area of forest surrounding the orphanage. Within
a few years, as they grew in size and strength, we would be
forced to confine them to the cage, a confinement that would
arrest their development at a crucial stage.

Kola's group needed to be introduced into a larger forest
territory where, supported by familiar human figures initially,
they could spread their wings towards a life independent of man.
The skills they were mastering as infants now, like nest-
building, foraging for food and climbing, not to mention the
social complexities of life in a group, would determine their
chances of survival in the wild.

Steve and Mark spent as much time as they could up in the
Lefini Reserve, learning more about the geography of the area,
the composition of the forests, their resident wildlife and the
surrounding human population. The results of their expeditions
made us more than ever convinced that we had found the ideal
site for the staged release of the gorillas.

The inner sanctum of the southern part of the Lefini Reserve, the very area we had glimpsed that fateful day a year before, contained forests rich in gorilla food, particularly the swamp-growing vegetation that provides the staple diet of wild gorillas. Within a core area of around 100 square kilometres, the gorillas would need to learn the composition of the forests, building up an internal map of the area to enable them to find food throughout the year. During this period of orientation to their new territory, they would still need the support of their human guardians, but if the rapid progress of Kola's group was anything to go by, they would soon find their feet.

Aware of the bad reputation of past projects in the interior – unfulfilled promises had left the local Batéké people cynical and mistrustful as projects folded, leaving them with nothing permanent – we were anxious not to make any promises that we could not be sure of keeping.

The small village of Mah with its 200 inhabitants stood to benefit the most. Located two kilometres from the main trade route – the North Road that led directly down to Brazzaville, some 120 kilometres south – Mah comprised a cluster of breeze-block and wattle huts, perched on a cliff top, overlooking the still, sinister waters of Lac Bleu in the valley below.

Some attempts by a local French entrepreneur had already been made to encourage weekend tourists from Brazzaville to visit the area. Four simple concrete villas on the outskirts of the village afforded a magnificent view of the patchwork of forests and grassland below. If our gorillas adapted successfully to life in these forests, this basic tourist accommodation might serve as a base for visitors, the small beginnings of a wildlife tourism programme that could bring employment and trade opportunities to the surrounding villages.

The local Batéké people survived at present on the sale or exchange of agricultural produce grown on the land, wild fruit

gathered from the forests below and bushmeat hunted in the
interior further north. This region of middle Congo, the Batéké
Plateaux, was still a political minefield of territorial squabbles
over ancient hunting grounds and bitter personal rivalries. A
complicated system of Chefs de Terre (Chiefs of the Land) and
Chefs de Village (Village Chiefs) divided the land into sections
and subsections. All were answerable to the tribal king of the
region, King Makoko, whose ancestors had been responsible,
over a hundred years before, for handing over the hereditary
rights of his people to the French. Although Makoko was now
only a cultural figurehead and not possessed of any officially
recognized political power, he would need to give his blessing
to any project proposed within his region. He could still, if he
wished, create a great deal of trouble.

The older generation of Batéké people were instantly recognizable by the distinctive tribal scarring of finely grooved lines the
length of their faces, as if drawn by a comb. The Marxist
government had discouraged this ancient tribal ritual, but this
had little effect on a people proud of their tribal identity. We
had often heard Congolese visitors to the zoo calling out 'Bateke'
as they pointed excitedly at the mandrills' striped, bright blue
and red faces. The caged mandrills responded by drawing back
their lips in sinister, one-sided sneers, revealing long, dagger-
like canines.

With its dwindling wildlife population, the southern part of
the Lefini Reserve was of little interest to serious hunters now.
Villagers did, however, still enter the forests to collect firewood
and wild fruits in season at certain times of the year. We would
need to negotiate a comprehensive agreement with both the
official Congolese government, based in Brazzaville, and King
Makoko and his cronies, that detailed the project's responsibilities to manage the area, whilst monitoring the progress of the

reintroduced gorillas, and agreed rights of land usage for the surrounding villages.

Late one afternoon we left Mah village after meeting with the village chief, a tiny, wizened old man with at least twenty children, and headed for the North Road. The road had not been repaired in decades and the tarmac which had been laid along this ancient trade route by the French now had deep pot-holes every fifty or so yards. Lorries hurtling down to Brazzaville from the North, their flatbeds crammed precariously to bursting point with sacks of manioc and passengers, would sway and bump over the potholes, a danger to smaller vehicles on the road and the cause of many accidents.

We had lingered in the village longer than intended and the light soon began to fade. Night had fallen by the time we reached the outskirts of the city. We slowed down, aware that there were likely to be children playing in the narrow, unlit streets. Open drains at the side of the streets overflowed with rank, brown water and a flotsam of paper and bottles. From our jeep we watched traders trudge wearily past, carrying their unsold goods back home, trailing straggling lines of still excitable children through the din of traffic and loud music blaring from candle-lit bars.

Spotting a group of children ahead of us playing with a ball we slowed even further, coming to a halt as the ball bounced into the road. A saloon car, driven by a Frenchman, which had been travelling fast behind us on its return to the city, careened around us to avoid hitting the back of the jeep. It clipped the side of the road, its bonnet smacking hard into a teenage boy who had been standing idly chatting with a friend. The boy's body reeled with the force of the blow, arcing into the air and falling to the ground limp as a rag doll. We stared in frozen, shocked silence as he emitted an animal groan, his body then seized in quivering, spastic death throes, the back of his skull horribly broken.

As soon as we had recovered we climbed out of our jeep to see if we could help. By this time the boy was already being carried to the Frenchman's car. The shocked silence of the onlookers was broken by murmurs which gathered strength and intensity as anger overcame shock. They looked around, needing to find someone to blame for the sheer injustice of what they had witnessed. Almost every expatriate we had met in Brazzaville had 'stories' to tell of someone who had unwittingly stopped to help at the scene of an accident and been stoned to death by a vengeance-seeking mob. The unofficial advice of the police to those witnessing or involved in a serious accident was to continue driving and report the incident to the nearest police station. We fled back to the jeep and drove on towards the zoo, the optimism we had felt earlier that day wiped out.

Back at the orphanage the silence that evening seemed deafening. With the brutal image of the dying boy heavy on our minds, Mark and I barely spoke over the next few days.

Chapter Fifteen

A Fledgling Democracy

At the end of 1991 a tank sat stationed outside the zoo entrance, its sinister grey metal bulk warning of troubles to come. The wide avenue that separated the zoo from the Parliament Building opposite was lined twenty-four hours a day by heavily armed military guards. Morning and evening, they raised themselves wearily from slumber to salute the coming and going politicians and generals travelling in a cortège of spanking new Mercedes saloons, tailed by rusty, rattling Russian cars housing their bodyguards.

As the relative riches of the years that followed the discovery of oil off the coast of Point Noire dwindled, Sassou found himself unable to pay his government. Civil servants had united in random general strikes over the past year, causing water and electricity cuts throughout the town. They had demanded a National Conference that would bring Sassou's rule to an end. Power was changing hands. President Sassou-Ngeusso's twelve-year military Marxist reign was drawing to a close. In progress now, the National Conference would conclude with the setting up of an interim government to rule the Congo until democratic elections could be carried out.

But the end of Sassou's reign would unleash tribal tensions

that his military dictatorship had effectively held in check. Key players would emerge in the next few months as political parties based on tribal lines vied for votes and power for their people.

Little spoken of until now were the two major contenders in the forthcoming power struggle: Bernard Kolelas, head of the Lari people, whose stronghold was the Bacongo Quartier of town behind the orphanage, and Pascal Lissouba of the Duma tribe, whose land was the fertile Niari region of the Congo between Pointe Noire and Brazzaville. Brazzaville would soon become a battlefield as both sides flexed their muscles and armed themselves in preparation for the elections.

Most of our staff, we discovered, were Laris. They discussed politics openly, exercising their newly won freedom of speech. Tribal tensions had begun to simmer everywhere. Fierce debates raged on street corners and in bars throughout the different quartiers of town. Ethnic identities were now proudly proclaimed and hopes were raised as each faction of the previously peaceful town dreamed that power lay within reach.

The regular guards soon became familiar with our comings and goings, not even bothering to check our identity papers or question our movements, regarding us simply as a source of harmless entertainment.

After several weeks, the Conference concluded; Andre Milongo was put in place as interim President of the newly named Republic of Congo, a new national anthem was adopted and the old red Marxist flag was replaced by the green, yellow and red stripes of a fledgling democracy. This was an uneasy period of peace which no one expected to last for long.

Mark and I at last moved into the small bungalow near the orphanage that we had found some months earlier. Despite losing the relative tranquillity of the zoo, we were relieved to finally have our own living space. It was part of a compound that housed a large Congolese family and the small office of a business that renovated Japanese cars for resale as taxis, whose clients turned up at all hours of the day and night. Directly in front of the compound was a petrol station. The impatient honking of car horns and noisy banter of queuing taxi drivers woke us early each morning as the market traders made their way to stalls at the end of the street, their wares piled high on their heads.

We set about converting our previous living space at the orphanage into rooms that could house the gorilla groups at night. We reserved one room as a small office where we could apply ourselves to the increasing amounts of paperwork regarding employment of staff, their salaries and pensions, tax payments, funding proposals and government contracts, as well as the records we kept of all animals resident at the orphanage, their progress and any medical treatment they received.

More gorilla orphans continued to arrive. They came from all sorts of places. For instance, Jean had heard rumours in his home quartier of 'Poto-Poto' (the local word for mud) that a baggage handler at the airport, who had been stationed up north for a while as a soldier, was attempting to export a gorilla using his work contacts. Having discovered the address of the man in question, Jean asked our permission to take one of NDinga's wildlife agents from the government offices next to the zoo, and pay a visit to the man's house. On their arrival they found a fairly large female gorilla in a makeshift cage amongst the filthy chaos of the backyard.

Deep in shanty-town was not the ideal place to attempt a confiscation. They knew they would have to coax the man and his gorilla out into the open in town, where he would be forced to give up the animal without a fight. Outnumbered by his friends and relatives, they returned to the orphanage, frustrated.

Unnerved by this semi-official visit and anxious to get rid of his illegal merchandise, the soldier appeared at the orphanage the following day, asking if we would like to buy his gorilla. Depositing her in our office he confidently suggested a price of four hundred pounds, a figure that betrayed some prior experience of this sort of transaction. As we engaged him in conversation in the office, two uniformed wildlife agents appeared at the door, pursued by an excited, breathless Nkodia, who had run the short distance from the orphanage to the wildlife offices to fetch assistance as soon as he spotted the trader making his way down the path some minutes earlier. Informing him that he was breaking the law, the wildlife agents frog-marched the soldier off towards NDinga's office. He turned back towards us as he left, scowling and muttering threats of returning to claim 'his gorilla' by force.

We took the crate in which Djembo, as we named her, was crammed, into one of the rooms behind the office and prised open the door. It was secured with a large rusty nail and some wire. Bolting straight out of the cage without a moment's hesitation, she stood upright, cupped her hands over her chest, and launched into a continuous, rapid chest-beating display, trapping air against her muscular chest to produce a 'pok-a-pok-a-pok' sound that carried some distance. We waited for this display to subside but she persisted, beating her chest frantically in an exaggerated and ridiculous travesty of a normal gorilla threat display that signalled her confusion and fear. Unsure, but fairly convinced that we were a threat, she kept up her display of bluff confidence.

Considerably older than any previous arrivals, she had a thick coat of charcoal black hair, long rangy limbs, and a curiously flat face, rendered even more bizarre by the fact that she was cross-eyed. Later, when left alone, her threat displays subsided. When we reappeared she merely squinted at us through the steel grille window of the bedroom.

We decided she should join Sid and Rupert's group. Jean,

feeling a particular responsibility for her, asked if he could help her settle into her new surroundings before she made this transition. They bonded quickly and by the time Djembo was ready to meet Sid and Rupert she regarded Jean as a friend. When she later suffered from a bout of amoebic dysentery Jean was the only person she would trust. Even so, injecting her with the necessary antibiotics was no easy task and involved Jean lying on top of a terrified Djembo, pinning her to the ground and immobilizing her with his considerable bulk, whilst we grabbed a leg and plunged the needle into her thigh muscle. She never once tried to bite Jean despite the fact that his face was pressed close against hers within easy striking distance of her impressive canines.

Djembo's old captor returned a few days following his arrest, dressed in full army regalia, armed with a machine gun and accompanied by a straggly entourage of sullen adolescent boys. He strode past the worried faces of Nkodia and Albertine, and stopped outside the office, adjusting his gun in a barely disguised threat.

'I understand now that I have broken the law,' he announced, 'and I want to make amends for my actions. I am reclaiming my gorilla so that I can return her to the forest when I resume my post in the interior!'

We could hardly contain ourselves as we imagined the first ever gorilla reintroduction being effected by this character. In the end we couldn't help but laugh in his face. He stood staring in perplexed silence as Nkodia ran to the wildlife offices in search of NDinga. A few minutes later NDinga's car screeched noisily down the dirt track in a cloud of dust and he emerged, steaming with anger, obviously having taken a dislike to the man on their previous encounter some days earlier. As he stormed into the office, the soldier's previously arrogant attitude dissolved, his shoulders hunched and he became meek as a child.

NDinga bundled him into the car in silence and drove him away. The soldier was barred from ever setting foot in the orphanage grounds again by the minister responsible for the wildlife authorities, who was also a military general.

It wasn't long before Djembo was confident enough to explore the forest with Sid, Rupert and Max. Jean was immensely proud of 'his group', and reported excitedly to us at the end of each day any new developments in their behaviour. One afternoon he came rushing back from the forest, trembling with anxiety, tears pouring down his cheeks. He explained breathlessly to Mark that whilst his attention was distracted, Max had somehow got hold of a discarded medicine bottle in the forest and had drunk the contents. Max was now hiding for fear of being punished. Unaware of the unfolding drama, I watched, intrigued, as Mark and Jean screamed angrily at one another in their panic and then rushed off into the forest. Half an hour later they returned with an embarrassed Max walking between them, one hand held firmly by each of them. I went over to find out what was going on, but the two men were now laughing together with relief, bending down occasionally to cuff the mischievous bonobo affectionately over the head. As they reached the cage Max looked fearfully up at them, expecting angry words. When none came he raced off towards Sid and Rupert, squealing loudly, and all were soon in an enthusiastic embrace.

One afternoon Sid's group were out with Mark and Jean in the forest. They had grown quite large by this time and could present an intimidating sight to any stranger who unexpectedly came across them on their explorations. Although we knew better, Sid's impressive physical bulk and pronounced orbital crest – which all but obscured his tiny eyes – made him a particularly menacing sight. Further, his limited intelligence and underlying insecurities made him a risk in unfamiliar situations. He might jump to the wrong conclusions and, imagining his group presented with a threat, leap loyally to their defence.

Two young men from out of town were in the forest that afternoon, unaware of the gorillas' nearby presence. They had come to collect giant snails in the very patch of scrub the gorillas had chosen to spend their afternoon. Max saw them first and rushed over, bursting with curiosity and excitement. Had Max not spotted the strangers, the gorillas would probably have kept their distance. The two bewildered youths had no idea whether Max's advances were hostile or not and they shoved him away in panic, only succeeding in frightening Max whose friendly squeaks now became screams of fear. Hearing Max in distress, Sid thundered to the rescue.

Seeing Sid explode out of the undergrowth, bristling and stiff-legged, coughing and barking aggressively, the older of the two panicking men pulled a rusty six-inch knife from his pocket. As Sid approached he stabbed it frantically into the gorilla's chest. It glanced off his shoulder blade and plunged deep in through his chest wall. The younger man seized his opportunity to run from the forest as fast as his legs could carry him. By the time Mark and Jean realized what was happening Rupert and Djembo were on their way to the scene with serious intentions.

'Get Sid back to the orphanage,' Mark screamed at Jean, 'and call Dr Bettini.' He then ran off in pursuit of the man with the knife who was now heading for the nearest tree, imagining that up it he might be safe from the irate gorillas. Convinced that he was about to die, and screeching abuse at Rupert and Djembo as they thundered close behind him, coughing and screaming, the man started climbing. They followed him up, much faster, trapping him in the branches.

Mark reached the tree and started up it, grabbing the man. 'Hold on to me,' he said with calm authority, 'we're going to jump.'

As they hit the ground Mark could see that the man was about to make a run for it. 'If you run,' he warned, 'they will probably kill you.'

Rupert and Djembo were indeed circling them like sharks whilst Max danced around, screaming maniacally. Clinging to Mark as if he was drowning, the terrified man allowed himself to be led back to the orphanage where Mark locked him in one of the empty gorilla cages, 'for your own safety' he explained with barely disguised pleasure. The youth crouched in the cage, paralysed with fear, for the rest of the day.

Once the gorillas had settled for the night we unlocked the door and told him to leave. He made a hasty escape, fleeing the zoo in search of his companion who by now probably imagined his friend lay dead on the forest floor.

We waited for Dr Bettini to arrive. She was a well-known figure in the Brazzaville community. Her exotic, dark good looks and wild behaviour at social events belied an exceptionally skilled and serious medical professional whose energy and compassion seemed boundless. Her ability to react quickly and calmly in any emergency with little if any technical back-up had saved many lives in Brazzaville. We hoped against hope this ability would translate to treating a gorilla. Arriving at the orphanage as we attempted to assess Sid's wounds, Flore was unfazed to discover that the emergency she had been called to was a gorilla stabbing. She entered Sid's cage without a moment's hesitation, cooing softly and reassuringly. It was exactly the right approach and Sid reached out towards her, planting his huge clumsy hands on her chic white mini dress, his tiny confused eyes searching hers for reassurance as he allowed her to gently examine him.

'The knife has narrowly missed his lung,' she told us. 'He has been very lucky. He just needs antibiotics to ensure that the wound doesn't become infected.' She pulled an anti-tetanus jab out of her bag and Sid watched quietly while she drew the injection up. Only at the point of the sharp needle's impact with his thigh did he react, shrieking with pain and the shock of betrayal. Flore made a run for the door while Jean attempted to distract Sid.

Sid enjoyed his convalescence and the break from the responsibility of being leader of his group, which now included Kambala, another of Madame Leroy's original four gorillas. Rupert and Djembo came to visit him in his sick room, but we thought it better to keep Max away until Sid was completely recovered. He savoured the peaceful mealtimes, grumbling and singing in anticipation and then sitting lazily, taking his time over every tasty morsel. Relieved of the pressure of guarding his food from Max he was able to leave his bananas to the last, delaying that final moment of pleasure which only a banana could bring.

When he was finally fit to rejoin the others he greeted the prospect of ending his spell of intensive care and attention with reluctance. Back in the cage with his group, he spent his first morning in a very bad mood, coughing irritably at Max who was overjoyed and determined to be reunited with his best friend. Rupert and Djembo hung back more diplomatically, waiting for Sid's mood to improve while Max, ignoring all attempts to repel him, screamed ecstatically and flung his arms tightly around an increasingly irritated Sid.

Although Mark and I were as good as married, with more parental responsibilities than most couples of our age, we wanted to make our commitment to one another public and official. A passionate proposal in an intimate moment within a few weeks of meeting one another had been buried by events that had for a while thrown into question our future together. After proving beyond any measure of doubt that we wanted the same things from life, we saw no reason to delay getting married. Our relationship had, if anything, been strengthened by the past few years in Brazzaville. Perhaps we even felt that our marriage would also be a celebration of our newly acquired gorilla family.

Anyway, we were now seized with a sudden urgency to get married and arranged to fly to England within a matter of weeks, leaving Steve in charge once again. It looked like we had a hard year ahead with preparations for the reintroduction, continuing work at the orphanage and the likelihood of escalating civil unrest in Brazzaville. This might be our last chance of a break for some time.

One balmy summer day in June, we were pronounced man and wife in a short civil ceremony in South London. Mark's wedding present to me was a night at the Savoy Hotel.

The following morning I opened my eyes, rubbing them as I took in the opulent three-room suite. I turned to look at Mark lying, still sound asleep, beside me, his presence reminding me of a very different world back in Brazzaville.

Leaving him to sleep on, I clambered out of the king-size, four-poster bed and wandered through the suite, stopping at the window to gaze dreamily across the Thames at the copper green, curved roof of the Festival Hall beyond. We had come so far and our attachment to one another was stronger than ever. I shivered as a cloud darkened the sky above and I felt suddenly cold. I wondered what the next few years would bring.

△ With Sid, fully convalesced following
the stabbing incident.

▷ What a difference a
few years make! Young
Sid investigating a
bucket of water, 1989.

△ Rupert, feeling defiant, 1989.

◁ Rupert meeting up with Kola.

▽ A portrait of Rupert taken in 1990.

△ Mboukou in the grounds of the orphanage, 1992.

▽ Clinging on for comfort.

△ Djembo climbing in the
orphanage forest.

▽ Titi out in the forest with
Albertine, 1989.

△ Albertine supervises
Kola's group. Clockwise from
left: Dinga, a newcomer, Titi,
Bilinga, Kola, Boko and
Nzambi.

▷ The original team at
Brazzaville in March 1989 –
a local electrician, Joseph, Mark
and Nkodia.

Madingo on watch in the
orphanage forest, 1992.

▷ Our extended family: Dolly, the Pel's Fishing Owl . . .

▽ . . . the kidnapped Nigel the mandrill . . .

▷ . . . and Queenie, the Lizard Buzzard.

Signing the marriage register in London, 1991.

Chapter Sixteen

A Killer in
Our Midst

Baxter was the first of a string of bonobos to arrive in Brazzaville as a result of riots on the streets of Kinshasa. One night, shortly before his arrival, Mark and I had driven down to the shores of the river and looked across the smooth moonlit waters at the city opposite. We listened as a rat-a-tat-a-tat of machine-gun fire, punctuated by single sharp pistol shots, broke the silence of the still night. The flash of tracer bullets shot through the dark sky above us.

'Look at that,' Mark had whispered, 'imagine living in Kinshasa now.' Little did we realize that within a few months Brazzaville would find itself engulfed in the same bewildering chaos.

The Kinshasa riots lasted for several days, with looters plundering shops and houses, ripping out even electric plugs and sockets, light bulbs and toilet seats. We heard reports of marauding gangs of civilians and militia soldiers who crawled like ants over the city, invading people's homes, shooting indiscriminately and emerging burdened with loot, struggling in pairs to carry fridges and other household appliances down the chaotic streets. It was rumoured that there were more deaths from electrocution as looters ripped electrical appliances from their sockets, than from actual gunfire. Ferries and pirogues brought thousands of fleeing refugees across the river every day, expatriates and Zairois alike crammed onto unstable floating contraptions. The Zairois hurled themselves into the water as they approached the riverbank, throwing their belongings into the river before them, then splashing about and screaming in panic as they attempted to stay afloat and retrieve their belongings as they bobbed away downstream. Few of them could swim and many drowned. Those who reached dry land would make a run for it to avoid interrogation by the Congolese shore police, who were anxious to keep the chaos of Kinshasa from spreading to sleepy Brazzaville, and in any case loathed their Zairois neighbours. They proudly proclaimed that this sort of shameful anarchy would never occur in Brazzaville as the Congolese were sophisticated and able to resolve their differences by verbal means. 'Well, what do you expect of the Zairois?' was the standard retort when discussing the behaviour of their neighbours.

Baxter must have travelled across river on one of these boats with his captor. We had heard from our contacts in town that there was a chimpanzee being offered for sale outside the supermarket and had already made attempts to track the trader down. In the end he came to us, unaware that he was breaking any laws and convinced that we would buy his chimpanzee. Jean got to him first as he appeared at the orphanage gates and, asking for a peek into his hold-all, he realized that inside was a bonobo. Excited, he stuck close by the man as he made his way to our office. 'Hélène,' he whispered in my ear, barely able to contain his excitement, 'it's a Max!'

While Nkodia rushed off to get help from the wildlife agents' office, I opened the hold-all and peered in. A gentle pair of dark brown eyes stared anxiously back into mine. I couldn't help feeling happy for Max that he might have a companion of his own species at last, despite the tragic circumstances of this orphan's arrival. The appearance of this bonobo orphan sadly signalled an increase in bonobo hunting in the Zaire interior as armed refugees fled Kinshasa and travelled deep into the forest in search of food.

The trader seemed genuinely confused as the wildlife agents appeared and escorted him off to NDinga's office. He returned to the orphanage later in the week for an explanation. He was not angry, merely intrigued, and surprisingly receptive to the story of our work in Brazzaville. He chatted and joked with the local staff and asked if he could return to visit regularly. Had circumstances been different and we needed local help at this point he might even have worked well with us. He never re-offended, although we would often see him in town selling legal merchandise such as rabbits, chickens and ducks. But more infant ape traders from Kinshasa appeared on the streets of Brazzaville, forced further afield by adverse conditions at home.

Baxter was a miniature version of Max, right down to the long black hair that sat, neatly coiffed, on his head like a helmet and his large hairy ears. His skin, apart from a boot-polish black face, was pale beneath the wisps of soft black hair that covered his body. He squeaked at first with tentative pleasure as we presented a plate of wild fruit known locally as tondolo, the squeaks becoming louder and more confident as we responded by mimicking his friendly, excited chatter. Reaching out a small hand questioningly towards the food, he looked up at us, lips pulled back, teeth clenched in an anxious grin. Reassured by our benign expressions he then stretched out one long, spindly arm and delicately plucked one of the fruits from the plate. The serious business of pulling apart the outer skin to reach the thirst-quenching pulp and small black pips inside soon distracted any fear. He bit into the tough skin with his small sharp teeth, concentrating, intent on the task. Now sure of his ground, he rapidly demolished the entire plateful of fruit, then sat back, the fragile, hairless skin of his now distended belly stretched uncomfortably taut. With his appetite satisfied, he returned his attention to his surroundings, gazing around the garden at the gorillas and people, confused and curious, until his eyelids started to droop and he gave in to an exhausted sleep.

The daily routine of orphanage life by now ran like clockwork. Jean took proud responsibility for Sid's group and Albertine had taken charge of Kola's group of nine, managing them with exceptional, intuitive skill, undaunted by the macho barging of the older boys and reprimanding them when they needed it like any good parent. Catherine had taken responsibility for a third group of six nursery age orphans all under one year old who had arrived over the past six months. She was particularly observant and often detected the early tell-tale signs of sickness in these babies who seemed to be plagued by a never-ending round of coughs and colds just like human children at nursery school. We considered these colds a necessary part of the process of gaining an immunity that would equip them for survival in adult life. We were very proud of this group. It was the first time we had run so many youngsters of roughly the same age as one group and we were nervous that a serious disease outbreak within the group might have disastrous consequences. This was the group Baxter was to join until he was large enough to cope with Max's boisterous but well-intentioned attentions. Mayoko, Steve's ex room-mate, was the oldest lead female of this group. Initially she had not taken kindly to these new arrivals who competed for the exclusive attention she had been assured of until now, but eventually the advantages of having new gorilla playmates overcame her reservations.

Under Catherine's watchful eye, this nursery group spent their days in a small patch of forest bordering the garden. Here they began their explorations of the forest world, chewing laboriously with tiny, budding teeth the thick stems of ground vegetation whilst the older, more adventurous ones, led by Mayoko, ventured further afield to test their strength and balance on the smaller trees.

As the weeks passed Baxter's confidence grew and his appetite remained healthy. His belly expanded but his tiny arms and legs remained thin and stick-like. After some experimental contact between the two bonobos through the bars of the cage, we brought Max into the garden for an official introduction. Intimidated by Max's size, Baxter clung tightly to my chest but eventually overcame his fear and cautiously held one hand out towards Max in a gesture of friendship, squeaking quietly, his teeth clenched in a subservient grin.

Max welcomed his approach, squeaking back reassuringly and holding out both arms to this tiny vulnerable figure. Having confirmed their mutually friendly responses, piercing squeals of delight from the two bonobos now rang out and Baxter leapt out of my arms and into Max's tight embrace. There followed a long period of mutual grooming, punctuated by tender squeaks and sighs as they relaxed and got to know each other.

Before long, however, Max, realizing that Baxter was not up to much in the way of games, started to look around for something more challenging. Spotting the telephone wire, which was suspended precariously above our heads from the office door to the main zoo phone line, he released Baxter and within seconds was swinging along the wire excitedly until it broke with a resounding snap. He plummeted to the ground, taking the phone line with him. We knew from bitter experience that it would take months to repair the damage and the sight of our angry faces sent Max hurtling off into the forest.

He returned some hours later when he hoped our tempers had subsided. Mark lured him into the office with the promise of one of his favourite fruit yoghurts and a game of hide and seek.

Once inside he let Max know how angry he was. While Mark ranted and raved Max sat with his hands over his eyes, grimacing submissively and peeking through his fingers every now and then to check when the lecture was finished. He then took Mark's hand and meekly allowed himself to be led back to the cage.

We realized that the age gap between the two bonobos was too great for them to be regular playmates, so Max remained with Sid's group and Baxter with Mayoko's nursery group, where he was able to recover his strength in the more peaceful company of the gorillas.

The rainy season drew to a climactic end as heavy sheets of rain poured day after day from black skies, lowering the air temperature before the dry season began. We had come to fear this season as the drop in temperature at night brought a plague of colds and bronchitis.

It was at this time of year that the latest addition to Mayoko's group arrived. Mboukou was a fearless little character, full of angry defiance from day one. As I bent down to pick her up, my hands cautiously placed around her waist from behind, she turned with lightning speed and sank her small, sharp teeth into the flesh of my fingertips, hanging on until she felt she had made her point. Unwilling to give humans a chance, she would wait for the moment when our attention lapsed and creep stealthily towards the outskirts of the forest, where she then gathered speed, plunging into the dense undergrowth in search of Mayoko's group.

Achieving a balance between protecting already-established, healthy gorillas at the orphanage from disease possibly carried by new arrivals, and allowing new arrivals the undoubted reassurance of other gorilla companions, was always difficult. In Mboukou's case, she appeared healthy and it was obvious that depriving her of gorilla company would only increase her stress levels, with likely repercussions on her physical health. We gave in to her desire to be part of Mayoko's group without putting her through the usual lengthy period of quarantine.

Within weeks of her arrival a run-of-the-mill cold virus started to do the rounds of the group. It seemed at first no more serious than the many other colds the group had suffered. However, ten days later we noticed that Baxter and one of the gorillas, Sembe, were unusually inactive. Approaching them in the forest, we realized something was seriously wrong. Joining them as they squatted, hunched on the forest floor near Catherine, we listened as they wheezed, their tiny chests heaving in a struggle to draw breath.

The rest of the group continued their usual daily forest routine, occasionally pausing to glance over to where Sembe and Baxter crouched, breathless and unwilling to play. Realizing that they needed more rest than group life would allow we took the two sick babies back to the house. It was already too late to prevent the spread of whatever we were dealing with. Each and every individual in Mayoko's group could already be infected with this mysterious virus. Mark and I started to argue furiously, our distress and guilt spilling over into vicious counter accusations that we had not been sufficiently vigilant or that we could have acted earlier. It was becoming obvious that if we didn't find medical help Sembe and Baxter would be dead within twenty-four hours. Slamming out of the house Mark climbed into the jeep and screeched off into town to find Flore Bettini.

As she examined the babies, Flore's expression grew grave. They barely reacted to the cold metal stethoscope she placed on their tiny heaving chests, merely looking up at her with soulful, dull eyes, resigned to their fate.

'Their lungs,' she explained, 'are completely dull, filled with fluid, useless. Listen.'

She replaced the stethoscope on Baxter's chest and I listened to the ominous gurgling sounds. We sat back, feeling helpless as they fought for breath. Had they been human babies we would have flown them to Europe for specialized intensive care. Their status as a protected species, ironically, prevented them from leaving the Congo. We would have to do the best we could with the basic facilities at hand. Flore took blood samples for basic tests at the local laboratory and more to be sent urgently on to France by courier, where we hoped specialists would be able to identify the virus.

'There's probably a bacterial infection of some kind in the lungs,' she explained, 'but the real problem is that they are suffering from heart failure, perhaps a virus affecting the heart muscle. We'll have to give minute doses of powerful cardiac drugs to help the heart pump efficiently and diuretics to act on the kidneys and flush out as much of the fluid congesting their lungs as possible. This may just relieve the symptoms, but we need to cure the underlying cause. There are so many viruses in this part of the world, we're unlikely to have a diagnosis to work with in the little time they have left. We need to start antibiotic treatment and work out a suitable dose of cardiac drugs urgently if we are to stand any chance of saving their lives.'

I rushed frantically around the dusty streets of shanty-town Brazzaville under the intense glare of the sun that afternoon, attempting to find the drugs Flore had prescribed in different pharmacies. The pharmacists all took one look at my anxious face and assumed my own child must be gravely ill. I didn't bother to disillusion them and rushed on, arriving some time later back at the orphanage with an assortment of plastic bags filled to bursting point with different medicines. Mark and I set about carefully calculating the minute doses of these potentially lethal drugs required for two patients weighing less than four kilos. We checked and double-checked before administering the drugs, feeling a growing hopelessness. We had seen too many orphans die not to recognize their already resigned posture as they barely reacted to the painful injections, only turning to look at us with dull eyes. I remained at the house to watch over the two babies while Mark returned to the orphanage to check on the rest of Mayoko's group.

The drugs seemed to have no effect and by evening of the following day we could see that they were unlikely to make it through the night. Flore returned to the house to let us know that the local blood tests had shown nothing helpful and the French ones would take at least another week to come through. As we had done before when confronted by hopelessly ill orphans, we wondered if it would be kinder to hasten their deaths rather than watch them linger. These babies had fought so hard in the weeks following their confiscation. It seemed too cruel that they should now suffer like this. But we simply couldn't deny them that last chance. They died in the early hours of the morning and we found them, peaceful at last, wrapped in one another's arms. Our sadness was only relieved by the thought that at least the suffering of their short tragic lives was now at an end.

Mboukou, the newcomer, was the next to die, her illness mercifully short-lived but the symptoms the same. We were now certain that Mayoko's group was in the grips of a killer disease which threatened to wipe it out entirely, possibly even spreading beyond the nursery group to the other gorillas and bonobos. We were no nearer to a diagnosis, although an as yet unidentified viral pneumonia seemed likely. We had no time to reflect that we might be vulnerable to this disease in the same way as the gorillas.

Two more of the nursery group died the following week and an eight-month-old female called Dolly was fighting the same symptoms. Watching her, cradled pathetically in Catherine's arms in a shady corner of the garden, I was suddenly seized with desperate determination. Sweeping her up and wrapping her hastily in a blanket, I leapt into the jeep and drove into town in search of Flore.

She was seeing her last patient of the morning and I managed to slip in without anyone realizing the bundle I clutched was a gorilla not a human baby. After a brief examination Flore's face grew determined. 'I refuse to lose this one too.' Her words echoed my thoughts. 'We're going to take a risk and try her on a very powerful antibiotic not recommended for children. What do you think?'

I agreed we had nothing to lose, took the details and rushed off to the pharmacy opposite her surgery. Back at the orphanage I handed Dolly back to Catherine while I prepared the first injection of oily liquid. Reluctantly I forced the thick, yellow liquid into her skinny thigh. She squealed in pain and, at that moment, I despised myself for my incompetence, my inability to relieve her suffering as she looked up at me, her trusting eyes bewildered.

Two days later a miracle seemed to have occurred. Dolly's lungs were significantly clearer and her breathing less laboured. She had even started to show some interest in the pots of mushy baby food I offered her. I could scarcely believe my eyes and immediately felt guilty that we hadn't tried harder to save the others. I took her to see Flore in triumph, along with a bottle of champagne to celebrate. But some days later, back at the orphanage, when the antibiotic course had been completed, the symptoms returned with a vengeance and Dolly died before my eyes.

I told Flore the tragic news. We both sat in reflective silence, thinking of the six infants we had lost in just three short weeks, and feeling a heavy burden of guilt for not having been able to save them. Their sad eyes would haunt my dreams for months.

Mark and I were unable to talk about what had happened. Instead of uniting us, our sadness alienated us from one another.

Her group decimated, Catherine was left with just Mayoko, whose tough, egotistical nature helped her to adjust quickly to the loss of her playmates after a brief period of mourning. She was a natural survivor and basked in the attention she now received as we tried to compensate her for the terrible loss we imagined she must feel. I forced myself out to the forest glade that had been their playground, now an eerie, silent place. Standing small in this cathedral of trees I understood in that moment the Congolese belief that the forest was possessed by spirits. The warm, damp air seemed thick with the wandering souls of the six dead infant gorillas and the past generations of their ancestors who had been killed over the centuries in the Central African forests.

Chapter Seventeen

Kola's Devastating Loss

While Mark and I remained preoccupied with the tragic fate of the nursery group, Steve had made the decision to leave Brazzaville to take up a place at Edinburgh University.

He planned to do a Masters degree and return to the Congo to pursue his thesis in the largely unexplored region of North-West Congo, the Likouala swamps. There he hoped to find a relatively healthy population of western lowland gorillas thriving on the abundant, succulent swamp vegetation and protected from heavy hunting pressure by the impenetrable nature of the terrain. Leaving the orphanage was not an easy decision to make, though, and he hoped to return at a later date to see how the gorillas were adapting to life in the wild. We were all sad to see him go and would miss his humour, hard work and level-headedness.

He was replaced by John Buchan, a gorilla keeper from London Zoo. Arriving in Brazzaville, John was thrown straight in at the deep end. He started full of energy and enthusiasm for the adventure that lay ahead. But within minutes of shaking our hands in the sweltering heat of the airport, he had proudly announced, 'I got married last week'. My heart sank. Although I knew he had a girlfriend, we weren't aware that marriage was so imminent! I didn't imagine he would be able to survive separation from a new wife for long, and it sounded as though from what he said that it would be unlikely she would be joining him in Brazzaville. He didn't appear to notice our disappointment as Mark and I muttered tersely to one another in the front seats of the jeep on the short trip from the airport to the orphanage.

He wasted no time in getting stuck into the work, completely undaunted by the larger gorillas and eager to take on as much responsibility as we were willing to give him. He worked incredibly hard, scarcely ever taking a day off, and showed enormous patience with the more time-consuming new orphans. His tolerant nature and relaxed manner made him an immediate favourite with the staff. The girls were soon bringing home-baked cakes in to work to feed him up, perplexed by the fact that his wife had refused to accompany him to Brazzaville.

Mark had just recovered from an attack of appendicitis. A high-dose course of antibiotics had narrowly averted the necessity of an operation in the hazardous conditions of Brazzaville Military Hospital, an institution which even the Congolese avoided. As we waited anxiously to see whether the antibiotics would work, I trawled the local pharmacies in an effort to put together a medical kit that would be essential if an operation was needed. A large hold-all was crammed full of sheets, infusion fluids, dressings, drugs – in short every piece of disposable equipment needed for an operation apart from the surgeon himself and his instruments – and sat in our sitting room ready for use as we prepared for the worst.

The infection subsided in time, but Mark was warned that he should return to England as soon as possible to have the offending appendix removed whilst free of infection. A recurrence in Brazzaville could be fatal. As John had only just arrived in Brazzaville we decided it was too soon to leave him to cope alone, so Mark continued to work with a potentially fatal time-bomb ticking away inside him. I was concerned, though, especially as I also needed to get back to England for a minor operation to deal with something that had been brewing over the past year and now needed urgent attention. Then, as I had feared, within a matter of weeks John Buchan seemed unhappy. He announced that his wife was missing him and he would have to return to England in the next few months. We were confronted with the task of finding another replacement.

Mark had first met Hans Otto Kopff in the early 1980s. Hans had come to Howletts to study captive gorillas as part of his university degree course, and had shared Mark's obsessive desire to work with gorillas in Africa. It seemed fated that their next meeting, many years later, was to be in Africa itself.

Hans had already visited the orphanage in 1991, on his way home to Berlin having completed a lengthy tour of Zaire. Despite the fact that they disagreed on many things, the friendship between him and Mark was still strong, so when John announced his resignation Mark immediately thought of Hans.

Hans had been captivated by the gorillas during his brief stay, and he was overjoyed to be offered the job. But from Berlin he explained that he had recently fallen in love and he would have to ask his girlfriend, Christiane, what she felt about coming to the Congo before he could accept our offer. When she accepted his suggestion none of us could believe our luck; suddenly life seemed blessed with a surfeit of good fortune. This was soon to be snatched cruelly away.

By the time Hans arrived in Brazzaville in May 1992, Mark and I had left for England to deal with our respective medical problems. We also hoped that a break from Brazzaville would help us over our sadness at the loss of our nursery group. John held the fort for a couple of days until Hans arrived. We firmly believed our parting words as we assured him before waving goodbye at the airport, that nothing worse than the past few months could happen.

Mark and I were sitting in John Aspinall's plush office opposite Harrods, when Sue Hunt, his personal assistant of many years, rushed in.

'Hans has just phoned from Brazzaville,' she shrieked. 'He says that two of the gorillas are paralysed. He needs to get in touch with Chris immediately!'

After speaking briefly to Hans on the phone I knew that the one thing I had always feared had happened. A polio epidemic had hit the orphanage, threatening every one of the gorillas and bonobos we had rescued over the past three years.

I insisted repeatedly to Sue Hunt and Chris Furley, the Howletts Zoo vet, that this was the only possible explanation and that vaccines should be flown out to the Congo as soon as possible, preferably accompanied by Chris himself. We knew all too well how quickly epidemics could spread there. They decided to wait for a few days and arrange veterinary cover for the two zoos in Chris's absence. In the meantime Hans and John did their best to control the spread of whatever they were dealing with.

Although I knew I had done my best to put in motion plans for a vaccination programme for the gorillas over a year before, I still felt terrible guilt for not having pushed harder or simply taken the matter into my own hands, had the vaccines sent over and administered them myself, regardless of the unlikely but possible risk of a fatal allergic reaction. It had been all too easy to push the matter to the back of my mind.

*

Bilinga was already completely paralysed, Hans and John told us, not even able to raise her head to drink or eat. Boko's legs were paralysed. Both of them had suffered terrible fevers in the first few days of the illness which spiked and fell with equal speed, leaving their bodies exhausted.

The following morning Kambala was also found paralysed. Chris Furley instructed Hans to put him to sleep. If Bilinga didn't improve during the next few days they would be forced to do the same for her, but there was greater reluctance to do this as we had already lost so many females in the nursery group a couple of months previously. By the time Chris arrived in Brazzaville it was obvious that she would never recover the use of her arms or legs, so one of his first tasks was to put her to sleep.

By this time Sid was sick too, off his food, feverish and showing signs of weakness in his left leg. He was also making strange movements with his mouth. Although Sid recovered from the acute feverish stage of the illness, he was left with the legacy of a handicapped left leg and seriously weakened jaw muscles. Physiotherapy and gentle exercise ensured that some of the strength returned to his affected leg in time, but he remained unable to bite with any strength. We had had such high hopes for him, of his eventual return to the wild. It was now going to be a hundred times harder. He would be unlikely to recover enough strength in the weak leg to climb competently and find food in the higher trees, and his inability to bite with any force and chew his way through the required quantity and variety of tough vegetation which forms such an essential part of a wild gorilla's diet would make his survival that much more unlikely.

Reassured by the familiar surroundings of the room he had occupied some months before, following his last narrow escape with death, Sid slowly recovered. But we noticed he had developed a bizarre method of feeding himself in an attempt to cope with his handicap. This involved placing one large fist under his chin and pushing upwards to assist his weak jaw muscles to bite into the tougher-skinned fruits. Even when his jaw regained a little of its former strength he retained this peculiar mannerism, the skin under his chin becoming hard and calloused with wear.

He was a survivor, it seemed. Having endured a terrible capture and imprisonment of many months, a stabbing and now polio, we came to feel we simply couldn't deny him the chance of a life in the wild, even though it would be risky and require careful surveillance to ensure that he was able to forage adequately and keep up with the rest of his group as they roamed the forest.

As Mark and I recovered from our respective operations in different wards in the same hospital back in London, the news from Brazzaville was that Madingo also now showed a slight weakness in one leg, had lost his appetite and become weak and inactive. He went on to make a reasonable recovery, but the experience of the illness itself and his awareness of his weak, handicapped leg left his confidence seriously dented. And it seemed the bad news kept pouring in.

Mark and I debated as whether to return immediately. Then the epidemic halted as suddenly as it had begun. No more animals seemed to be at risk so we decided to remain in England to convalesce.

But on our return a week later, the orphanage was a sad place, its numbers so diminished it seemed impossible that just three months before we had been planning to expand its holding capacity. Sid was back in his convalescent's room, looking weak and thin and in need of a great deal of affection, reassurance and encouragement to begin his long recovery. Boko was being seen daily by a French physiotherapist who had declined to treat the rather larger, more daunting Sid, but reports were not encouraging. Boko was a sad mockery of her former active, bright, socially successful little self. She never recovered the use of her legs, which now hung like useless appendages, and was resigned to a life where she struggled to keep up with her group in the forest, dragging her limp legs along the ground as she moved forward using her strong arms as crutches. She tired long before the others and was soon left behind, whimpering and hooting as they disappeared from view. Nzambi, her closest playmate in the group, would climb the high trees with the others and bring down handfuls of fruit and leaves which he would then hand to Boko, ensuring that she had at least a share of the food they found. The rest of the group bore her no animosity for her slowness, but they ignored her now, quickly bored by her inability to play and join them in their explorations.

Unable to watch Boko's distress any longer, we decided to remove her from her group and create a new group with her, Mayoko and Kabo. Without Bilinga's protective presence, Kabo suffered from bullying in Kola's group, now containing only males much older than himself. Kola was preoccupied with his loss of Bilinga and not his usual observant self, failing to notice the in-fighting that now unsettled his group. For the first few days Boko sat in the forest hooting plaintively for her old friends and family. It was an unbearably sad, haunting sound that echoed throughout the forest, carrying its message to Kola's group some distance away. But as the months passed, she did form new friendships with the youngsters Kabo and Mayoko, establishing herself as a sort of gorilla 'aunt' to these younger orphans.

Kola coped with his loss of Bilinga with as much dignity as his years allowed, but at times he still hooted, calling for her. At night in the cage his poignant cries carried in the humid night, his message understood by all the gorillas. However, a challenge lay before him which would test his skills of leadership once again. He needed to control and reform the ranks of his group, unsettled by the events and changes of the previous few weeks.

Chapter Eighteen

Mabafi and Dimonika

Hans had passed his demanding initiation into orphanage life with flying colours. We had high hopes that we had found someone who shared our commitment to the gorillas and who would stick by the project through thick and thin.

The local staff, however, always wary of new expatriates to the project, were unnerved by Hans' abrupt, Germanic manner, misinterpreting it for arrogance or simple disrespect. We were obliged to call a meeting during which they aired their feelings. Asking them to give him time, we assured them that Hans liked and respected them all immensely even if his manner did not seem to reflect this. It was a cultural problem, we explained, and they needed to show tolerance. They sloped off to reflect and there seemed to be an improvement in relations, apart from with Jean who always had difficulty with male authority figures.

The staff had accepted Mark and me, and now held us up as shining examples to any new expatriate staff, our qualities grossly exaggerated and impossible to match. Although the high standard of work we demanded still occasionally caused complaint, as time passed they had grown to realize that these high standards reflected well on themselves. They had become like family to us. We infuriated one another at times, at others we enjoyed happy moments, a common sense of humour and the confidence of one another's loyalty. Despite the importance placed on children in African society, none of them ever asked us the question which most expatriates seemed to get round to sooner rather than later – why did we not have children of our own? Their unspoken acceptance of our way of life was greatly appreciated.

Nkodia was our trusted link with the rest of the staff during unsettled periods. Whenever we sensed disquiet, noticing them shuffling despondently about their work feeling misunderstood or abused, he would explain their complaints to us. At first he was reluctant to do so, worried by conflicting loyalties, but he soon understood that unless we knew about any problems and understood them, we could not hope to solve them. In the evenings, as darkness fell, we would sit with the youngest gorillas playing lazily on our laps whilst Nkodia chattered on about everything and anything. We danced around sensitive subjects and learnt to respect and understand better one another's cultures and points of view.

A new addition to the staff was a friend of Albertine called Bernadette Mahoungou. She was about my own age, already a mother of three children, and she instantly struck a natural rapport with the gorillas. She was petite, and coy in a way many African women appear at first, but we discovered she could erupt with surprising fury if provoked. The animals appreciated her gentle manner, sensitivity and sense of humour. She even succeeded in breaking through Titi's defences where no one else had been able to.

One day, as Bernadette sat in the forest with Kola's group under the tutelage of Albertine, Titi plucked up the courage to approach the unthreatening female newcomer. Sitting with his broad back to her, he extended one long arm backwards and left his hand open, palm upwards beside Bernadette in a tentative gesture of friendship, daring her to touch his hand but his bodily posture of apparent indifference allowing his pride to remain undented if his invitation was refused. When she put her hand in his, he maintained the contact for some minutes, returning her trust. This simple routine continued for a few days until he decided to take a bigger risk and with little warning plonked himself down clumsily on her lap. Her face creased in a mixture of surprise, delight and discomfort, and she responded by whispering softly to him, repeating his name, 'Titi, Titi'. His heart beat rapidly at first but his face soon relaxed its mask of feigned indifference, softening as his confidence grew and he started to grumble with pleasure.

Bernadette swelled with pride at her conquest when, a few days later, Albertine recounted her story to the other staff who smiled and congratulated her, assuring her that she had won a very special friend that day. Titi was also proud of his new friend and would sit possessively on Bernadette's lap most days, only prepared to give up his place diplomatically for Kola.

In September 1992 Bernadette's sister had her first baby, a boy, by Caesarean section in the local hospital. A few days later she started to complain of abdominal pain which grew worse day by day. She was eventually readmitted to hospital and died shortly afterwards. An autopsy revealed that she had died of peritonitis – that the surgeon who had performed the Caesarean section had left a pair of surgical scissors inside her abdomen. Bernadette was inconsolable. I had witnessed the expressions of dumb pain etched on the tragic faces of our staff when family members died and our neighbours' wild sorrow as they wailed throughout the night at wakes that often lasted a week, but Bernadette's agony did not seem to pass with the weeks. She appeared late for work every day, her eyes dull and hopeless, her body leaden with grief. Her doctor had given her a cocktail of sedatives and sleeping pills which rendered her virtually unable to walk.

I took her aside one morning and we talked. My attempts to persuade her that her sister's death was not her fault met with stubborn resistance at first, but eventually she listened. I took advantage of this moment to explain that the pills were only confusing her thoughts and postponing the time when she had to confront her feelings and find a way of coping with them. Support from someone outside her family, who were busy blaming one another for the death, seemed to help. Like most of the Congolese she was convinced that death never struck randomly, but that her sister had died under the spell of an as yet unrevealed sorcerer. She became convinced that she would be the next in line to die.

Hans' girlfriend, Christiane, settled smoothly into life in Brazzaville and her presence put Hans into even higher spirits. It was impossible not to notice, the constant gestures of intimacy and reassurance between them that signalled their complete absorption in one another. They moved into the bungalow with us until they could find a place of their own. Hans had just taken over care of his first bonobo baby, Blixa, a tiny female, and his life now seemed complete. But Hans and Christiane's relationship was soon to be put to the test just as ours had been with Max.

Dimonika had been confiscated in Pointe Noire by Madame Jamart and arrived at the orphanage curled into a tight, impenetrable ball. She screamed her heart out in protest, her little fists and feet clenched so tightly that the skin stretched taut on her knuckles, her body rigid with fear. Her screams of fear and rage continued, unremitting and impossible to ignore. When we placed her in her basket late at night, a routine which most new orphans quickly grew familiar with, she re-lived each and every time the feelings of panic and abandonment she must have felt when her mother was killed in the forest. She woke with monotonous regularity every two hours throughout the night, screaming in panic.

We took turns to rescue her, offering warm milk and waiting for the panic to subside and sleep to overwhelm her exhausted body. As the months progressed we realized that her mental faculties were not developing as they should. She was backward in both co-ordination and development, and we began to wonder whether her strange Mongoloid eyes and unusually flat, round face might be an indication of Down's syndrome, if such a thing existed in gorillas.

Within weeks of her arrival, Dimonika was seriously ill with amoebic dysentery. Her already high stress levels were exacerbated by physical pain now and she bluntly refused all fluids, her entire body gripped by rigid muscle spasms. The diarrhoea improved and her fever fell as a result of antibiotics, but we noticed that her nappy had remained dry throughout the day and began to worry about urinary retention. We called on Flore Bettini once again.

Flore confirmed our fears and said she would have to puncture Dimonika's bladder. We presumed that Dimonika's spasms of panic had caused the muscles at the neck of the bladder to contract. It now risked rupturing with fatal consequences.

'I 'ave never punctured a gorilla's bladder before,' Flore wailed, 'I'm not even sure exactly where it is.'

'Assume she's a human baby?' I proffered, as she selected the smallest bore needle she could find in her medical bag, crossed her fingers and we all held our breath. She cautiously pushed the sharp tip through the fragile skin of Dimonika's belly and immediately thick, yellow, misty fluid flowed from the needle. We all heaved a sigh of relief.

She was still, however, dehydrated and any oral fluids we

managed to get down her came straight back up in a stream of projectile vomit. Flore suggested we sedate her and administer the fluids subcutaneously.

New to this business, Christiane was obviously distressed and left the room in tears to the sound of Dimonika's angry squeals as the sedative was injected. Suddenly all was blissfully quiet as she drifted off to sleep. We injected the required amount of glucose solution which formed painful-looking bumps under the skin of her thin arms and legs, but the welts had dispersed by the time she came round and she began to make surprisingly fast progress.

Within the next few days her bowels slowed down to the point where she was soon painfully constipated. We gave her a dose of laxative and waited for the result. That evening we all gathered expectantly round her tiny figure as she crouched in the centre of the living room, straining, pushing and squealing as we cheered her determined efforts on. Eventually the dam burst and after much cursing and cleaning we sat back, relieved, and Dimonika fell fast asleep.

When Hans and Christiane found a flat about a hundred yards down the road and moved out of our crowded bungalow, Dimonika moved with them. We took over the care of Blixa, who had now developed some strength in her spindly legs and would spend hours in the office chair bobbing up and down, squeaking excitedly as we attempted to work. We felt a little guilty about landing them with Dimonika, but were confident that Christiane's patient, loving nature would provide exactly the right degree of consistent care she required.

Blixa, like Max, soon discovered the joys of sex. As soon as she was strong enough to sit upright we noticed her rocking back and forth on the chair, rubbing her groin against the rough surface of her nappy, grinning and squeaking in a crescendo of excitement.

Mabafi, the next gorilla arrival, was a complete contrast to Dimonika. As we lifted her from the cardboard box she had arrived in and had lain in for maybe a week, we were horrified to see her back covered in pustulating sores. Mango flies had laid their eggs in the damp cloth on the base of the box, embedded themselves in her skin and hatched into larvae which fed on her, growing larger daily and causing sores which quickly became infected. We had seen sores like this in other babies, and indeed suffered from them ourselves, and knew how painful they could be. Thankfully Mabafi seemed barely conscious. Translucent, fragile skin sunk into bone, her skull resembled that of an old man.

As Mark cradled her tiny body to his chest she miraculously responded, pursing her dry lips to make pathetic, token sucking motions. Her unfocused eyes gazed out at the world through a haze of pain and confusion. I quickly prepared a bottle of re-hydration fluid, searching frantically for a rubber feeding teat small enough. Mark and I exchanged despairing looks, convinced we had arrived on the scene too late. Her lips pursed and clasped themselves around the teat, sucking feebly at first but with gathering strength as the cool liquid soothed her parched throat. Soon she was sucking with the strength of desperate thirst and Mark had to forcibly remove the teat from her mouth before she overloaded her tiny body. With a sucking reflex this strong, we thought, she must stand a chance.

Having consumed the rest of the bottle, her skeletal body started to convulse, then lay suddenly still and lifeless. Her heart had stopped. Mark gave her chest a quick thud and applied two fingers in a gentle pumping motion. We held our breath and watched in disbelief as the colour returned to her lips. Through-out the course of the day she consumed three more bottles and by the evening we felt surprisingly optimistic.

Her strength returned in bounds. Before long Mabafi had

outgrown Dimonika to become a surprisingly sturdy, well-balanced young gorilla. Despite their differences in character and ability, the two became firm friends. But the extent of Dimonika's retardation became increasingly obvious as the year progressed and she failed to achieve even the most basic milestones of infant gorilla development. Catherine had to choose and peel fruit for her and even place it in her mouth. She seemed simply incapable of learning even the most basic skills. When placed on the tiled nursery feeding platform which we used for hygiene purposes as it could easily be scrubbed clean, she never once attempted to climb down to the lush grass below as the others did, to explore and play. She remained paralysed by confusion on the platform, unable to work out how to get off and join in the fun below. Once lifted down by Catherine she would immediately rush off giggling and grumbling with pleasure. The art of climbing remained just as much of a mystery to her. Our attempts to encourage her to begin climbing by hooking her hands onto a low branch and leaving her dangling failed. She would remain hanging motionless, giggle for a few moments, then panic and, stretching her arms and legs rigid, she would fall to the ground. As she landed on the soft earth she would curl into a tight ball and scream angrily, waiting for Catherine or myself to rescue her and spend the next fifteen minutes cradling her in our arms, walking around the garden murmuring reassuring noises and waiting patiently until the panic subsided.

We feared for Dimonika's future as the rest of her group grew and developed, leaving her increasingly alienated and clinging stubbornly to her own safe, monotonous routine.

Mabafi, however, was showing great promise. She was quick to learn, curious but cautious. She had already won a special place in our hearts.

Kola's group would need female company one day. By chance

the early years of the orphanage had brought us mostly male orphans. The females that had arrived had, sadly, died in the two devastating disease outbreaks of the past year. Mabafi and Mayoko were at this point our only hope.

Chapter Nineteen

Monkey Business

In October 1992, at the end of the long dry season, the forest was dry and brittle, thirsty for rain. Clouds of dust erupted wherever we walked and temperatures soared beneath the scorching sun. Our erratic water supply had been cut off for days, a health risk as well as an inconvenience.

When the rain finally fell, we all stood luxuriating under the warm, bulging droplets. Once the staff had left for the day Mark and I stripped off our filthy clothes and stood beneath the gutter. Clean rainwater poured over our hot bodies. Cool and refreshing, it washed away the dirt and sweat of the past few days. After a few minutes I started to shiver as the air cooled and I ran into the flat to find dry clothes. The aftermath of the storm brought mud, and more mud. It steamed under the hot sun early the next morning and by evening was parched, cracked and dry. While it lasted, Djembo loved to play in the muddy water, plunging into puddles and beating her chest ecstatically while Sid and Rupert crouched under shelter, their heads cradled in their arms. The younger gorillas squealed as the first drops of rain fell and ran for cover beneath Albertine's maternal bulk. On the wettest days they would all stay in and when the rain abated they would burst from their rooms, the younger ones trailing behind, grizzling and trying to climb onto the backs of the older gorillas to avoid the boggy ground as they made their way out to the forest. Even Kola's group headed back to the shelter of the orphanage when the rain fell heavily.

Kola's group were now confident and competent in the forest, and would wait impatiently in the early morning to be free from the confines of their overnight room, bursting out and off towards the undergrowth to begin their search for food. If their morning drinks of milk were delayed, the confinement of their small bedroom would lead to petty disputes and bad temper. Nzambi, in particular, would scream with the uncontrolled impatience of a baby, sorely testing the tolerance of the others who were waiting with more mature patience for their drinks to arrive, exchanging looks of contempt for Nzambi, whose behaviour they considered unbecoming for a gorilla.

As Albertine opened the heavy wooden door they would explode out in a chaotic bundle, spreading out and thundering off to the outskirts of the forest where they would sit politely waiting for her as she ambled along behind them carrying the bucket that contained their drinks. They would then group around her as she sat, ladling milk from the bucket into individual mugs and handing them around. Again it would be Nzambi who would become impatient if he wasn't served first. Titi would become so irritated by Nzambi's wilful screams that he could no longer restrain himself and would barge past him, deliberately knocking his mug flying and spilling his precious milk.

The moment they had finished they would drop their mugs, leaving Albertine to clean up, and disappear into the forest, chasing one another and tunnelling into the dense undergrowth as they made for whatever area they had chosen for the day, with Albertine eventually following behind. Once there they would haul themselves with heavy grace up the tall trees in search of fruit and leaves, stopping to rest occasionally on a convenient forked branch to munch contentedly. Nzambi often remained on the ground, close to Albertine, fidgeting aimlessly, grabbing the odd leafy stem nearby and stuffing it into his mouth. As the morning progressed and they had satisfied their appetites, Titi and Madingo would descend to the forest floor to chase one another around the broad tree trunks until one or other of them lost interest and they sat quietly catching their breath before setting off again.

Albertine would sit on the forest floor as they explored around and above her, sometimes lost from view, the sound of her knitting needles furiously clacking in the still air. Occasionally one or other, usually Madingo or Titi, would try to provoke a reaction from her, grabbing her colourful head-scarf and running off into the undergrowth with it, hoping to be pursued. Her knitting output was prolific – she sold the blankets and clothing she made for extra cash or gave them as gifts for weddings or funerals. She would tolerate their playful attentions, amused for the most part, until they overstepped the boundaries of polite behaviour and unleashed her considerable wrath. She would then shout their names with obvious irritation and they would move off in search of a more receptive victim. On one occasion Titi grabbed at the shiny, gold-plated chain around her neck. It snapped and he ran off with it, sitting a little way off, pouring the shiny object, intrigued, through his big fingers and looking up every now and then to see whether Albertine would react. She was furious and rushed over, grabbing it off him, shouting angrily, then retiring to sulk, nursing her sore neck and broken chain. She remained angry with Titi the next day, feeling injured by his disregard for her prized possession. Although we replaced the necklace, we warned her not to wear jewellery when out with the gorillas – she was lucky the chain had broken and not garrotted her. That afternoon she returned from the forest with a nasty bite wound on her foot. We never quite got to the bottom of the story but suspected that, still angry and resentful, she had provoked Titi and he, frightened, confused and unable to understand the gravity of his intended joke, had bitten her. Thankfully, the incident blew over.

As the late afternoon light faded, the gorillas would start to wind down, descending the trees to sit in comfortable silence with one another before setting off to build night nests, an evening ritual they performed even though they would return later to their cage to sleep for the night. Kola would stir first, disentangling himself from the group and moving off to stand proudly for a few minutes, posing with languid grace, swaying his head from side to side and raising it to sniff the air before turning to beckon his group and moving off.

The group would then lazily rouse themselves and follow Kola up into the trees in search of suitable platforms of branches where they would squat, rotating in circles while they methodically pulled branches in and under with both hands, crushing them with their feet into a densely woven mattress.

The orphanage forest had been transformed over the previous couple of years to a luxuriant green mass as the gorillas pruned by foraging, and dispersed seeds in their dung as they wandered. We needed more information on what they were consuming and any input this might have on the balance and diversity of plant species in the small forest.

Abel Mpassi, a Congolese botany student from Brazzaville University, was keen to undertake this study. Having worked with Dr Kuroda's team up north, he felt confident of his competence for the task. However, the gorillas were not always polite or tolerant as he followed their every move in the forest, collecting samples of everything they ate for identification. The younger gorillas were not a problem, but Sid's group occasionally got irritated by Abel's presence. When his attention was distracted they would barge past, flattening him head-first into the mud and running off with his precious notebook, sitting at a safe distance, their clumsy, muddy hands obliterating his morning's hard work.

Abel's first study was, however, against the odds, a success. He produced a comprehensive list of plant foods consumed by the gorillas, even noting that they would treat themselves for diarrhoea and intestinal parasite infestations by consuming certain plant species known locally for their medicinal properties. Through a combination of innate and learnt knowledge, it seemed that our gorillas were able to find and identify the appropriate food sources available within this limited area. As a result of their exploitation of the forest, Abel confirmed, there was an increased density of plant species favoured by the gorillas in the regularly used areas.

Spurred on by the success of his first study, Abel insisted on undertaking a second, this time assessing the speed of regeneration of these same plant species. To the delight of Sid's group, this required Abel to bring with him a three-metre wooden measuring stick. His efforts were soon made impossible as he found himself unwillingly engaged in a tug of war with Sid. He was a good-natured, tolerant person, but this enthusiastic, unwelcome help proved too much. We were not surprised when he finally admitted defeat, but we thanked him for the valuable information he had given the project – information that convinced us further that the gorillas would soon need to move to a new and much larger territory if they were to continue their progress towards a wild future.

As their play became more boisterous, Kola's group needed a regular human male presence. Juislain Mvila proved the perfect solution. Sixteen years old, he had already been employed at the orphanage for the past six months doing cleaning duties. He was keen to work with Kola's group and jumped at this opportunity, anxious to show how capable he was. Kola took to this adolescent male, similar to himself in many ways and, being short and thick set, Juislain was the ideal build to cope with the physical rigours of a group of macho male gorillas. He soon made himself indispensable, his skills a close match for Albertine's.

One afternoon we were sitting in the forest as Kola's group fed in the canopy above. As we discussed their progress I was impressed by Juislain's observations and uncanny understanding of his charges.

'Madame,' he said as I made to leave the forest, 'you know why I am so happy with the gorillas?'

'No, Juislain. Tell me,' I responded, intrigued.

'My grandmother told me,' he explained gravely, 'before she died, that I would work in the forest with animals. This is my fate.'

I smiled, unable to restrain my pleasure at his pride. It was lucky that he felt so at home with the gorillas: he would need this emotional grounding in the coming months.

The orphanage also now housed a motley collection of non-primate creatures. There were a couple of ducks we had ordered for our Christmas dinner. As Christmas approached, Jean plucked up the courage to confront us with what he saw as our hypocrisy. Marching into the office one morning, he took a deep breath and launched into an impassioned speech about animal cruelty.

'We are an animal sanctuary, Monsieur Marc,' he said. 'We cannot kill these ducks. Look at them,' he pointed as they waddled happily past the office door looking for food. 'How can we kill them? We could eat their eggs instead.'

Stunned by his defence and the logic of his argument, we gave in, defeated and ashamed. The fact that Mark had procrastinated over killing them made me suspect that he was secretly relieved. The case was closed. We bought an imported frozen duck, at great expense, from a French butcher in town and the ducks settled in to orphanage life. Soon we were overrun with ducklings that waddled in single file behind us wherever we went.

The gorillas would occasionally muster the energy to chase them, delighted by the way they flapped their wings and fled in panic. True to form, it took Dimonika several months to register the ducks' existence and when she did her eyes grew wide with the revelation. She launched herself onto the back of one of the larger birds, then panicked when it flapped its wings and fled as she clung tightly to its tail feathers, dragged through the mud behind it, unable to work out that she should simply let go.

We had also inherited two monkeys. Kiki, a female spot-nosed monkey, had been released into the orphanage forest by an elderly French nun leaving the Congo. She had been named Kiki by the orphanage staff – all monkeys in the Congo were called Kiki, an onomatopoeic reference to their chattering. Virtually wild and shy of humans, she lived in the refuge of the forest, only emerging occasionally at dusk to snatch pieces of fruit left by the gorillas in the garden. As the weeks passed, she became curious and would sit on the wooden fence that surrounded the garden, watching as the gorillas gathered round us for their midday meal. In the forest she watched, silently at first, from the tree-tops whilst the gorillas explored, until one day she plucked up the courage to approach them, inviting them to play with gentle play-bites, pulling them towards her with long, spindly arms. Soon she was jumping enthusiastically on their backs as they grumbled contentedly, enjoying her gentle attentions.

As their friendship grew, Kiki assumed the role of sentry guard for the gorillas. She would chatter furiously at any human intruders approaching them in the forest, leaping at their legs from behind and biting with all her strength. On a more serious level, her alarm calls alerted the staff and gorillas to the presence of venomous snakes which she spotted from her vigil in the trees above.

This gentle introduction to monkeys did not prepare us for the next arrival. Pétain was a vervet monkey, an altogether more aggressive and territorial species. Spoilt by his previous owner, the French Ambassador's wife, he arrived incapacitated by a plaster leg cast. He was a political refugee, shot in the leg as a direct provocation to the French Ambassador. So it wasn't until we removed the cast some weeks later that we realized what we had taken on. Pétain, as we called him in reference to his French origins, wasted no time in asserting himself. His confidence grew to ludicrous proportions. Although he did have his moments of calm, when grooming or being groomed, he enjoyed provoking a reaction. He would steal Mark's cigarettes from under his nose and wait for Mark to pursue him, when he would scoot up a nearby tree out of reach. As Mark ranted and raved at the foot of the tree, he would pluck the cigarettes one by one from the box, snapping them smugly in half and nimbly dodging the missiles Mark hurled up from below. When challenged, he would hop up and down, eyebrows raised menacingly, impossible to subdue. He effectively intimidated all but Jean and Mark, who he kept a wary eye on.

At mealtimes, he would steal food from the younger gorillas, biting them hard and making off with his 'prize', to their screams of pain. The older gorillas, for the most part, treated him with lazy contempt, swatting him aside when he got in their way. Only occasionally, when he pushed the boundaries of what they considered to be fair play with the youngsters, would they pin him to the ground and bite hard, sending him screaming and chattering in rage back into the forest.

The ducks' eggs soon became a bone of contention between Pétain and Alphonse, the night guard, each assuming rights over these delicacies. We were often greeted in the early morning by an irate Alphonse, cursing the fleeing figure of Pétain as he made off with one of the prized eggs. The ducklings were also on Pétain's menus and started to disappear one by one.

A pygmy goat called Bob, another creature originally intended for human consumption, also provided a good deal of entertainment for both the monkeys and the gorillas. Kiki and Pétain were fascinated by him and would reach up on two legs to stroke his velvety ears before leaping onto his back, clinging on like rodeo riders as Bob reared and bucked in his attempts to throw them off.

The gorillas were more circumspect in their initial reaction to this strange, hoofed creature. As Bob tugged against the rope that tethered him to the gatepost – a precaution to stop him wandering off and ending up in some hungry passer-by's cooking pot – the gorillas spotted him on their return from the forest and huddled together in a tight group, perplexed and unsure what to make of him. Max fled up a nearby tree to watch, uncharacteristically quiet, followed by Djembo. As Rupert craned his neck forward to take a closer look and Sid thundered around, stiff-legged, at a safe distance behind him, Bob reared up on his hind legs and swiftly butted Rupert in the stomach. He recoiled in shock, but curiosity soon got the better of him and he tried again, advancing towards Bob and this time, as he reared, moving away just in time. He had discovered a new game, but Sid, Djembo and Max remained unconvinced. Bob didn't appear worried by this encounter, which only briefly distracted him from the business of eating.

Food was Bob's main motivation in life. Having eaten his way through every succulent leaf within reach, he would strain against the rope, choking himself to reach further afield. One afternoon we returned from town to find him hanging, noosed, from a thick branch, saliva drooling from his frothing mouth as he fought for breath. We rushed over, released him and within seconds he trotted purposefully off in search of more food, oblivious to his narrow brush with death.

At night feral dogs roamed the grounds, scavenging for food. One morning out in the forest we came across an old dog chained to a tree. A sinister cloth purse hung round his neck, probably an evil charm. As we approached, he raised himself on trembling legs from the deep bowl of cool earth he had dug to escape the burning heat of the sun. His skin hung from his bones like an over-sized coat but he snarled, frightened and aggressive. Anxious to put him out of his misery, Mark went back to the orphanage to fetch our tranquillizer blowpipe. He returned with the blowpipe loaded with a dose of the anaesthetic Ketamine big enough to kill a horse. The old dog yelped as the dart hit home and was soon unconscious, his torture ended. We released his neck from the noose and walked back to the orphanage. The next day as we drove to work we spotted him crossing the road. He slunk into the shadows and disappeared from sight. Perhaps he did indeed possess magical powers.

Alphonse, the night watchman, had recently developed heart trouble and would often arrive at work puffy-faced and breathless, his condition not helped by the amount of his salary he spent on drink. I had attempted countless times to explain to him that he must take his medication regularly, but without success. The more confused he became the less likely he was to do so. He began to claim that he was possessed of powers of sorcery. The staff were terrified by his sinister rantings as he threatened to cast spells over them all. Explanations about senility did nothing to assuage their fears. In the end we were forced to retire him, replacing him with a night-guard from the zoo whose reliability had impressed us and who was keen to move to a job that promised a greater and more reliable salary.

We offered Alphonse the option of a lump cash sum or

smaller regular payments each month to help him pay for medical treatment. He took the cash, and we bade him an affectionate goodbye as he left the orphanage and Brazzaville for good.

That night, back at the house, a wake took place nearby. I listened in the dark to the beat of drums, their rhythms like a heart beat in the quiet night. The murmured incantations of mourners accompanied the drums, an undulating lament that erupted every now and then into tragic animal moans and strange, unworldly cries. I thought of Alphonse returning to his village in the interior to die.

As 1992 drew to a close, we hoped to receive a visit from a Professor Hayama, a pathologist from Kyoto University, who had been recommended to us by Dr Kuroda. He had agreed to perform autopsies on the deceased gorillas whose frozen corpses we had stored specifically for this purpose. We needed a greater insight into the reasons for their deaths, information that might help us deal more effectively with their health problems on arrival and to understand the physiological processes involved. As our budget couldn't stretch to the purchase of a freezer for this purpose, the gorilla cadavers had been stored in the fairly large ice-making compartment of our own domestic fridge. Occasionally a recognizable hand or foot would push its way out of the fridge as the ice built up. The unexpected, gruesome sight of these corpses as we opened the door for some milk or butter provoked horrified reactions from visitors to the house. To us it had seemed simply a practical solution.

The Chandleys became very concerned for our health after all our various bouts of illness, and donated their chest freezer to the orphanage as they prepared to close down the British Embassy and leave Brazzaville for good.

It was only such reactions of outsiders that reminded us how bizarre life had become. Back at the orphanage flat in the early days of the project a French doctor had called to treat me for malaria. The moment he walked into the flat he was confronted with the enormous bulk of Magne hanging from our kitchen window, a steel lattice grille that directly bordered onto the gorilla cage, trying to force a huge hand through the narrow bars. Rendered speechless, the doctor stopped still, rooted to the spot, his mouth gaping wide open.

Recovering himself, he asked in a small voice if we might move to another room. We moved, only to find Mark and Max involved in a noisy game of hide and seek in the sitting room. He wrote out the prescription and fled.

Professor Hayama arrived unexpectedly with his young assistant one evening, his letter announcing his plans to arrive in Brazzaville having never reached us. In his sixties, he was short and slight with greying hair and thick glasses, behind which his lively, curious eyes burned intensely. He spoke only Japanese and so we resorted to sign language to communicate. This proved particularly inadequate when, within a few days, his poorly controlled diabetes took a turn for the worse and he teetered on the brink of hypoglycaemia. His attempts at explanation left us none the wiser but luckily Dr Kuroda paid a chance visit and was able to act as interpreter.

One afternoon, after an arduous morning's work in the intense airless heat of the orphanage building, Hayama walked out into the garden and sat quietly in the shade of a large tree. I asked if he was feeling unwell.

'Gorilla . . . banana.' He smiled at me, his eyes rolling wildly. He stood up and staggered towards the gorillas' fruit store. Plucking a banana from one of the bunches hanging overhead he looked questioningly at me. I realized that he needed the sweet fruit to boost his plummeting blood glucose levels, but was too polite to simply help himself. We laughed and the ice was broken. From then on our relationship relaxed. He worked extremely hard for the rest of the week, in difficult conditions, using toxic chemicals that burned his eyes and throat in a room with no air conditioning. We were very grateful for his determination to finish the task.

Thanks to Hayama's work, we confirmed that Mayoko's group had all fallen victim to the same illness. However, it was still impossible to identify the mysterious disease. Autopsies done on individual orphans who had died only a few days following confiscation revealed a legacy of acute gastro-enteritis and in some cases evidence of severe infestations of intestinal worms, particularly hookworm. But the professor left Brazzaville convinced that the psychological trauma these orphans had suffered prior to their arrival at the orphanage had played a major part in their susceptibility to disease.

Hayama had confirmed the conclusions we had drawn from our experiences to date: that the gorilla's two main areas of vulnerability were his complex, finely tuned digestive system, that could be easily and fatally disrupted, and his fragile emotional make-up. We had seen, time and time again, the effects of emotional stress, not only in new arrivals, but also in well-established individuals like Kola.

Emotional stress, exposure to human disease and malnutrition that resulted in the breakdown of a fine balance of intestinal parasites held in check under natural conditions, made the survival of newly arrived orphans unlikely.

What had become clear to us over the past few years was how fragile these complex creatures were. At times it seemed to me that as a species in the wild they were doomed Psychologically they were dinosaurs in the modern age, ill-equipped to cope with change, clinging stubbornly to their peaceful existence in the forest, determined to die rather than adapt.

Chapter Twenty

Escalating Chaos

The installation of an interim government meant that the post of wildlife director, a political one, changed hands. The new man was called Raphael Tsila. We hoped he could match NDinga's authority and went to meet him in his office for the first time. A great deal rested on our relationship with the Water and Forests Ministry. We were now working to improve the original orphanage agreement made with John Aspinall in 1987. More importantly, we still needed to agree on an all-encompassing co-operative contract with the Congolese government for the planned gorilla reintroduction to the Lefini Reserve. Aspinall had recently approved our plans for the reintroduction and urged us to proceed within the limits prescribed by funding and civil unrest in Brazzaville. He was unable to provide further funding at this stage, and while the absence of money from elsewhere would effectively limit the potential for progress, it made sense to proceed with clearing the legal hurdles at least.

The wildlife director's office was even more sparsely furnished than usual. Thieves had stolen the typewriters, most of the office furniture and even the office telephone. Tsila looked up as we entered, peering over the mounds of paper piled high on his wooden desk. Recognizing us for who we were, he stood to greet us. Short and stocky, he would have made a good rugby-player. His hair was silver-grey and he wore thick glasses. Physically, he presented a complete contrast to NDinga. He beckoned us forward, offering us seats on the thread-bare armchairs.

Any worries about him evaporated as he started to talk enthusiastically about our project, full of hopes for the future as he embarked on his new task. We couldn't help wondering how on earth he would fulfil these dreams, or function at all with so little office back-up. At one stage in the meeting he popped his head round the door to wake one of his three unashamedly slumbering secretaries whose heads lolled over their empty desks. He roused the senior one and asked her to find the telephone number of a colleague he thought we should contact. She finally appeared with a phone number scrawled on a tatty scrap of paper which she handed to him, then shuffled back to her sleeping colleagues in the dingy outer-office. Tsila cleared his throat, ready to dictate the number to us, but stopped, incredulous as he realized that written on the paper was his own phone number. His face then broke into a smile and, shrugging his broad shoulders, he gave us a knowing look. We all burst out laughing.

Tsila made valiant efforts to work hard despite such handicaps, even bringing his own phone in from home each morning, taking it back with him at night. He toiled industriously, writing all his correspondence laboriously in long-hand. He would prove an ally in the months to come when tribal tensions increased, especially as he was of the same ethnic group as 90 per cent of the orphanage staff.

Two years earlier, at the end of 1991, a team of environmental consultants working for the World Bank had arrived in the Congo to do a preliminary investigation into protected areas of the country that might be suitable recipients of funds from the World Bank's newly formed Global Environmental Facility. Amongst the areas proposed as potential recipients of this fund had been the Lefini Reserve. This had given us the perfect opportunity to submit our gorilla reintroduction proposal for scrutiny. The reintroduction stage of the project was ambitious and would be expensive. Realistically, we could not be sure that any individual or independent source of funding could cover these costs alone, if at all. But even if granted, World Bank funding could take years to materialize as it would be channelled through the Congolese government and rigorous constraints would be needed to protect the system of payment from abuse.

Although officially declared a protected area in 1951, the Lefini Reserve had in reality received no protection, resulting in heavy hunting pressure and general chaos. With its diverse landscape of gallery forest and grassland, unique in the Congo, it met the necessary criteria to qualify for funding. The gorilla project could bring funding, management and protection to this previously abandoned area.

Dr Kuroda and Mike Fay had both completed brief botanical studies of the proposed reintroduction site and agreed it was ideal for the reintroduction. We were edging slowly closer to the fulfilment of our dream.

In April of 1993 we finally reached an agreement on the first contract. On the appointed date we made our way across the road from the orphanage to the parliament building to formally sign the first official project agreement between the Howletts and Port Lympne Foundation, funders of the gorilla project, and the Congolese government. We were now calling ourselves the Gorilla Protection Project to encompass our new, broader goals. We stood gravely to attention during an austere signing ceremony attended by the local press and posed stiffly afterwards for photographs with the Minister of Foreign Affairs on the grand steps of the parliament building, our hands clasped in a firm theatrical handshake for the benefit of the cameras. The more complex second agreement, essential before any practical

work could be undertaken, would concern the project's responsibilities for the Southern Lefini Reserve, the release site now
named the Lesio-Louna Sanctuary, after the two rivers that
snaked through the forests. The sanctuary would be entitled to
specific protection and restricted land usage by the local population. The area surrounding it, the buffer zone, could still be
exploited in agreed ways by the villagers. This agreement was
going to take a great deal longer to finalize.

Out in the forest with Kola's group one morning, we heard the
distant sound of rhythmic chanting. It was some sort of proces-
sion or demonstration. As the marchers gathered and advanced
towards the zoo, the chanting gathered strength. Sensing our
unease the gorillas were relieved when we led them back to the
orphanage, huddling behind Mark as we walked.

At the orphanage Nkodia explained that there had been
rumours circulating for days of a pro-democracy demonstration
motivated by mounting public frustration with the constant
delays in preparation for the promised democratic elections. Back
in the office I realized that Mark had disappeared and Nkodia
started to panic, both of us knowing that Mark's insatiable
curiosity, coupled with his belief in his own invincibility, meant
that he had probably joined the march.

'Madame, he should not have done this,' Nkodia said, stern-
faced. 'It's dangerous out there.'

We looked at one another and shrugged, knowing that there
was nothing we could do about it. In the meantime Sid's group,
whose cage bordered the patch of forest that overlooked the
parliament building, had sensed the mob's ugly mood and fled
to the roof where they cowered in fear.

Eventually Mark sauntered back. He had found himself welcomed into the crowd, the only white face present, on a wave of

brotherly solidarity. A group of armed civilians, however, had pulled him aside and demanded that he identify himself. When he showed them his British passport they offered to escort him back to the orphanage, warning him that he might be mistaken for a Frenchman and that as the French were perceived as collaborators with the previous government he might be at risk. Heeding their concern, he returned. Despite their worries for his safety, the staff were proud of Mark's show of support for their cause.

In the days that followed, the demonstrations escalated into violence and the gorillas remained grounded in their cages. We all learnt to identify the different sounds of gunfire: the single shots of civilian hand pistols responding to the rat-a-tat-tat of machine-gun fire from the military guards defending the parliament building opposite the zoo. Then there followed an uneasy lull, as the crowds melted back to their separate quartiers of town and we resumed our normal forest routine with the gorillas. We needed to be constantly alert to danger on these days of sinister calm which were to continue for another five months. Outbursts of sporadic gunfire punctuated the hum of the humid tropical night, a reminder that the violence had been only temporarily quelled, awaiting the July 1993 elections.

During the past year Max had developed a new obsession. When the feral dogs of the orphanage forest left their new-born puppies in search of food, he would raid their nests, gathering the pups up in his arms and bringing them excitedly back to the orphanage where he would scoot up a high tree and sit, hugging them possessively to his chest, grinning maniacally and squeaking, his feelings torn between paternal protectiveness and sexual frenzy. It would take hours of patient persuasion to extricate the crying pups from his tight embrace, but boredom finally set in when the pups' hungry whimpers became irritating.

He would then hand them over, leaving us with the task of finding homes for them amongst the staff. Predictably there was one we couldn't resist. He was brindle brown with a black patch over one eye. We decided to call him Mutley, and took him home. Before long he had grown and established himself as guardian of the household and the young gorillas in it. Any well-intentioned visitors who decided to approach the gorillas would find themselves face to face with a snarling mut with a fearsome set of teeth. He would have made an excellent working dog but, unfortunately, neither of us had the time to train him or give him the attention he needed. We couldn't take him to the orphanage because too many of the older gorillas had bad memories of the dogs which hunters used in the forest, bells tied round their necks as they tracked down prey for their masters. So Mutley was left alone in the house for long periods during the day and set his active mind to finding his own entertainment. Mark was particularly unamused when Mutley took a shine to a mandrill skull, part of his prized collection of primate skulls rescued from the zoo forest, and reduced what he saw as simply 'a bone' to a pile of chewed remains.

When Mutley's playmate, a neighbouring dog called Ox, moved with his Congolese owners to a new home some distance away, his life became even lonelier. Our housekeeper, Denise, would take him out occasionally and I watched one day as she left the house with Mutley shadowing her. For a brief moment I wondered whether I should shout after her to put him on the lead, but I dismissed the thought, knowing that he had good road sense. A few minutes later I heard a loud thud, followed by a piercing squeal and my heart leapt. As I ran out of the house up the slope towards the petrol station I met one of the pump attendants rushing down towards me.

'Madame Marc,' he gasped breathlessly, 'I think your dog has been hit by a car! He was thrown into the air.'

'Where is he? I asked, desperate to find him.

'Sorry, I don't know. He ran off.'

Guessing he would have returned home to lick his wounds I went back to the house and peered through the wooden stilts that supported the bungalow about four foot above the muddy ground. Mutley lay in the mud, a whimpering, bloody mess, fearful to emerge from the shadows but pathetically wagging his tail at the sight of my familiar face. When he eventually dragged himself towards me my heart sank. He couldn't possibly survive such horrific head wounds. None of the local vets would be equipped to operate on such an injury. I was faced with the choice of either watching helplessly as he died a slow, painful death or putting him to sleep with the Ketamine we kept at the orphanage. I held him in my arms as the lethal injection took effect and he slowly slipped into unconsciousness, his eyes focused trustingly all the time on mine. I remained for some time cradling his lifeless body in the silence of the creaking house. Then grief, which had remained stubbornly imprisoned throughout the terrible year, welled up inside me, gathering strength like a wave and erupting as my body heaved and shook, physically possessed with the force of it.

Eventually the sobbing waves subsided, leaving only the welcome numbness of exhaustion. Mark arrived home and put his arms around me. 'Don't cry,' he said, 'you'll make me start.'

I buried my head in his neck, feeling the strength of his comforting arms grounding me. I knew that he understood and shared my pain, and was frightened that if he let go he would be unable to carry on.

Ox continued to return to our house from time to time after Mutley's death to visit his former playmate whenever he managed to escape his owners' compound some distance away. At first we wondered whether he returned for food, but the meat we left lay untouched. One afternoon, spotting him in the garden, we invited him into the house. Having searched every room for his friend he understood our message and never returned.

That evening I felt violently sick and vomited blood. I feared I might have a stomach ulcer. Taking a dose of Valium I slept heavily and the next day went to see a French doctor who confirmed my fears and urged me to start immediate treatment.

'You must have an endoscopy soon,' she said and suggested the name of a Congolese doctor who could do it in his own private clinic. Too tired to think about the risks involved in such a procedure, I agreed. The following day Mark took me to the clinic and sat with me in a long queue of Congolese patients in a dimly lit waiting area. As I waited my panic increased and I started to regret my decision not to return to England for treatment. My thoughts were interrupted as I heard my name being called. Stepping forward robotically, I entered the tiny clinical room.

Glancing round the room I spotted a plastic bucket on the floor, filled with what I hoped was disinfecting bleach. Inside the bucket lay what looked like a garden hose. I lay back on the stretcher bed and, having given my throat a token spray with local anaesthetic, the doctor loomed over me with the tube.

'Take some deep breaths,' he instructed, then shoved the tube forcefully down my throat. I retched loudly and violently, turning my head to look at Mark seated on the other side of the room. His expression mirrored my shock and disbelief. The doctor confirmed the presence of an ulcer and advised me that I should follow a course of treatment for at least six weeks.

'And,' he added, 'you must avoid situations of stress!'

Chapter Twenty-One

Election Day

In March 1993, as the dry season approached, Hans started to complain of stomach pains. Assuming it to be the onset of amoebic dysentery he treated himself with the appropriate antibiotic but the pain persisted. Dr Bettini did some tests, but could not find a satisfactory explanation.

Despite his escalating anxiety, Hans continued to put his usual enthusiasm into his work, although I did notice that at times he uncharacteristically lost his patience with the gorillas.

He changed his diet to see whether this would have any effect on the pain, but nothing relieved it. By the time Christiane left for Berlin in April to make arrangements for their forthcoming marriage, he had become gaunt, shrunken, a sad contrast to the thick-set figure who had arrived in Brazzaville the previous year. His sallow, jaundiced complexion made us think of hepatitis, a virus endemic in Central Africa and known to be carried by apes. We attempted to carry on as normally as possible, reassured that Hans would be able to seek expert medical advice when he returned to Berlin for the wedding. In the days leading up to his departure the pain became severe and he could no longer work. We finally waved goodbye to him, feeling a mixture of anxiety and relief that he was on his way to Europe where a diagnosis could be made.

There followed a long silence and we assumed that Hans was now well and enjoying preparations for his marriage. But as the day of his return to Brazzaville neared and we heard nothing we began to worry. Finally, the evening of his expected arrival we discovered a fax from Berlin waiting at the house as we returned from the orphanage. I tore it off and read it out loud to Mark.

'After many weeks of tests,' Hans wrote, 'the doctors have today found a pancreatic tumour which has already spread to my liver.' My voice stumbled as I read on. He was due to start a course of chemotherapy the following day. He asked us not to inform Howletts of this development, fearing that he would lose his job the moment the word cancer was mentioned. We hoped against hope that the chemotherapy would work. We would have to resign ourselves to severe under-staffing problems, just as escalating civil unrest made daily life even more complicated than usual.

A week later Hans phoned the house to ask for news of the gorillas, his words slurred with the effect of heavy painkilling drugs. Both he and Christiane tried to disguise their panic and distress for each other's sake, forcing brave, hopeless words of optimism. We could only imagine what torture they were going through.

A few days later his condition deteriorated and he was readmitted to hospital in a coma. Christiane phoned with the news late at night, her voice brittle. I felt hopelessly lost for words. Hans died that night and she called again the next morning. We shared a numb silence, thousands of miles apart and I wished I could put my arms around her. Mark agreed that despite the problems in Brazzaville I had to get to Berlin to see her as soon as possible. Although she had her immediate family and old friends in Berlin, I knew how intense the feeling of alienation could be on leaving Africa and hoped my presence might help. Not only had she lost Hans and a lifestyle in which she had become completely immersed during the past year, she was also separated from her beloved Dimonika.

Two weeks later, despite the heavy workload and unstable political situation, Mark saw me off on a plane to Berlin. Christiane met me at the airport and we walked in silence to her car to drive the short distance to her flat. We shared the same bed that long night, talking at times and sharing silent memories at others. Long after she had waved me goodbye, her tragic face remained in my thoughts.

Returning to Brazzaville was a welcome distraction. The city was now factionalized between the various political parties formed along tribal lines. Coalitions were made for brief periods in the hope that their combined strengths would lead them to power. When we asked the staff who they would vote for they named Bernard Kolelas, leader of the party whose tribal origins they shared. The Laris had called their forces the 'Ninjas', Lissouba's people the 'Niboleks' (the name deriving from the Niari, Borenza and LeKoumou regions), and Sassou's troops the infamous 'Cobras'. Each party gathered its forces, arming them in preparation for the elections.

July and election day finally arrived and all foreigners were instructed by their embassies to stay at home. We prepared to leave for work as usual. 'Ville morte' (literally translated 'dead town') was declared and no vehicles were allowed to circulate in town without a government pass clearly pasted on their windscreen, so we left on foot early that morning with our two youngest ape charges in tow. Mabafi travelled on Mark's back in typical gorilla fashion, her arms clasped tightly around his neck, her feet gripping the fabric of his shirt, and Blixa, the bonobo, perched pertly in the raffia basket I carried on my arm, a smug expression on her minx-like face.

The silence in the deserted streets was disturbing, the white sun already bright in the sky. But crossing a couple of armed barricades we elicited nothing more than bemused stares. The day passed uneventfully and we walked home that evening barely able to believe that this long awaited event had apparently gone so smoothly. When the votes were totalled an announcement was made. Pascal Lissouba was pronounced the new, democratically elected, President of the Republic of Congo. Back at the house we settled Mabafi and Blixa down for the night, ate a brief dinner and collapsed into bed. Then, as we drifted into an exhausted sleep, a burst of rapid gunfire broke the quiet humming of the night. Pushing me off and under the bed Mark leapt to his feet. I lay still, listening in the darkness for some time before emerging to crawl down the cool tiled floor of the corridor that led to the sitting room. My hands trembled as I picked up the phone and dialled the number of the American Embassy.

'This is Gorillas speaking,' I whispered, using our pre-arranged code name for the marine security guard who had answered the phone. 'I'm reporting several close rounds of machine-gun fire in the Marche de Plateau area.' As I said this, further pistol shots rang out close by.

'Are they in your house?' the guard shouted, concerned.

'No,' I assured him, 'they're outside.' I hung up the phone and everything went silent once more. We waited, crouched low in the corridor between two thick brick walls. Eventually Mark, his curiosity getting the better of him, crept out of the house and up to the petrol station to find out what had happened. The orange glow of an overturned jeep in flames illuminated the dark sky and the pungent smell of cordite hung in the air. We assumed there had been an assassination attempt on the prominent Lari figure who lived nearby in the old British Embassy building, vacated some months earlier by the Chandleys. We returned to bed, succumbing to light, disturbed sleep.

Emerging from the house early the next morning we encountered a barricade of logs, manned by armed guards, fifty yards
from our front door. A pump attendant rushed over to tell us
conspiratorially that there had indeed been an assassination
attempt on the occupants of the former British embassy by
Lissouba's government troops. They had also accidentally shot
dead a visiting dignitary from the World Health Organisation,
and seriously injured the politician's wife – she had already left
for medical treatment in Paris earlier that morning. The attack-
ers had been shot dead by the politician's bodyguards and the
smoking carcass of their jeep was left in the road as a deliberate
warning to others. As he finished his story with florid gestures,
he noticed the guards staring at him and slunk back to the
petrol station.

As a result of the night's activities the American Embassy
issued us with a radio walkie-talkie so that we could provide
them with information as we went about our daily work in areas
of town designated unsafe, information that might contribute to
any decisions made to evacuate the wives and children of their
nationals. The embassy political advisor, Walt Hughey, was
sharp and had a good grasp of the situation. There was a great
deal of pressure on him to help quell the escalating violence and
resolve the conflict. He could be seen cycling around town in his
shorts and trainers, a peaked baseball cap perched jauntily on his
balding head, stopping to talk with the various factions of the
military on both sides.

The orphanage sat on the border between the Lari stronghold
of Bacongo and the government-controlled area of town in which
our house was located. We needed to cross the border zone daily
to continue our work.

Later that day we returned home for a much-needed siesta,
but within minutes of our heads hitting the pillow we heard the
distant sound of an advancing mob, heading our way. The Laris

wanted revenge for the events of the previous night, seeing the assassination attempt as a direct provocation. Reluctantly leaving the cool comfort of the bed, we opened the front door to see a mob of wild-eyed civilians pouring out of battered old buses, scouring the street for victims on whom to vent their anger. These armed bandits were mainly untrained Lari youths from Bacongo whose frustration and anger had been fuelled by a newly strengthened sense of ethnic identity. Armed by their tribal leaders, they now possessed the means for mass destruction. There was wild panic as people fled down narrow side streets to escape the mob who were headed for the headquarters of the new President Elect's political party about a hundred yards from our house. We went back into the house to await events.

Minutes later the government military arrived and sprayed the crowd with bullets. The brutal sound of machine-gun fire stuttered over the noisy rabble and then there was silence. The previously confident mob fled back to Bacongo. Bodies lay on the road, their limbs splayed out in the convulsive last moments of life.

It was no great surprise that Pascal Lissouba had been declared the new President but the Laris, led by Kolelas, claimed that the official election results were fraudulent. Brazzaville, once a peaceful town of mixed ethnic groups living side by side and often inter-married, became a violent, sinister place. Tribal strongholds formed in different quartiers of town, protected by their own armed civilian vigilantes. Those who had made mixed marriages used their adopted dialect to conceal their true ethnic identity. Brutal violence erupted between those who had once been trusting neighbours.

Rumours circulated of the killing and decapitation of children of party officials on both sides. It was claimed that the bodies of these children had been dumped as a public warning behind the hospital about 200 yards from the orphanage. It was whispered that Pascal Lissouba's special troops, the much feared Aubervillois, possessed magical powers which made them invisible to their enemies. One of these soldiers, it was said, had managed to pass through two of the heavily armed military barriers on the approach to Sassou's Brazzaville residence, but as he approached the third barrier his fetiche suddenly lost its power and he was spotted by Sassou's bodyguards and kidnapped. He was released a few days later with gruesome injuries as a warning to others.

Renewed rioting in Kinshasa at this time led to a further influx of bonobo orphans. Three arrived in quick succession, a three-year-old male called Axel and two older females, Alexa and Trixie. They quickly settled in and were soon exploring the forest as a group, accompanied by a new member of staff, eighteen-year-old Peggy Koudiabouna, whose extrovert personality matched their own.

Max's reaction to the new females on the scene was not a surprise. Within minutes of introduction he had copulated with both Alexa and Trixie. The younger bonobos, Blixa and Axel, were anxious not to be left out of the general excitement and jumped up and down on Max's back as he mounted the females, turning the event into an acrobatic pyramid. Females, however, are dominant in bonobo society and Max soon felt overwhelmed by the precocious, sexually demanding newcomers. Fleeing to the top of the cage, he squeaked at us, grinning in confusion. Despite the pull of this group of his own species he would soon lose interest when out in the forest with them and head off to look for his loyal gorilla friends.

As the situation continued to deteriorate in town, it became more dangerous for the staff to get to work. Peggy arrived late one morning, pale and shaken. She had been beaten and threatened with rape by armed civilians of her own tribe as she made her way to work. Worried that she might have been raped but was ashamed to admit it, I took her to see Flore Bettini. Flore's calm manner seemed to help and we returned to the orphanage where she spent the rest of the day asleep on the camp bed in the back room. The staff left in a group that evening for protection.

Realizing how hard it was becoming for them to get past the armed barricades, we assured them that they would still get paid even if they were unable to get to work. They exceeded our expectations, however, by going to extraordinary lengths to reach the orphanage, often walking many miles in the relentless heat from villages out of town that their families had fled to and where they were living in overcrowded, refugee conditions. We offered them refuge at the orphanage or our house, but they insisted on continuing their lives as normally as possible, confronting the armed barricades with feigned courage and a firm belief that the gorillas gave them a magic fetiche charm which would assure their safety.

We were equally determined to ignore embassy advice and continue our normal routine, essential to the gorillas' well-being and safety. Our relationship with the staff deepened with our shared dangers as we spent the days comparing our night-time experiences in different parts of town.

We now lived in a strange twilight world, constantly alert for the sound of gunfire. The streets were deserted day and night. At night we made sure we were always home by the seven o'clock curfew. We drove in strict silence, the windows down so that we could listen for gunfire or a voice from the shadows ordering us to 'halt!'. Sometimes this order was deliberately inaudible, the guards hoping that the driver would not hear and would continue driving, providing the perfect excuse to open fire. The procedure at each barricade was to slow down, stop, switch off the car engine and headlights and switch on the cabin light, so that the guards could identify the occupants of the vehicle and check whether or not they were armed. Failure to do so might make these edgy guards open fire. The greatest threat however was of coming across a group of drunken guards itching for a fight, or simply encountering an individual who bore a grudge against whites in general. Our presence would be tolerated as long as we were seen to be politically neutral.

Chapter Twenty-Two

Juislain's Story

As the conflict continued to escalate we decided we should listen to official embassy advice and leave our house, since it was on the border zone between government and opposition strongholds. After some discussion we agreed that Mark should camp out at the orphanage and do his best to look after the older gorillas with the help of any staff who could reach work, and that I would move into the Hugheys' walled-in residence in the centre of town, along with the youngest animals, Blixa, Mabafi and Dimonika. I was particularly grateful to Walt who, it had been obvious from previous encounters with our gorillas, was not at ease with apes.

I arrived at their residence loaded down with nappies, bottles, baskets, cans of milk formula and my three ape infants. Walt's wife, Diane, welcomed us, responding with instinctive motherly concern to the babies. Within no time at all Blixa and Dimonika were competing for her attention and the comfort of her large, reassuring bosom. Mabafi, younger and more wary, insisted on clinging to my legs throughout the entire stay.

Seeing his wife so relaxed in their company, Walt finally plucked up the courage to take Blixa in his arms. His body tensed visibly for the first few minutes but he found himself unable to resist her invitations to play, and was soon completely absorbed and fascinated by her. During the next three days he seized every spare moment to come out into the garden and sit with us as the babies played contentedly, ravaging his carefully nurtured flower beds and plucking the heads off the daisies on the front lawn.

After three days' constant gunfire the streets were finally quiet. Both Mark and I decided to make an attempt to resume our normal routine, but within hours of my arrival at the orphanage we heard the sound of tanks approaching, the ground rumbling as they crawled past. Silence descended as people stopped in their tracks and listened as the tanks rolled on towards the opposition Lari stronghold just behind the orphanage. The silence was abruptly broken by heavy gunfire and the resonant boom of mortar raining down on shanty town Bacongo. Government troops were demonstrating in no uncertain terms their superior strength over the opposition who had erected a heavily armed barricade at the entrance to Bacongo, a clear message declaring their independence from the rest of town and their refusal to recognize the elected government.

The gorillas sensed our fear. Kola's group remained huddled together in the shelter of their overnight room, their screams of raw fear ringing out in the ominous silence that followed each explosion.

Dimonika climbed onto my lap, plastered in the sticky remnant of her last meal and leaving a trail of mud and fruit the length of my jeans. She tucked herself close under my chin, her expression anxious as the familiar rat-a-tat-tat of automatic gunfire resounded in the still, damp air. The responding pock . . . pock . . . pock of single, sharp pistol shots responded. It was midday. I feared for the staff, most of whom had failed to reach the orphanage that morning.

My lap was soon a crowded place. Mayoko and Mabafi piled

onto me, the latest burst of gunfire leaving them trembling, their tiny hands squeezed tight as they clung to my body. Sid's group, restricted to the cage and unable to pursue their usual daily explorations of the forest had climbed to the highest point of the cage and looked down at us as we sat hunched against the brick wall. As another burst of gunfire rang out, followed by the boom-boom of a mortar, they screamed, their lips drawn back in a grimace of terror. Mark moved away to enter the cage and the gorillas descended silently from its roof and were soon huddled in the refuge of his arms, gazing questioningly into his eyes.

If this sort of stress continued for long, it would start to affect the gorillas' health, making them vulnerable to sickness that we were ill equipped to cope with, since imported goods, medicines included, remained blocked at the airport.

It was rumoured that there might be a counterattack by the opposition on the government controlled area of town that night. Bodyguards stationed outside the government residences that surrounded our bungalow were tense and jumpy, their guns poised for action, their eyes wide and watchful in the shadowy darkness. When we finally arrived at the petrol station outside our house that evening, we free-wheeled down the slip road with our headlights off and cabin light switched on, anticipating the guards' suspicious reaction to a vehicle approaching in the darkness. They visibly relaxed when they realized it was just their neighbours continuing their bizarre business as usual.

We fed Mabafi, Dimonika and Blixa their evening drinks and settled them down for the night before sinking wearily into the armchairs. We were soon plunged into blackness. Electricity cuts in various quartiers of the city were a common event but with the threat of a counterattack from Bacongo, the darkness seemed pregnant with menace. We sat alert in the eerie silence. I could hear my heart thud and my watch ticked loudly as the minutes slowly passed. Outside there were no glowing lights visible across the ravine, no signs of human activity. The entire town had been switched off.

In the morning the sun rose as usual. The attack had never materialized. As we made our way to the orphanage we passed an exodus of refugees leaving Bacongo, non-Laris fleeing their homes with whatever possessions they could carry, shuffling in funereal lines across the border to safer zones of town. Ethnic cleansing of the quartiers began. A criss-cross migration of refugees was occurring across the city as families grouped into safe areas. Tribal strongholds formed and reinforced their borders with armed vigilantes. Over the next few days the staff emerged from their homes, reaching the orphanage with terrible tales to tell. Juislain did not appear. With rumoured round-ups and executions we feared for his safety.

Ten days later, when we had almost given up hope, he finally appeared at the gates, his face gaunt, his eyes dull, unable to speak about whatever had happened to him. His thin body trembled as I led him into the office and offered him a seat. He refused to sit, he refused the food we offered, but he at least accepted our offer of refuge in the relative safety of the orphanage. As the days passed Kola's group drew him out of his introspection. He started taking them out to the forest on the safer days when gunfire was only intermittent and distant. The gorillas sensed his distress and restrained their desire to play, instead gathering protectively around him as he sat in reflective silence. Kola would amble over to sit on his lap and, leaning back, clasp his arms tenderly round Juislain's neck, his lips nuzzling Juislain's chin. Dinga would sit back to back with him in supportive silence and Mbinda would squat by his side with one long arm placed gently around his shoulders. Together they tried to ease him tenderly out of his introspection, gently pulling his hands in an effort to interest him in play and, when he responded, playing with deliberate gentleness, sensing his physical fragility. They recognized a common bond of suffering as he sat, initially withdrawn and unresponsive, as they had done on their arrival at the orphanage some years earlier, and eventually they managed to coax him skilfully back to life.

Gradually his story emerged. He had been rounded up whilst trying to escape government troops who had invaded his home quartier. With fifty other people from his township he had been marched to the military camp behind the airport where they had been locked, packed like sardines, in a container to await their execution. After two days, as they began to drift into unconsciousness from dehydration, they were unexpectedly released and told to leave. Bernard Kolelas, the Lari leader, had spoken publicly, declaring an intent to peace. Juislain's brother had been shot before his eyes as he fled the family home, leaving Juislain consumed with guilt, wondering why he alone had survived. His hatred of the 'Niboleks' as they were called was now profound.

A few weeks later he insisted on venturing out from the orphanage. Leaving the zoo grounds he encountered a gang of unarmed Nibolek youths who seized his precious ghetto-blaster and tried to make off with it. He reacted with the brute strength of anger and fought them off, grabbing back his ghetto-blaster and making a run for the orphanage. We found the machine, some days later, smashed into tiny pieces in the grounds. When we showed it to him he just shook his head and Nkodia explained that Juislain had done this himself because the 'Niboleks had laid their filthy hands on it'.

Arriving back at the house one afternoon we found Don Webster, who had helped us so much with the initial building work, his wife Thérèse and their three children sitting on the steps. Don looked ashen grey and exhausted. Thérèse looked shattered. Their normally peaceful quartier of town had erupted into violence and their previously friendly neighbours had seized on the fact that Thérèse was from a minority ethnic group in the area and chased them from their house to take up residence themselves. Don had lost everything, even the only remaining photographs of his dead parents. They asked if they could stay with us until they could make their way to Thérèse's mother in a safer area of the city. We could only offer them temporary refuge as three noisy children in a small house would have disturbed the already unsettled gorillas with probable repercussions on their health. We were already pushed to the limits. The embassies had evacuated all wives, children and inessential personnel from Brazzaville and the British Foreign Office had banned travel to the Congo until further notice. We considered using Hans' flat down the road as a temporary solution, but armed barricades made it impossible to reach. The chaos in Brazzaville since Hans' death had prevented us from packing up his possessions and sending them on to Berlin. In the end Don and Thérèse decided to continue their journey on to her mother that same day. We watched them trudge down the road, hoping they would reach their destination before the seven o'clock curfew.

When security relaxed a few days later we made our way to Hans' flat, finding it exactly as he had left it when he set off to marry the girl of his dreams. I felt like an intruder as we sorted through all his hand-written notes on the gorillas and his plans for the future, the legacy of a life full of hope and optimism.

When we asked Howletts for funds to repatriate his belongings to Christiane, they told us that we should contact her and ask her to pay for it herself. Shocked by their response and knowing that she was out of work, having given up a secure job to follow Hans to the Congo, we decided we would take the necessary sum from the orphanage funds and settle it with Howletts later. However, as the airport remained strictly out of bonds, the packed boxes remained in the flat.

Discovering the Lefini for the first time.
Mark on the cliffs surrounding the reserve.

△ A view of the cliffs surrounding what was to be the gorilla reintroduction site.

▽ Mark surveying the forests before the gorillas' arrival.

◁ Forest buffalo in the
Nouabale-Ndoki
National Park, Northern
Congo.

▽ Approaching
a Northern Congo village.

△ Addressing the press after signing
the last agreement with the Congolese
Government in 1993.

▽ Lac Bleu and the Lefini forests.

△ The gorilla holding cage, set up
in the Lefini.

▽ The barge constructed to cross
the Lesio River.

△ Juslain and Kola in his new
home, 1995.

▽ Titi and Despina relaxing
in the Lefini forests, 1995.

△ The Sangha River in the
Northern Congo.

▽ Derelict barges on the
Sangha River.

△ Kola peering from
his forest home, 1995.

▷ Titi at rest, 1995.

Not only were lack of available funds and staff preventing any progress on the Lefini reintroduction site, but we were unable to leave the city and were struggling to keep even the orphanage afloat.

With the flat cleared, we offered it to a German researcher, Martina Witzlack, who had started helping out at the orphanage on a voluntary basis, her intended study of the gorillas rendered impossible by the unstable political situation. Howletts had asked their zoo staff back in England if anyone would be willing to travel to Brazzaville to help and had been met with blunt refusals from all, so we were grateful for Martina's help. Both Martina and I, having trained as nurses, harboured the fear that Hans' cancer might have been provoked in some way by an ape-borne virus, an idea Mark dismissed.

We urgently needed a contingency plan to evacuate the gorillas to safety if it became impossible to find food for them in Brazzaville. We suggested to Howletts that they constructed holding crates for the gorillas which they could fly in from Aspinall's residence in South Africa should the situation in Brazzaville become untenable. In an emergency the gorillas could then be crated up and flown to safety. They agreed to the plan, much to our relief, and we coped better knowing that we had an escape route planned should things get worse.

By now familiarity with the situation had indeed bred contempt. Our initial feelings of fear and nervous excitement had turned to resigned irritation. Even the odd stray bullet pinging off our tin roof as we lay in bed elicited little response.

We lived in the worst affected part of the city and were surprised when we ventured into the city centre to shop by how quiet it was. Pandemonium broke out in the supermarket at the sound of gunfire, something we now considered tedious but normal. We refused to move to the centre of town, fearing that if we did we might end up being cut off from the orphanage.

Food was now imported through Kinshasa as Brazzaville airport was considered too dangerous for international air traffic. Shortages might soon become serious.

As we travelled between the house and orphanage we were often stopped and questioned by nervous armed guards. We drove past soldiers intimidating civilians, presumably Laris, who kneeled, stripped naked and begging for mercy in the road, and averted our eyes to spare their humiliation and ensure that we didn't engage the interest of the soldiers ourselves.

Four-wheel drive Toyotas belonging to the United Nations and American Embassy were hi-jacked by gangs of armed civilians. They were rarely recovered. They would be used to transport partisan gangs, and could be seen careening around town at great speed, their flat-beds crammed full of armed civilians. We often found ourselves driving behind these trucks that bumped over potholes, the bandits' guns aimed lazily at our windscreen as they bounced precariously up and down on the flatbed.

The phone at the orphanage had ceased to function many months earlier, but we still had a line at the house which allowed us to maintain contact with the outside world. We listened to World Service on the radio for news and were surprised by the little press coverage given to this apparently insignificant country.

With so little international interest shown by the press about the situation in Brazzaville we were able to keep our families in blissful ignorance, until one day my mother phoned and, during the course of the conversation, I was forced to hang up as a burst of loud machine-gun fire rang out. When I phoned back a little while later I tried my best to explain the situation, assuring her that we were not personally in any real danger. I don't for a minute think she believed me.

Chapter Twenty-Three

The Fever Hospital

I had little time to reflect on the death, disease and disaster that seemed to pursue us. At times I felt as if the harder we tried, the greater were the obstacles placed in our path. Reeling from the effects of one crisis, we confronted the next. It seemed as if a shadowy presence stalked all those involved in the lives of the gorillas, drawing us all deeper into the tragic fate of this vulnerable, endangered species. I felt myself being sucked into the murky mind-games of Congolese witchcraft. I began to wonder whether sorcery was a hidden, sinister force behind the events of the past year – we had upset a lot of people in the course of our work.

But there was never any question of giving up. The gorillas' future lay in our hands. If we abandoned them now we could be accused of worse than the poachers whose actions had brought them to the orphanage. We were emotionally committed, caught up for better or worse in a chain of events that we had set in motion when we confiscated our first orphan in 1989. Our complete absorption in our own gorilla-centric world was probably what kept us going.

In this extreme, confrontational world, nothing could be judged by the values I had learnt at home, something that was hard to explain to friends and family back in England. By now I had lived for so long on an emotional roller-coaster of highs and lows, that when I was not under stress or experiencing an emotional extreme of one sort or another, I no longer really felt alive. I suppose I had adapted well to my circumstances.

Prepared for worse to come but with our goal still firmly in mind, we pressed on with everyday life in Brazzaville.

One morning Albertine arrived late for work and tearfully explained that Bernadette had been admitted to the local hospital in Bacongo with suspected tuberculosis. For the past year poor Bernadette had been battling with her demons, convinced that she had Aids and would die, the second victim of the family curse which had claimed her beloved sister. This new illness would undoubtedly reinforce her belief in the power of sorcery.

Bernadette's family believed in 'traditional' cures. She had once appeared at work in obvious pain. When asked if she was sick, she had revealed a vicious-looking wound on her shoulder, a 'cure' inflicted by the feticheur with a razor blade. Deep grooves cut into the skin had been packed with a herbal remedy that promised relief from arthritic pain. We had warned her, as gently as possible, that dirty razor blades used for this treatment were an Aids risk and that if she returned to the feticheur she should take her own sterile, unused razor blades.

Bernadette was a sunny character most of the time, a pleasure to work with, her coy sense of humour and sensitivity appreciated by both ourselves and the gorillas, but recently she had suffered terrible moods, plunged into the depths of introspective depression for days on end for no apparent reason. We guessed at family troubles. There were constant fierce family disputes over money that she earned. Albertine, her closest friend, was anxious that if anything should happen to Bernadette, any monies paid to her family should be shared equally, ensuring that her three children did not lose out. She assured us that if we dealt with Bernadette's family through her she would protect the children's interests.

That morning I asked Paul to drive me into Bacongo to visit Bernadette in hospital, hoping that his presence would ensure me safe passage through the barricades. We drove slowly past the deserted market place and the shells of buildings destroyed by mortar. Litter blew in swirling, erratic patterns around the empty stalls. The simple breeze-block shacks which lined both sides of the broad main avenue were bleak and lifeless, the doors firmly shut. It was a sad contrast to the colour, bustle and noise of the Brazzaville street scenes we had known when we first arrived.

The hospital, supervised by a French doctor who specialized in tuberculosis, lay down a maze of murky back streets in the heart of the quartier. The patio outside the building was like a makeshift village with people preparing food in huge saucepans over wood fires and sleeping bodies spread-eagled in exhaustion from long vigils over sick relatives, their slumped bodies oblivious to the noisy, agitated debates raging around them.

We made our way through the dark cavernous corridors, eventually emerging into a tiny ward at the far end of the building. Bright sunlight shone through the large open window and into the small room. Sunken, hopeless eyes stared from bodies that seemed to have collapsed in on themselves, lying weightless, barely leaving an impression on the sheets. Anxious faces lined the lower frame of the window, staring in at us, surprised to see a white face enter this death chamber.

Bernadette lay, apparently comatose, at the end of the ward. An old woman, her mother I presumed, stood wiping her daughter's glistening, sweat-drenched face. She paused and turned at the sound of voices, staring at me half embarrassed and half surprised as I introduced myself.

As I touched Bernadette's spindly hand a flicker of life sparked momentarily in her dull eyes and she attempted to raise her head from the bed in recognition.

'Restes tranquille,' I murmured, and she fell back, relieved. She had lain in the bed for many days, her mother explained, slipping in and out of consciousness, feverish and hallucinating at times. I couldn't imagine her emaciated body would withstand much more. Although Aids was probably responsible for her succumbing to tuberculosis, the word was taboo, yet fear of it was visible in the anxious faces of her family and boyfriend who kept vigil outside the window. The idea of Bernadette having Aids would be disrespectful to her character, so no one acknowledged it. Paul and I left in silence, unable to find any words of consolation for one another.

The implications of Bernadette's illness were grave for the gorillas. They could easily have contracted tuberculosis from their daily contact with her over the past year. We would have to test every ape at the orphanage. If they proved positive, our plans for reintroduction would be over. We could not possibly release gorillas carrying TB. Chris Furley, the Howletts' vet, was able to make an urgent visit and tested every human and animal resident at the orphanage – the results came back negative.

Some weeks later we received the surprising news from Albertine that Bernadette had been discharged from hospital and was at home on a strict drug regime. We could only hope that she would stick to the treatment, but we doubted that her family would support her in doing so.

The rainy season began in September 1993, and new gorillas arrived, steadily replenishing the numbers and bringing with them a host of new health problems. After several years of exploitation by the gorillas, the orphanage forest was rich in gorilla food plant species, its floor densely carpeted with the thick stems of marantaceae and affromomum that erupted like bamboo from the saturated earth. The gorillas' favourite foraging grounds, depleted at the end of the last dry season, sprang back to life as the rains fell, bloating new shoots that pushed through the damp earth reaching for sunlight, and bringing yellow and red fruits that appeared like bright lights in a blanket of rich green foliage. We persisted most days with our usual routine and the gorillas rushed eagerly out to the forest to feast on the succulent fruits that the rains had brought.

A new bonobo arrival, eighteen-month-old Xanthe, had recently joined forces with Blixa, now two years old, to form a troublesome duo that kept Peggy constantly on her toes.

Initially terrified and submissive, Xanthe soon revealed a surprisingly confident, assertive character. She was tiny for her age and, despite a voracious appetite, remained painfully thin. This fragile appearance and her coy, timid approach to humans, gave no warning of the arrogant, obnoxious little tyrant she became in bonobo company. She soon had Max wound round her little finger, her relationship with him dominating and sexually precocious. Perhaps the advantage of her experience of wild bonobo society prior to capture gave her this resilience and self-assurance that Blixa would never possess. We observed her transformation with incredulity, feeling at times sorry for poor Blixa, who seemed completely intimidated initially and then attempted to follow Xanthe's example in her own awkward fashion.

With practical work towards the setting up of the reintroduction in the Lefini Reserve still made impossible by roadblocks sealing the city, the only progress we could make at this point was to attempt to finalize and sign the second agreement with the Congolese government. This would allow us, when the political situation calmed, to start preparing the Lefini site for the arrival of Kola's group, who were starting to become bored and frustrated as we had anticipated by the confines of the small forest. When the time came to return to the orphanage at the end of the day Kola would now often challenge Juislain's authority by leading the group away from the cage at the last minute, purely to make his point, well aware that they would follow him unquestioningly, even if the idea of returning to the cage for a milk drink was tempting. Juislain would saunter out of the forest, confidently calling the group that followed behind him, only to arrive at base to find himself alone, the group having split off behind him to follow Kola as he strode back to the forest, where he now stood, leaning lazily on one muscular shoulder, biting his lip in a nonchalant, half-serious gesture of challenge. This Mexican stand-off could continue for up to an hour and would only resolve when Kola felt he had made his point – namely, that the group would only follow Juislain if Kola gave them his permission to do so. Occasionally he would even lead the group right up to the door of the cage and then, when Juislain was just about to breathe a sigh of relief and close the door behind them, he would suddenly pull back and charge off again into the forest, the confused group thundering after him.

An exclusively male group of gorillas made for a complex hierarchy within which there were constant jostlings and attempts to out-macho one another. We realized that the delicate balance maintained at the orphanage would be upset by the future move to the Lefini, a change in routine that would inevitably raise their stress levels and possibly result in serious in-fighting. We feared that the more ambitious group members might use the opportunity to bolster or improve their status at the expense of the younger, more vulnerable members. The move would need to be very carefully handled. Although in the familiar surroundings of the orphanage Kola handled his group extremely well, a move to new territory might reveal his confident leadership as fairly fragile. We couldn't deny that there was a real risk involved in relocation, but without it the gorillas would be condemned to captive life in Brazzaville for the rest of their days. Not only could we not justify them ending their days confined in Brazzaville, there would be no room to continue taking in newly-confiscated gorillas.

There would be certain risks along the way – predictable ones we could forearm ourselves against and unpredictable ones such as disease. Our work with the gorillas even up to this point left us in no doubt that however well we prepared the path for Kola's group, this next phase might harbour sudden, devastating complications. But these were risks that had to be taken if the project was to progress at all. Some of this risk-taking was to pay off; some left us questioning the price that had to be paid. Losing the nursery group over a year before had been hard to bear, but fear of further loss couldn't be allowed to hamper what was, after all, progress towards securing the gorillas' long-term survival in the wild.

Kola's group were the ideal pioneers. His exceptional leadership qualities stood a good chance of carrying these gorillas through the potentially stressful changes that lay ahead, and paving the way for future successful reintroductions from the orphanage. It would be tough on them, but there was no other choice.

Eventually, the week before Christmas, we finalized the Lefini agreement with the government. The vast majority of cabinet members for the Ministry of Water and Forests originated from the Batéké Plateaux and were anxious to establish our project in their region. We fixed a date to sign the agreement on 28 December 1993.

Despite the outbreak of renewed violence in the Bacongo quartier we drove to the Minister's gloomy offices. To a background of distant gunfire, we greeted the cabinet members, most of whom bore the ritual facial scarring of the Téké tribe. With the signing ceremony completed, local radio and television journalists rushed forward with questions.

'What could such a project promise, at this difficult time, to a disillusioned Congolese public?' one man asked, shoving a microphone in my face.

Blinded by the bright lights I took a deep breath and spoke of employment opportunities and future revenue from gorilla tourism.

Finally the interview session drew to an end. Gathering my papers, I grabbed Mark, the precious agreement for the next stage of the gorillas' future safely tucked under my arm, and we headed for the bar next to the zoo for a celebratory beer. That evening, to our surprise, we were the first item on the TV Congo news. Presumably the government-controlled television station was relieved to have some good news that might distract the public and assure them that their newly elected government was working for them, helping create jobs and a future.

As the new year approached peace talks started to promise results. Bernard Kolelas, the leader of the opposition, made a rousing speech on local radio to the effect that a solution had been reached. His people should lay down their arms, he announced, and make efforts to co-operate with the new government now that various concessions to the Lari population of Brazzaville had been promised. He was soon declared the new Mayor of Brazzaville. We listened to his speech at Martina's flat in the early hours of the evening. As the speech drew to a close, the silence of the night broke with the sound of heavy gunfire, and tracer bullets painted a criss-cross of haphazard lines in the dark sky. We looked at one another, initially confused, then realized that this was the ecstatic response of the Lari people to their leader's address, a celebration of peace. The din continued for some time and then there was silence. The musky smell of

gunfire hung suspended in the damp air as we walked back
down the road to our bungalow. We slept heavily that night
and woke in the morning with only a dreamlike memory of the
previous evening.

Over the next few days Brazzaville came to life as people
emerged from their homes to test the truth of the declared cease-
fire. The street in front of our house resumed business as usual
with taxis queuing noisily once again at the petrol station and
the market sellers from Bacongo labouring their way up the
street in the hope of re-establishing trade.

Mike Fay returned to Brazzaville from the tranquillity of the
northern forests and we headed into town to test the waters for
ourselves. The curfew had been extended to 9 p.m. in an attempt
to gradually return the town to some sort of normality.

Business had suffered at the Central Bar, once the popular
haunt of expatriates and rich Congolese, as well as a honeypot
for the town's more aggressive prostitutes. Approaching through
the deserted streets we were surprised to find most of the tables
outside the bar occupied. On closer inspection we realized they
were full of dubious-looking characters and local hookers desperate for trade. Their usual targets, young, lonely white males or
balding, overweight old timers, were now hard to come by and
they were driven to fierce competition with one another over the
few potential clients on offer.

We claimed an empty table at one end of the pavement, our
subdued conversation soon drowned out by the drunken procla-
mations of an Ethiopian businessman at the neighbouring table.
Expatriates who had remained in town were now subjected to a
fair amount of anti-white resentment. We sat quietly chatting,
drinking and minding our own business, attempting to ignore
the provocative comments being thrown in our direction.

As the evening wore on, our conversation was drowned out
by the din of an increasingly vociferous dispute between two

prostitutes. A fight broke out right behind us. The two women were locked in combat, spitting and scratching like cats. The younger woman's apparently luxuriant head of hair was wrenched from her head and flung through the air, revealing wispy curls of short black hair beneath. Further enraged by this loss of her dignity, she grabbed a half-empty beer bottle from our table and lurched towards the older woman. As she smashed the bottle over her head they fell, entwined, to the pavement with a resounding 'smack'.

At this point one of the on-lookers leapt to his feet to intervene, pulling the younger woman off the older one, who now lay bleeding from the head. Dazed, but undeterred, she raised herself to her feet, still cursing loudly as he held them apart, standing between them with his arms outstretched, ordering them to behave themselves or go elsewhere. The younger woman stormed off across the street in search of her wig, leaving the older woman to gather herself together and leave the bar with as much dignity as she could muster. We decided we had seen enough for one night and left.

On New Year's Eve, as the midnight hour struck, bullets filled the sky as every soldier in possession of a weapon and fuelled by alcohol, joined in the celebration. It seemed there might be peace at last.

Chapter Twenty-Four

Taking Some
Practical Steps

Martina had been happy to fill Hans' post at the orphanage as a full-time member of staff, so Mark and I seized the opportunity of the tentative calm to take a break in England. We left her in charge with Andy Fifield, a gorilla keeper from Howletts who had been sent over to help but was finding the reality of life in the Congo overwhelming. Martina now had a boyfriend, Matthew Hatchwell, who worked for the Wildlife Conservation Society's Noubale-Ndoki project in Northern Congo. He was based at the project's office in Brazzaville and, brought together by adversity, their relationship went from strength to strength.

Two weeks into our break we received a call from a distraught Matthew, telling us that Martina had fallen into a coma. Flore and the American Embassy doctor, Ernie Davies, had rushed her to their makeshift intensive care unit, he explained, assuming that she had cerebral malaria. We hoped that the high doses of intravenous quinine they were giving her would not prove too late.

Later in the day he rang again to let us know that she had recovered consciousness and they were making urgent plans to evacuate her to Europe. Andy was doing his best to manage the orphanage alone, but it was obvious we would have to cut short our leave and return as soon as we could secure a flight.

We crossed paths with Andy as he hurriedly left Brazzaville on the flight which brought us in. Back at the orphanage we found the staff relieved to see us. It was always a shock to the Congolese when a 'mondele' became seriously ill or died.

Albertine explained that in our absence she had had fierce disputes with Bernadette's family over her medical treatment. Bernadette turned up at the orphanage looking pathetically fragile and unsteady on her feet, but declaring herself ready to return to work. We explained that we didn't think this was a good idea, and assured her that she would continue receiving her salary whether she returned to work or not. She seemed relieved, but hung around a little longer. It was obvious she missed the gorillas and the sense of purpose and camaraderie of the orphanage. Despite their initial welcome of Bernadette, the staff soon wished she would leave. Her pathetic appearance was that of an Aids victim and they felt embarrassed, as if the shameful disease in some way reflected on themselves.

Bernadette complained that her treatment was making her horribly sick and asked me whether it was really necessary to continue. I did my best to persuade her that it was absolutely essential. If she stopped taking it she risked a relapse of the TB that would be unlikely to respond to further treatment. She didn't seem to listen, her eyes staring vacantly at me from her cavernous skull. A couple of days later her boyfriend came to tell us that she had died.

Albertine erupted in a display of wild fury. She wailed, screamed and sobbed, blaming Bernadette's family for persuading her to ditch the prescribed treatment and seek a traditional cure with the feticheur.

We continued our usual routine that day, but our sad silence was felt by the gorillas who went about their usual business in the forest in respectful hush. Although the burial of Bernadette's body would take place within the week, there would follow a three-month mourning period before the celebratory ritual of 'soul-burial'. The Congolese believed, Nkodia explained, that the spirit of a deceased person remained on earth amongst the living for a period of three months following their death and could only finally rest in peace if its departure was celebrated by the living. I had once asked Hélène, one of our wild fruit suppliers, why she had worn nothing but black since the day we first met her two years before. She had explained that she was condemned to remain in mourning in respect of her deceased husband until she had the money to perform the burial ritual of his soul.

'Life and Death are but shadows of the soul,' Nkodia explained to me, 'and it is our responsibility to send the soul-spirit of Bernadette to the other side in as much style as we can afford.'

We agreed to host the celebrations in the bar next to the zoo. The staff, who I suspected sometimes spared us the full extent of their involvement in sorcery, included us as honorary guests. We had shared so much with these people, so many difficult times, so many joys and sorrows in the lives of the gorillas, the deaths of Hans and Bernadette and the anxieties of the recent political upheavals. These common experiences linked us now inextricably, bridging the cultural gap which had once divided us. After the long period of grave mourning, during which those closest to Bernadette wore only black, the mood of the ritual was one of cheerful release, bordering on ecstasy.

They each brought a local dish which they had prepared at home. The vast spread of food was more than their entire families would consume in a week, the quantity being a mark of respect to Bernadette. Having eaten and drunk to excess they proceeded to dance hypnotically to the soulful sounds that throbbed fuzzily from the cassette player in our car, parked just beside the bar. The older members of staff swayed serenely whilst the younger ones gyrated their hips suggestively, their arms raised high above their heads. I felt emotionally overwhelmed, caught up in their exuberant mood. Only when tiredness set in towards the late evening did tears finally smart in my eyes as I looked around at the familiar faces whose loyalty and friendship had meant so much over the past few years. The evening was brought to a premature close, even though the curfew had now been extended to eleven o'clock, as the girls started to worry about getting home late, fearful of encountering the armed bandit gangs who still roamed the streets of Bacongo.

Martina returned from Berlin in early March 1994, anxious to rejoin Matthew and hoping to resume her work as soon as she was fit. She still suffered from some residual weakness on one side of her body, but her strength steadily returned. By the time she had fully recovered she discovered she was pregnant with Matthew's baby. We were pleased for Martina and Matthew, both so obviously delighted by the news, but sad that we would lose yet another valuable member of staff within months of her arrival, just when her experience could have been put to full use.

Losing Martina from the orphanage staff would also further ground us in Brazzaville, as there would not be enough of a team to leave behind if we were to go to Lefini. What was ironic – and frustrating – was that by this time, New Year 1994, new funding was starting to look like a reality, and resolutions in the political climate made leaving Brazzaville look like a possibility. The bureaucracy of World Bank procedure had ensured delays from that quarter, but we learned that funds *were* earmarked for the Lefini, and we hoped that by the end of the year the Bank would liberate them. In the meantime, however, Aspinall had agreed to employ an extra pair of hands in Leo Mastromatteo, and was providing money to enable practical work to begin.

Given the boggy, inhospitable nature of the Lefini terrain, as well as other logistical problems, Leo had his work cut out.

Leo, a tall, bear-like man, had spent the past few years working with the wildlife film-maker, Alan Root, in Zaire. Prior to that he had been employed by the Mountain Gorilla Project to help set up their infrastructure in the Virunga mountains. We needed someone with Leo's skills and experience. The swampy terrain of the Lefini, so ideal for the gorillas, was less ideal for human habitation. He came well recommended and we had high hopes as we watched him struggle off the plane, weighed down with baggage, his pockets crammed with electronic gadgetry.

Within months he had established a temporary camp in the Lefini with basic facilities powered by solar energy, only appearing in Brazzaville when building materials needed to be purchased. His tent was like a workshop, his precious electronic gadgetry stored on makeshift shelves which lined the sides, leaving him barely enough space to sleep. He would spend hours fiddling with tiny pieces of electronic equipment, only to lose his patience before completion. The camp was littered with mysterious looking contraptions which were rarely put to any practical use.

He worked hard to complete a system of walkways across the swampy land that led from the open grasslands, where the building materials were stored under cover, to the base camp located the other side of a patch of dense forest. A simple barge mechanism made from a platform of wooden planks nailed together, attached to a floating bed of empty oil drums and operated by a wire cable pulley, made it possible to transport heavy loads of building materials across the Lesio river which intersected the forest.

But before long, Leo found himself embroiled in the machinations of the local Téké population. He complained of their obstinate, lazy attitude to work, an attitude that sapped his optimism, causing him to lose his temper frequently. Then he would be shocked by his own outburst and fearful of the repercussions. He inevitably ended up giving in to the unreasonable demands of his crew. He had spent many years working alone in Central Africa and his workforce seemed to recognize his vulnerability to threats and sorcery, using it to manipulate him and extract higher salaries and often ridiculous concessions. It probably didn't help that for the most part he was alone up in the Lefini. Mark did his best to escape from the demands of the thirty apes still resident in Brazzaville, but with the many calls on his time it was hard not to leave Leo without supervision or support. We were still trying to find a suitable candidate for the post of Lefini animal manager.

It was soon July 1994, and we had hoped to complete the base camp and gorilla holding cage before the end of the dry season. The rains would only make the work more problematic. With a basic camp established, Leo set to work on the cage foundations, no easy task on the inundated grassland.

In Brazzaville, he managed to find a reliable, conscientious team of chauffeur and assistant, Lecko and Emmanuel, who could confidently be left in charge of transporting building materials to the base camp from Brazzaville in the huge ex-NATO four-wheel drive truck we had purchased for the purpose, which had been boldly hand-painted with the words 'Projet de Protection des Gorilles'.

Lecko had friends in the Lefini region and often stayed overnight in Mah village. The truck was always welcomed as it rumbled over the dusty village main street. Children ran towards it the moment it appeared, waving, shouting and hurling themselves at the flatbed in an attempt to get in, hanging precariously off the sides. Lecko's maturity and level-headedness did much to resolve potential conflicts between the project staff and the village. The staff often went to him with their private troubles, knowing that he would give good advice.

Having completed the arduous first stage, Leo's pace of work declined as he became bogged down by the bickering, intrigues and threats of his staff. His mood would swing from zealous enthusiasm to apathetic depression. When in optimistic spirits, his excitement was contagious and he was affectionate and loveable, but when in the grips of depression he seemed sulky and indifferent to the impact of his mood on his work and those around him. Ground down he started to appear more often in Brazzaville, which inevitably caused delays to the construction programme. He needed more support and unfortunately we were not in a position to provide it.

Mark and I found ourselves fully occupied with the demands of a continuing influx of new orphans as well as those of our rapidly growing and challenging older gorillas. With the rainy season fast approaching, we had just secured Aspinall's agreement to employ Geoff Creswell as the Lefini animal manager. Although Geoff's arrival was imminent, he would have little time to acquaint himself with the gorillas and to complete work on the holding cage before the transfer of Kola's group. Martina's post at the orphanage remained unfilled.

We were aware that Aspinall was negotiating filming rights with the BBC and a Japanese film crew and, although we did not object to this in principle (in fact we welcomed the additional funding it could bring), we hoped that the timing of any filming and the inevitable disruption this would cause would not jeopardize the actual move of Kola's group and their positive reaction to their new surroundings. We had agreed with Aspinall to move ahead as fast as possible within the limits of our staffing.

As the pressure mounted I was becoming increasingly anxious about Mark's health. He slept very little at night, remaining awake in reflective thought until the early hours of each morning before giving in to fitful sleep disturbed by vivid dreams. His face was etched with deep lines of tiredness and he had started to develop regular high malarial fevers, barely recovering from one attack before another struck. He worried about Leo, about finding staff, and about the increasingly pushy communications from Howletts which showed a growing impatience to move Kola's group as soon as possible in order to co-operate with filming schedules they had agreed with the two film crews.

To outsiders, Kola's group appeared confident, but we knew that this could crumble with the stress of new surroundings. Kola in particular would need a great deal of support in the early weeks when he led his group into a new and consequently threatening environment. He could easily lose his nerve with resulting anarchy within the group. The gorillas had shown, time and time again, their vulnerability to stress through change in their physical or social environment. This long-awaited move needed careful timing and handling in order that the unavoidable stresses were kept to a minimum. Even then it was risky. We felt it should not be compromised by human impatience and filming schedules.

Chapter Twenty-Five

Feathered Friends

The majority of civil servants had now been unpaid for months. As a result, the zoo staff turned to other means of finding food, setting vicious wire snares in the orphanage forest.

Alerted by Juislain's frantic cries one morning, Mark rushed off to the forest. Locating Kola's group he saw Titi, confused, frightened and angry, pulling desperately at a tight wire noose which trapped his hand. Kola hovered close by, his expression one of concern, whilst the rest of the group huddled behind him, their eyes wide with fear. Feeling that as the leader he should know what to do, Kola was relieved when Mark appeared and hoped that he would be able to solve the confusing problem.

'Go back and fetch the wire-cutters!' Mark shouted at Juislain as he tried to approach Titi and take a closer look at the thin, razor-sharp wire which had already sliced through the skin of his wrist as he pulled it desperately tighter and tighter. As Mark tried to calm him, younger members of the group, particularly Mbinda, started to cough aggressively, thundering stiff-legged past him. Kola, ignoring the threat display being performed behind him, strode slowly towards Mark to join him and take a closer look at the perplexing object he was focused on. Titi coughed a warning and stamped his feet, the ground resounding beneath his weight.

Juislain returned, handed the wire-cutters to Mark and attempted to distract Titi's attention. As Titi lunged at him, coughing angrily Mark grabbed his brief opportunity to cut the wire, releasing Titi's hand as he pulled. Now, miraculously freed, Titi rushed off to join Kola, who placed a reassuring arm around his trembling shoulders and took him off into the nearby undergrowth. Some minutes later they returned to the perplexing scene and were confused to find nothing.

The wound needed cleaning and antibiotic powder so, as the group emerged from their bedroom in the usual rush to get to the forest after their siesta, we separated Titi off and darted him. The wound on his wrist was not as bad as we had feared and we were not too worried as skin wounds and bone fractures had not proved a real problem for the gorillas in our experience so far.

Kola led his group of six confidently around the forest, deciding when and where to move to new foraging pastures. But the small forest was too restricting and they needed the move to the Lefini where their progress could continue unfettered. Although there would be a temptation to take them out into the forest shortly after their arrival in the Lefini, it would be essential that they remained in the holding cage until they settled and considered it home, a safe place they could return to at night or in the unlikely event that they panicked in the unfamiliar terrain of the nearby forest.

Occasionally now, Titi and Madingo would combine the weight of their respective influences on the group to overrule Kola when deciding which direction to take in the forest. This flexibility of hierarchy, that might change subtly from day to day, never however threatened Kola's overall position as leader and demonstrated to us their maturity as a group. A hierarchy which might at first have appeared rigid was revealing itself to be far more complex.

All male 'bachelor' groups are not uncommon in the wild. Black backs (sub-adult males) who have left their family groups once the dominant silver back is no longer willing to tolerate their presence, will set out on a solitary existence in the hope of poaching females from other groups to start family groups of their own. These young males may temporarily team up for company and protection. The previously unquestioned theory that gorilla groups are always composed of one dominant silver back male, his harem of females and their offspring, has been thrown more and more into doubt as researchers reveal the dynamism and flexibility of gorilla group sizing and composition. Our gorilla groups at the orphanage mirrored this flexibility.

Kola's languid, fluid grace and easy authority was now reinforced by his muscular physique, his broad back and shoulders warning of formidable strength. He would stand proudly in the forest before turning his head, slowly beckoning his group to follow, leaning lazily on shoulders whose size was accentuated by the natural slope formed by his long arms and shorter legs. He still retained his childishly eccentric manner of chest-beating, slapping his broad chest with flat hands rather than 'cupping' to trap air that would explode with a smack on impact against the drum-like muscles. Chest-beating was a ritual they all performed regularly. It was often purely an expression of high spirits, but it also effectively displaced tensions and energies that might otherwise have built up. Kola's chest-beating displays were, however, almost purely an expression of authority, a dominance display that was noted by his potential rivals within the group.

We first spotted Queenie and Rambo in a small chicken wire

cage perched precariously on top of a dog's kennel in the back
yard of our timber supplier's house. They were Lizard Buzzards.
The young dog below them barked constantly, resenting the
chain that tethered him to his kennel, and keeping the birds in
a constant state of nervous tension. There were no perches on
which they could preen or sleep and dirt obscured the delicate
grey and white barring of their breast plumage. Their clumsily
clipped wings bled from constant beating against the wire as
they panicked, unable to hide from prying eyes.

'What do you think of my eagles?' the merchant proudly
asked us. 'They are young as yet, but will grow.'

When we diplomatically informed him that they were not
eagles but Lizard Buzzards, unlikely to grow much larger than
they were at present, his face fell and, disappointed, he asked if
we would take them off his hands.

Mark caught the two birds up, hastily placing the protesting
bundles of feathered fury into one of the gorilla baskets we
carried in the car. Back at the house they emerged, glaring at us
haughtily, their amber eyes blazing defiance. Over the next few
days they continued to angrily resist our intrusive approaches,
their scornful expressions shaming us into retreat.

But as the weeks passed they settled and the 'manning' process
began. Training them to the fist was a battle of wills, but one
which we had to win if we were to allow them freedom from
their makeshift perches on the large window sill in our sitting
room. Initial attempts seemed hopeless as they flattened their
plumage and crouched, gripping the leather glove with vice-like
feet and diving headlong in a raging, terrified bid for freedom,
only to find themselves hanging like trussed chickens, suspended
by their leather ankle jesses, spinning and flapping wildly in
their attempts to right themselves and furious at the indignity
of the situation. In the face of such stubborn defiance I was
reminded of our attempts to conquer the gorillas' brave façade

on their arrival at the orphanage. They made us feel dispropor-
tionately grateful for the slightest sign of acknowledgement or
recognition. Eventually the birds capitulated and accepted the
fist as a necessary evil which usually resulted in food or a more
interesting perch. We had come to an understanding of some
sort.

They soon made it clear that the area around the sitting room
window was their domain. There they spent many contented
hours observing the insect, animal and bird life in the garden
through the mosquito net window. They would sit for the most
part, apparently catatonic, poised on one leg, the other leg
tucked up and under their downy breasts. When they spotted
something particularly interesting in the garden, they would
break their pose to crane their necks forward and hop excitedly
up and down the length of the window sill.

As they grew in confidence they became increasingly vocal,
singing exuberantly in the early mornings, sometimes for hours
on end, yodelling a musical series of cries descending in pitch,
the distinctive black stripe on their throats standing proud as
they raised their beaks to call.

The short journey from the house to work each morning
became a logistical feat with gorillas on our laps in the front
seats and Queenie and Rambo perched skilfully on wooden
perches secured to the back seat, watching the world go by with
beady eyes. Arriving at the orphanage we were confronted with
the task of getting the birds from the car to the office on our
fists whilst the monkeys, Kiki and Pétain, danced round our
feet, curious and challenged by the birds' apparent arrogance.

Once safely inside the office they released their grip and
settled on the highest shelf of the bookcase above my desk where
they spent the morning surveying the office activities from a safe
vantage point, perched on one leg, one eye open, one shut. If a
stranger entered the office they would tense, sitting bolt upright,

and assume scornful expressions that made it clear they resented the intrusion, occasionally shifting on their thrones to eject a projectile stream of bird shit which would land with a noisy splat on my desk or the unfortunate intruder's head.

Some visitors would point at them and enquire if they were stuffed, at which they would swell indignantly to their full size, puffing out their feathers, insulted by the offensive pointing finger.

They were fed on a combination of beef, cockroaches, and any mice or rats which the staff caught around the orphanage, a bounty having been placed on their heads. We kept a rusty old tin in one corner of our sitting room that often housed up to ten live cockroaches or a clutch of small rodents from which a victim could be chosen at meal times, stunned and placed on the window sill to await its death in the vice-like clutches of the two hungry birds. Although most of my squeamishness had been obliterated by now, I still recoiled at the sight of a tin full of cockroaches!

As Queenie appeared the more assertive of the two we assumed that she was female and Rambo was male, females being dominant in raptor pairs. It wasn't until some time later that we discovered they were, in fact, both males. Their silvery grey plumage was now glossy, the barring of their breast feathers precisely defined. But we were disappointed when their first moult of feathers confirmed our fears that they would never be able to fly. The damage done to their primary flight feathers by the poacher's ignorant hacking had been so severe that at times they still bled from the amputated stumps.

In the afternoons they were blocked out on perches in the garden where they watched with intense raptor concentration the insect life in the long grass, occasionally trapping with powerful feet the odd cricket that wandered too close. We had cut down a large plastic bucket to provide a water bath in which they would often sit together, flapping their wings excitedly and dipping their smooth, silvery heads quickly in and out of the water to send the cool drops splashing over their hot backs, or simply standing on one foot enjoying the sensation of the cool water on their feet.

Mabafi, Dimonika and Blixa had accepted the Lizard Buzzards as part of the scenery. Instinct must have warned them not to mess with these predatory creatures as they did the ducks. The Buzzards were equally unbothered by the gorillas, but bonobos were a different matter, their shrieks and generally manic behaviour greeted with scornful expressions by the birds.

Denise, our house keeper, initially wary of the birds, soon became curious, mimicking their calls and delighted when they responded. She had quickly become fond of the younger gorillas at the house and even arrived at work one morning, breathless with excitement, to recount in detail her dream of the previous night in which she walked in the forest hand-in-hand with the gorillas. The arrival of a somewhat larger bird of prey was to test her new-found enthusiasm to its limits.

Since our arrival in Brazzaville in 1989, Mark had hoped that one day the zoo would allow us to take over care of the Pel's Fishing Owl they owned, living at present a miserable existence in a chicken wire cage. Five years later the Zoo Director had finally agreed and we erected a large enclosure that housed an artificial pool we intended to stock with live fish. Once released into the enclosure, Dolly, as we named her, shook herself and gazed around wide-eyed before swooping silently the length of the cage and up to perch on top of a tree stump. From her vantage point she gazed intently at the water, her eyes alert to every ripple that betrayed the catfish writhing and flicking eel-like beneath the surface. She and Mark formed an immediate attachment. Whenever Mark disappeared I knew I would find him with Dolly. She would coo softly at him through the wire netting the moment he appeared. As he entered the enclosure, her huge, marble-like black eyes would fix on him and she would swoosh down towards him, her nut-brown and cream barred wings spreading silently to their full span of five feet and fanning the still air as she landed delicately on his head and proceeded to gently pad up and down in affectionate greeting. This ritual completed she would fly back to her perch. When Mark approached, his face level with her eagle-sized frame, she would lean forward and gently nibble his cheek. Soon she was broody and could be seen scraping and scratching at the hard ground in one corner of her cage, preparing a nest in which to lay Mark's eggs.

She rediscovered her fishing skills the first afternoon. Her head swivelled as she watched the water ripple. Suddenly she dropped from her perch and, surprisingly clumsy, plopped into the water, her feet clamped round a squirming catfish. She stared down at the protesting fish in her grip, as if surprised to see it move, then hauled her wet self out of the water, spreading her wings to fly back to her log perch where she tore off lumps of orange flesh, carefully avoiding the dagger-like spines around the catfish's head. When the supply of live catfish temporarily dried up, we introduced a live rabbit into the cage, but she showed no interest in this mammalian prey. Each day we returned expecting her to have eaten the rabbit, only to find that the rabbit had grown fatter and the vegetation in the cage sparser. Eventually it was reduced to nibbling the foliage at the water's edge, straining its neck towards the hyacinths that bobbed on the surface. One morning we found its bloated body floating on the surface of the pool next to a half-eaten lily. It had presumably stretched too far, fallen in and drowned. Dolly reacted at last, upset by the strange lifeless object bobbing in her pool and relieved when Mark removed it.

When her pool developed a leak we took her home to the

house while repairs were carried out. She seemed confused by this turn of events, but as long as Mark was around she meekly accepted the situation. She spent her nights in the shower, tethered to a wooden perch, and the days in the back garden, much to the indignation of Queenie and Rambo. She accepted the restraints of ankle jesses and leash, and made a strange, ungainly sight gripping Mark's leather-clad fist with her huge feet, looking to him for reassurance and only willing to accept morsels of beef from his mouth.

Denise was completely fazed by Dolly. The Congolese believe owls to be possessed by magical spirits, their silent flight and night vision signalling special powers. When we asked Denise not to go into the shower room because there was an owl there her eyes grew wide with alarm. We brought Dolly out in an attempt to prove that she was harmless and Denise gasped, recoiling to the far side of the room. But as she watched Dolly lower her head and gently nibble Mark's cheek, she started to relax. Although she was never entirely comfortable in the owl's presence, her own fear amused her and she would sneak out to the garden to watch, staring trance-like at Dolly, curious and fascinated, giggling to herself in disbelief and embarrassed when we caught her.

Dolly despised the monkeys. Pétain in particular would taunt her by leaping onto the roof of her cage and jumping menacingly, his eyebrows moving furiously up and down in an exaggerated threat display, whilst she made angry attempts to peck at him through the wire. Nearly every morning we would arrive at the orphanage to find her being taunted by either Pétain, Kiki or a group of complaining crows who perched on the roof of her cage cawing loudly. Pétain, however, was a nuisance to everyone, spending most of his time mugging visitors to the zoo and making off with their refreshments. He had discovered that the bar next to the zoo was the ideal place to hang out, somewhere he could find victims who were easy to intimidate and would quickly surrender their food. Eventually, he only ever visited the orphanage on Mondays when the bar was closed.

Chapter Twenty-Six

Tragedy Strikes Again

Bernadette's death was still painfully fresh in our minds when Jean fell ill with a fever. We presumed it was malaria, but he failed to recover as the days passed, remaining weak and unsteady on his feet, his balance apparently affected. After several weeks off work he turned up one morning accompanied by his wife, who supported him as his legs trembled, threatening to buckle when he attempted to walk, swaying as if drunk. I urged him to sit down, anxious to relieve his obvious embarrassment at my seeing him in this pathetic condition. I couldn't help but feel a sense of foreboding.

We insisted that he see Flore, assuring him that we would pay the costs. He agreed a little reluctantly, half relieved and half dreading the possibility that medical tests would reveal something he would rather remain in ignorance of.

A couple of days later Flore told us that, frustratingly, Jean's brain scan had failed to reveal the cause of his mysterious condition. She was at a loss to explain it and presumed it must be some form of encephalitis. His Aids test was negative, which was an enormous relief to everyone. Apart from treating him with antibiotics, a shot in the dark, we could do nothing but wait and see whether he would survive and recover.

Over the next couple of months he made a slow recovery and eventually returned to work. He still tired quickly and would spend hours with Sid's group, sitting in a corner of the cage, absorbed in thought. The gorillas welcomed him back in their usual low-key way, making it clear that they had missed him, but sensitive to his obvious mental and physical fragility. They sat circled around him as he squatted, his head in his hands, taking turns to stay with him when boredom set in and the urge to play and work off some energy became overwhelming. He slowly recovered his former strength and enthusiasm, resuming his usual macho front, but our bond had deepened with the experience.

Our agreement with the Congolese government signed eight months earlier stipulated that we must take on a Congolese counterpart for each key expatriate working on the Lefini project, a gesture of intent to train a Congolese management team for future responsibilities. These counterparts were to be chosen from the staff of the wildlife department. We needed three to work alongside Mark, Leo and animal manager Geoff Creswell, who would arrive shortly.

Marcel Nguimbi, Mark's counterpart, was bright and painfully meticulous in his work. He agreed submissively with whatever we said, leaning as far forward as he could without falling off his chair to catch Mark's every word, his head nodding up and down like a soft toy on a car dashboard. Any form of authority would reduce him to painful obsequiousness, but underneath boiled a cauldron of repressed anger which, when stirred up by Leo's counterpart, Gilbert Pongui, would erupt to the surface.

Gilbert would drag Marcel off to the zoo bar at lunch-times. He would return tanked up and wound up, itching to provoke an argument with anyone he found in the office, screaming hysterically in a high-pitched, piercing voice and gesticulating

wildly, fuelled by resentment over a grievance which the manipulative Gilbert had pointed out over lunch, a grievance no doubt
felt by Gilbert himself who was reluctant to air the matter and
risk open confrontation.

Gilbert considered himself an 'intellectuel', and therefore
above any sort of physical hardship or activity. He refused to
sleep, as the expatriates and local staff did, in a tent whilst
awaiting the completion of staff housing at the Lefini base camp.
I was reminded of a passage from Dr Albert Schweitzer's book,
More from the Primeval Forest:

> Suddenly I catch sight of a negro in a white suit sitting
> by a patient whom he has come to visit. 'Hullo friend,' I
> call out, 'won't you lend us a hand?' 'I am an intellectual
> and don't drag wood about,' came the answer. 'You're
> lucky,' I reply, 'I too wanted to become an intellectual,
> but I didn't succeed.'

It appeared to us that Gilbert wanted nothing more than to
spend his days sitting comfortably behind a desk in an air-
conditioned office in a suit that proclaimed his elevated status to
the world. He even wore the label of his designer sports jacket
on the outside for maximum effect. He simply refused to do his
share of the physical work we felt was required, and appeared as
adept at manipulating Leo as he was Marcel. We resented the
time spent dealing with problems we felt Gilbert had created
when other pressing problems needed our attention. In the end
we were forced to ground him in Brazzaville. He proved just as
disruptive in our office, but at least the repercussions of his
behaviour there were limited. In the Lefini his position of
authority had opened a treasure-trove of opportunities for making money for himself and bestowing it graciously on others in
return for favours. He presented himself to the villagers as a

local hero, someone who would protect their interests and extract as much money as possible for them, even at the expense of the project and the gorillas' well-being. Behind their backs he referred to them dismissively as 'simple villagers'.

Gilbert was a handsome man, well built with a fierce, large-featured face. At the age of thirty-two he had already fathered at least ten children, few of whom he took any responsibility for. He found it completely impossible to resist a pretty woman and as a result often turned up on Marcel's doorstep, banned from his own home for misconduct.

The third counterpart was Mbani Akangala, a Téké man who proved a positive delight in comparison to his colleagues. The tribal scarring on his face was completely at odds with his calm, gentle, understated manner, qualities which gained him imme-diate acceptance by Kola's group. He proved a valuable older and respected father figure for people like Juislain. He worked hard, demanding little recognition for his work. He was a fount of information and kept meticulous notes on everything that involved the gorillas, the forests and the local people, the scruffy notebook he carried everywhere filled with interesting and often enlightening facts and observations.

The orphanage office was now a noisy crowded place, Marcel and Gilbert's presence overloading a space barely large enough for the two of us. We considered it essential to keep the office door open at all times in order to stay in touch with what was going on with the gorillas and the staff, and as a result had not bothered to install air-conditioning. Gilbert complained con-stantly about the heat, insisting that he could not possibly work in such appalling conditions, apparently having forgotten that he had spent the previous five years in the stifling offices of the wildlife department. The atmosphere of our previously peaceful office was no longer conducive to work and we often found ourselves in the early hours of the morning doing paperwork that should have been completed during the day.

As Leo struggled to maintain progress on the cage in the Lefini, the orphanage had problems if its own. Dimonika was still sleeping overnight at the house, Mabafi having now taken the important step of joining two other recent new arrivals, Makoua and Ngoko, to sleep at the orphanage. Mabafi's boisterous, tom-boy approach to life made her an immediate favourite in this new nursery group. She had already joined them out in the forest during the day as they began exploring, testing their developing climbing skills. She gambolled after them as they tunnelled into the undergrowth in search of food, hooting when they disappeared from view, eager to keep up with her newly acquired older brothers.

Back at the house, Dimonika was a pathetic sight, her growing bulk squeezed tightly into her small overnight basket, that was beginning to split at the seams. She needed to find her feet in a gorilla group of her own, to leave behind the refuge and security of human arms and a cosy, unthreatening world she so stubbornly clung to. If we didn't try now to integrate her into a social group with other gorillas her age, she would fall behind, unlikely ever to catch up and certainly unlikely to survive one day in the wild.

An important step towards finding her feet in Makoua's nursery group was to sleep with them, alongside her friend, Mabafi, in their bedroom at the orphanage. Siesta time offered the ideal opportunity to begin this transition. This was a time of relaxation for the group. Their appetites satisfied by a busy morning foraging in the forest and a midday meal of fruit and vegetables, they retired willingly to the cool shade of their bedroom during the hottest hours of the day.

They tumbled lazily into the room, their drowsy eyes already

blinking involuntarily with beckoning sleep, their pendulous
bellies bulging and satiated with the contents of their recent
meal. Catherine followed behind, carrying Dimonika. She depos-
ited her on the springy bed of leaves alongside Mabafi and
turned to leave the room. Dimonika stared vacantly at her as she
closed the heavy, wooden door.

Outside we pressed our ears against the door and listened. All
was apparently peaceful. But as we turned to leave a piercing
scream broke the silence. Suddenly realizing that she had been
abandoned, Dimonika vented her rage in ear-splitting shrieks
that irritated the other, tired gorillas. They coughed loudly,
warning her of their annoyance at this unwelcome disturbance
of their normally peaceful siesta. Gentle attempts by Mabafi to
comfort her failed. As her screams persisted unabated, the other
gorillas lost patience and bit in an attempt to silence her cries.

One long piercing wail could be heard, subsiding, as exhaustion overwhelmed her panic, to plaintive hooting as she called
for Catherine to come and rescue her.

We persisted with this routine until she accepted the new
arrangement. Now was the time to start leaving her with the
group overnight. This hurdle proved to be as hard on Makoua's
group as it was on Dimonika. We left them that night to the
sound of her hooting calls. The next morning we opened the
bedroom door to unusual silence. Normally they would emerge
immediately into the bright morning sunlight, energetic and
grumbling with hunger for their first milk feed of the day. This
morning was different.

Peering into the darkness, we made out the tired faces of
Makoua, Ngoko and Mabafi, who looked as if they had not slept
a wink the entire night. Dimonika sat alone at the back of the
room, staring with dull eyes into space, her tragic face ravaged
with emotional exhaustion.

It was such a pitiful sight we couldn't help but laugh. If the others looked exhausted, then Dimonika looked positively ill as she squatted, immobile and dejected. Catherine picked her up and, emerging from the room, raised her eyebrows in despair at us as she took the pathetic, apparently lifeless Dimonika into a quiet corner of the garden. The rest of the group watched them leave in silence and then, after hungrily consuming their drinks, dragged themselves wearily off to the forest with Albertine.

Later that morning I approached the nursery group in the forest. I was met by a scene of devastation. The gorillas lay spread-eagled and slumbering heavily around Albertine, who explained that they had collapsed in this state a few minutes after arriving, too exhausted to begin their usual early morning routine of urgent, excited explorations of the nearby foliage.

Alerted by my footsteps, as dry leaves crunched and split like fire-crackers under my feet, Ngoko raised his head, grumbling with pleasure as he spotted the milk bottles in my hand. Roused by his deep, resonant voice, the others woke, lazily raising themselves to their feet and ambling towards me. Soon, three expectant, hungry faces were lined up in front of me, waiting politely for their bottles to be handed out. Makoua and Ngoko then fought over their bottles, spilling the precious milk as they tussled, one hanging onto the rubber teat and the other the plastic bottle, until it split apart and they watched, surprised, as the milk spilled out and was quickly absorbed by the parched earth below. Mabafi clung on tight to her bottle, repelling them both with fierce warning coughs, determined to stand her ground. Her rapid development and independence couldn't have been more of a contrast to Dimonika.

The dusty, hot days of the dry season finally broke at the end of September with an almighty storm that raged all night. The forest sprang back to life, new shoots pushing hungrily skyward, claiming the sunlight that filtered through breaks in the canopy, created by silvery-white trees struck dead by lightning. The rains brought with it an outbreak of amoebic dysentery amongst the gorillas which eventually reached Dimonika. Resisting all forms of treatment she coiled into a stubborn, bewildered ball and retreated into herself. The other gorillas easily accepted the Flagyl suspension, some positively relishing the sweet taste of the syrupy elixir, but Dimonika simply refused to co-operate and we were forced to immobilize her in a towel and squirt the syrup down her throat from a syringe. This apparently aggressive act made her even more tense and she vomited it back up immediately. It was hopeless. She reacted like a newly arrived orphan. Instead of attempting to ignore the crampy pains as the others did and carry on life as normal, she quickly spiralled into a state of depressed, introverted misery, losing interest in everything and everyone and regressing back to her original impenetrable state.

Injecting her with an anti-sickness drug had no effect. She continued to vomit. To help her keep the medicine down, we tried cradling her in our arms and walking around the garden in an attempt to distract her. Nothing worked.

Within two days she had gone from being a healthy young gorilla to a gaunt bag of bones, her diarrhoea nothing but gluey mucus flecked with blood as the amoebae multiplied in her intestines. She no longer reacted to either Catherine or myself and waited for death to end her miserable suffering in this bewildering world. She died on the third day of the illness. We tried to comfort ourselves with the thought that it was probably a merciful release from a life that would have become increasingly difficult the older she became, her child-like simplicity becoming less and less acceptable as the other gorillas matured, leaving her alone and abandoned as they pursued a wild future. I dreaded informing Christiane. Dimonika was her last remaining link with Hans and the Congo.

We tried hard not to have favourites amongst the gorillas, but since her arrival at the orphanage at barely three weeks old,

Mabafi had claimed a special place in Mark's heart. As she grew and matured, he took paternal pride in her progress. She was a tough little character, a very promising gorilla with a bright future ahead of her. When she developed the same symptoms as Dimonika and failed to respond to treatment, Mark became frantic. Initially she bravely shrugged off the inconvenience of painful stomach cramps and profuse diarrhoea, stoically trying to keep up with her group, making token attempts to play but tiring quickly. On the third day of her illness the diarrhoea had stopped, but she started to deteriorate rapidly and crouched, hunched on the forest floor, her hands clasped over her belly, only occasionally moving to stretch out on her back in an attempt to ease the agonizing pain. Her face was drawn with exhaustion, her eyes dull with pain. Seeing Mark approach she raised her head slowly and focused her brown eyes questioningly on his. As he crouched down beside her she moved slowly towards him and settled on his lap. As his reassuring hands gently stroked her head she exhaled a deep sigh, relaxing briefly before another spasm of pain wracked her body and she curled forward, whimpering softly. We were completely at a loss to explain why, when the diarrhoea had stopped, she had now developed this excruciating pain.

An anti-spasmodic injection, which she tolerated patiently, seemed to have little effect. She co-operated bravely, almost as if she understood that we were trying to make her well again, but she was becoming increasingly exhausted by the constant pain and soon started vomiting a vile green, sticky fluid, her weak body wracked by convulsive heaving as she retched until she had nothing left to bring up.

That night we took her home and remained awake with her until the early hours of morning. Her agony continued unabated, her belly now tense and distended, and she would only leave Mark when the pain became so unbearable that she was forced to crawl off his lap, wincing and whimpering with each movement to try different positions in an attempt to ease it.

As she turned her head and gazed pleadingly into Mark's eyes, I saw her agony reflected in his face. It was unbearable to watch. She died that morning in Mark's arms. He never spoke of her again, even the mention of her name was too painful. Already under pressure from England to press on urgently with the transfer of Kola's group, Mabafi's death was a blow he had few reserves to cope with. The events of the past year had forced us further into our own different coping mechanisms, alienating us from one another. We were unable to share our sadness or comfort one another.

Results of an eventual autopsy revealed that Mabafi had died from an intersussception, a condition which can occur in human infants as a complication of amoebic dysentery, when part of the bowel turns in on itself, causing complete and fatal obstruction of the intestine. The guilt we felt over her death was only marginally relieved by this news. Even had we known that this was the problem, there would have been nothing we could have done about it in Brazzaville.

Makoua, the leader of Mabafi's group, mourned her loss. His plaintive hooting carried in the still night. The other gorillas listened, subdued by his sad message.

In the early morning he would wait hopefully in the garden before the group ambled off to the forest. When Mabafi did not appear, he would reluctantly lead the others away, still turning his head from time to time to look, hoping to see her familiar form gambolling towards them, calling them to wait.

In the forest he searched, hooting more loudly as he moved through the dense tunnels of undergrowth that had been their playground. The group, sensing his distress, remained close to Catherine, subdued and never moving very far from her side to search for food, confused by their leader's anguish.

Chapter Twenty-Seven

Beyond Endurance

Mark buried his grief, becoming more and more withdrawn and throwing himself into his work with even greater determination in the hope that by physically exhausting himself he would find relief in sleep. He worked late into the night building a hardwood fence to provide much-needed security for Queenie and Rambo when they were blocked out in the garden. Having finished work at the orphanage, finding himself unable to unwind, unable to sleep and dreading the long hours of darkness alone with his thoughts, he would take his tools and wear himself out in the garden, working the heavy wood in the moonlit heat, sweating profusely until he could barely stand.

Returning to bed exhausted, he would finally give in to sleep. I would wake in the early hours, roused by his involuntary moans as he slept, animal groans of grief that broke my heart.

I became more and more worried. He had worked for so many years, uncomplaining and determined, whilst others, myself included, fell apart under the stress. I felt instinctively that he was nearing his breaking point.

The pressures were building up on all sides. We were now increasingly in conflict with Howletts over their intended filming schedules. Although aware that the filming would reap financial rewards that might benefit the project in the future, we could not agree that such a crucial, unpredictable event as the transfer of Kola's group be endangered by the presence of well-intentioned but inevitably interfering film crews, who would be complete strangers to the gorillas. Why not, we felt, film Kola's group in the orphanage forest before their relocation to the Lefini, then return at a later date to film their progress when they had settled and adapted to their new environment?

Apparently the dramatic potential of filming an entire group of gorillas being darted, crated up and loaded onto the project's ex-military truck to take them 120 kilometres up the North Road to their new home was irresistible. We remained, however, wary of the presence of film crews at this crucial time and made our feelings clear to Howletts. But, we feared, our behaviour was misinterpreted as sheer obstructiveness. Although our motive was purely to protect the gorillas at this crucial point in their lives, our objections seemed to be dismissed. Ironically, the very qualities of determination and pigheadedness that had got us this far now counted against us as we fought to protect the gorillas from what we firmly believed was unnecessary additional stress. They had enough in store for them in the next few months, and the presence of film crews would further unsettle them. These disputes did nothing to help us tackle the critical event ahead.

Geoff Creswell arrived in Brazzaville with his girlfriend, Liz Pearson, just weeks before the Japanese film crew appeared, unannounced, with a filming schedule agreed with John Aspinall in London. Faced with this fait accompli and feeling sorry for the film crew who knew nothing of the disputes, we sat down to try to work out how they could get good footage of the gorillas at the orphanage. We knew them from a previous visit in 1992 and they had proved themselves to be sensitive to the gorillas and capable of keeping a low profile. We suggested they filmed in the orphanage forest with the younger gorillas, but what they really wanted was footage of Kola's group. As Kola's group were becoming increasingly challenging even for ourselves recently, we did not think this a wise idea. They did not take kindly to the presence of strangers: it disrupted their behaviour in the forest and if not carefully managed could end in serious injury. Titi in particular was quick to jump to conclusions and panic, his screams provoking a protective reaction from the rest of the group, who would rush to his defence, intent on doing damage to the perceived aggressor. Geoff had little time to help Leo complete the Lefini holding cage, get to know Kola's group and get to grips with his job. We assumed that Howletts would agree with the two film crews a date for filming the transport of Kola's group that allowed sufficient time for the preparation of both the new expat staff and the Lefini holding cage. We did not realize at this point that dates had already been agreed with both crews.

The BBC film crew were due to arrive on the same flight as Naobi Okayasu, who would join the project staff with the aim of taking over responsibility for the daily running of the orphanage, allowing Mark the freedom to oversee both ends of the operation. Naobi had spent much of 1991 and 1992 studying the gorillas at the orphanage and we were confident that she was the ideal person for the job. Having suffered a near-fatal attack of cerebral malaria in 1991, her life only saved by Flore's rapid intervention, she had courageously returned after only a brief convalescence in Japan, intent on continuing her studies.

The night the BBC film crew was due to arrive in Brazzaville coincided with the Annual US Marine Ball, held at the MBamou Palace Hotel in the centre of town. Mark and I were hardly in a party mood when we finished work at 10 p.m. that day, but decided it would perhaps make a healthy change to escape for a night from our intense little world and loosen up. Mark had just finished his fence. It stood like a monument to his determination, symbolizing his self-punishment, and would probably still be there many years after the house had crumbled to dust.

We showered, dressed and made our way into town, my long, clingy dress and Mark's smart suit seeming incongruous until we reached the relative opulence of the hotel. We arrived shortly before eleven when the party was in full flow. Flore danced energetically next to the live band, her husky voice audible above the music as she abandoned herself to the throbbing rhythms.

A couple of drinks later Mark and I danced slowly to the soft music which brought calm to the previously frenzied room. I tightened my arms around him, remembering with sudden intensity the first weeks of our life together back in London many years earlier. I felt acutely aware of the estrangement caused by our mutual distress over the death of Mabafi, and an overwhelming sadness that the world we had shared now seemed to divide us.

As the music faded to a close Mark moved away from me and sank into a nearby chair, his pale face beaded with sweat.

'What's the matter? Do you want to leave?' I asked.

'Nothing, don't worry, I'm fine, just hot,' he replied quietly.

Ernie Davies, the American Embassy doctor, brushed by and whispered in my ear, 'Is Mark all right?'

Relieved that my anxieties had been noted by someone else I replied, 'Well, he insists he's fine but, you know Mark, I don't think he's fine at all.'

Ernie moved on into a noisy gathering of people and I talked distractedly with friends, preoccupied by Mark's unusual behaviour. As I drew up a chair beside him I noticed his chest heaving as if he was fighting for air. I asked again if he wanted to leave and this time he agreed. I took his arm, heading towards the door.

As we made for the exit his left leg knocked clumsily against Flore's chair. She turned around and made a passing joke, but when she saw Mark's pale face she looked at me, silently mouthing the same words as Ernie. Sensing Mark's unease I did not stop to respond to Flore's joke and, having reached the door and emerged into the long, cool corridor of the hotel, we both breathed a sigh of relief. The car was parked a short distance from the main entrance of the hotel and we walked to it in silence. I made my way round to the passenger door, waiting for Mark to unlock his side and let me in. As I stood there I watched him fall to the ground with a hard thud. Blood pulsing loudly in my ears, I ran frantically around the bonnet to find him lying, apparently unconscious, on the muddy ground, his eyes glazed and staring, his body lifeless.

I threw myself to the ground, clutched his head and screamed, 'Mark, Mark, can you hear me?'

There was no response. In the still silence I watched myself kneeling in the mud in my long dress in the loneliness of the tropical night, watching my husband die. His blank eyes stared back at me, unseeing. I felt the resigned inevitability of this final, tragic scene. Jerking myself out of this paralysed state, I pulled my dress up around my thighs and ran back to the hotel screaming, my words erupting in a meaningless jumble, until I reached the ballroom and found Flore's familiar figure. I pulled her with both arms, panting heavily from exertion, propelling her out of the room and down the corridor. She needed no explanation, the expression of horror on my face told her everything.

As we neared the car I saw with relief that some friends, the Greek Honorary Consul and his wife, Mr and Mrs Peres, knelt in the mud beside Mark's lifeless body, anxious to help and relieved to see Flore appear on the scene, Ernie Davies running close behind her. We stood round Mark in shocked silence, then, taking charge of the situation, Flore and Ernie exchanged urgent words and agreed to move him to the American Embassy Infirmary a few hundred metres down the road.

Mr Peres lifted Mark's dead weight over his shoulder and into the back seat of the car where he lay inert, his neck cricked freakishly to one side, his feet protruding stiffly from the narrow seat. I sat in the front with Flore, unable to speak.

Within a few minutes we were under the harsh lights of the infirmary. Mark's body lay on the stretcher-bed, his eyes staring blindly at the bright globe-like light above. I held his head, talking softly to him while Flore and Ernie barked orders at one another, their hands moving quickly and efficiently to open the sterile wrappers containing needles and infusion fluid. By now the American Ambassador, Bill Ramsey, had appeared on the scene and he rushed around trying to find the emergency resuscitation box. His reassuring presence registered somewhere in my mind. Flore passed me an infusion needle, asking me to do something with it. I raised my head to look at her, mumbling incoherently and unable to react despite my training as a nurse. We had all consumed a considerable amount of alcohol during the evening and found ourselves struggling, suddenly sobered as we gathered around Mark's inert form, all ridiculously overdressed.

Ernie and Flore both tried desperately to access a vein for infusion without success. When finally Flore appeared to have succeeded, blood shot back up towards the infusion bag. She had hit an artery, not a vein and rushed to retract the needle, leaving blood to pulse out and down my legs, splattering my now-ludicrous dress. I looked down at the red stain with numb detachment, hearing distant voices asking me whether Mark had complained of feeling unwell recently.

'I knew this would happen,' I spoke robotically, 'I'm not surprised. It had to happen.'

At this point we were distracted by a barely audible mumbo-jumbo of words from Mark. His eyes still stared blindly, his pupils dark and dilated. Arching his neck he exhaled a deep sigh. If this was death, he seemed to be saying, it was a relief. I placed my cheek against his and he spoke again.

'Don't worry, Helen, I'm not in pain.'

'Can you 'ear me, Mark?' Flore squawked in her stilted English, 'Wake up Mark!'

She had drawn up an injection of Valium, deducing by now that this was a fit of some sort. As she plunged the needle into his thigh muscle his body jerked and he instinctively moved his right hand towards the point of pain, grabbing Flore's hand to pull it away. He was mumbling again, moving his head now, his eyes focusing briefly before fading back again to black unconsciousness.

A few minutes later he made an aggressive attempt to free himself from the confusing situation. He seemed unable to move his left arm and leg. Flore and Ernie reassured him and he calmed down, unable to see their worried expressions. Ernie tested the neurological reflexes in Mark's arms and legs, and raised his head, his expression glum.

He looked at me, shrugging, aware that my medical training would not allow me the luxury of ignorance and, leaving Flore with Mark, he beckoned me to join him in the adjoining office.

He explained that Mark appeared to be paralysed on his left side and that at present they couldn't tell why. 'You need to return to Europe for diagnostic tests,' he said, 'tomorrow if possible.'

As the facts sank in I heard Flore's voice calling. 'Hélène, viens ici, viens voir Mark!'

I rushed into the room to see Mark raising himself shakily to his feet, the strength returned to his left arm and leg. He smiled gently at me and I moved closer to him. As I felt the warmth of his body against mine, my chest started to heave with involuntary sobs of relief. I looked up at the faces that surrounded us and smiled. At that moment I loved those people with an intensity I knew I would never forget.

Chapter Twenty-Eight

G-Day

Mark insisted on going home that night so Flore dropped us off at the house at two o'clock. She warned me to keep a watchful eye on him as fits were sometimes followed by a period of amnesiac wandering. After checking on his infusion she left. Despite a large dose of sedative, Mark remained agitated, pacing around the house in confusion. He was aggressive to my attempts to encourage him to come to bed. I was desperately tired and needed some sleep. He crashed around the sitting room, carelessly dislodging his infusion and I was forced to ring a very tired Ernie Davies at home and ask him to come over and reset the drip. Ernie left at about four o'clock and I continued to shadow Mark as he roamed the house until, exhausted, we both slept.

Waking the next morning still in my blood-splattered dress, I remembered the events of the previous night. If we were to leave for England, we needed to make arrangements to cover our absence. Geoff's girlfriend, Liz, was staying in Martina's old flat down the road. Her past work with the orphan chimps made her a valuable asset to the project. I phoned her, close to tears. Hearing her sympathetic voice unleashed convulsive sobs that left me unable to speak. She arrived at the house within minutes and we started to make urgent plans to cover our absence.

The newly arrived BBC crew phoned from their hotel. They had come with a schedule agreed with Howletts to film the transfer of Kola's group which they had the impression would happen within the week. I explained that Mark and I were leaving for the UK the next day and we arranged to meet them that evening in the Central Bar to discuss whether they wished to remain in Brazzaville and film at the orphanage or to cut their losses and return to the UK immediately. With Mark absent, the transfer of the gorillas was obviously impossible. In the end they decided to travel back to England with us and return at a later date to Brazzaville when we were ready to undertake the transfer. We hoped that Aspinall would now wait until Mark, Geoff and the Lefini were as prepared as possible for the move. Geoff needed more time with the gorillas and with Mark and, although the framework of the cage had been completed, he had had little time to furnish the interior.

Back in England Mark underwent a series of tests. I had been functioning like a robot for days, busying myself with the practicalities of getting us out of the Congo and making sure things kept running while we were away. I left Mark sleeping in his hospital bed and climbed into a cab to go the few miles to my sister's Wimbledon house. A love song played on the cabbie's radio and I found myself crying uncontrollably, my body shaking silently as I tried to stem my tears and save the taxi driver's embarrassment. I saw him glance in the mirror at my anguished face and avert his eyes. Arriving at last, my sister came out to pay the driver. She put her arms around me. 'I wondered when this would happen,' she said. 'Go ahead and cry, it'll do you good.'

I slept deeply that night, no more disturbing dreams or moments of wakeful panic. The next morning I made my way back to the hospital to await the results of Mark's brain scan. When the doctor finally spoke that afternoon, his distant voice seemed disembodied. As his words hit home, Mark and I looked at each other in relief. Nothing sinister had shown on the scan, and the doctor supposed that the fit must have been caused by sheer physical exhaustion. An hour later we were out of the hospital. A copy of the doctor's report was sent to Howletts.

We returned to our small apartment in Folkestone, feeling strangely flat despite the good news. Suddenly we found ourselves in the cold English winter with time on our hands. Mark's angry silence forced me to withdraw further into myself. He was angry with himself, angry with his body for letting him down and angry with Howletts.

We received a summons from Aspinall a few days later and drove to his mansion as the snow fell gently on the green Kentish hills. Ushered into a large, plushly furnished room we were offered a cup of tea. Aspinall enquired after Mark's health, adding in the same breath, 'Well, he looks in good condition!' To me, Mark looked exhausted. The conclusion of the meeting was that Mark should take several weeks' convalescence, before returning to Brazzaville to supervise and follow through the transfer of Kola's group.

The subject of film crews was studiously avoided, and we assumed they had been asked to delay more filming until Mark was back in Brazzaville and had the time to ensure that conditions in the Lefini were ready to receive Kola's group. However, a week later Aspinall phoned us, prompted by increasing impatience and pressure from the Japanese film crew, who had already paid for filming and were unable, for whatever reason, to delay any further. He informed us that Chris Furley would fly out to Brazzaville in a week's time, ten days before Christmas, to carry out the darting, crating and transfer to the Lefini of Kola's group. Tickets were booked for both of us on the same flight. We knew Aspinall well enough to realize that this was no bluff. If we did not return with Chris as suggested, we were told that the transfer would proceed without us. Challenging Aspinall would change nothing, it would only risk making him more determined to assert his authority. We were not being offered a choice because they knew we could not abandon the gorillas at this crucial point in their lives.

We were both shocked: Mark needed to recover his energy for the task ahead, and while we didn't know what the pressure and problems facing Aspinall were, it was difficult for us to understand why those who had always shared our concerns over the gorillas should seem to be letting film deadlines dictate the timing of the transfer. Mark was pivotal to the success of the move and to suggest going ahead without him seemed madness.

Despite a phone call from Geoff saying that he would back us up if we refused to co-operate with the proposed plan, we decided we would simply have to do the best we could under the circumstances. We were tired of fighting and in this instance it would not have made any difference – this had been made clear to us. We hoped that Geoff would be able to work on the holding cage interior in our absence.

A few days later we were back in the Congo with the BBC film crew. Geoff and Liz met us at the airport, Geoff looking thin and Liz tired and stressed. There was no time to make up for lost sleep, we needed to catch up on everything that had happened in our absence and prepare urgent plans for the transfer. The Japanese film crew were still there and became understandably less patient and sensitive when they realized that they were going to have to compete for the best film footage with the BBC.

Geoff was not happy with the deadline for the transfer and informed us that little progress had been made on the Lefini holding cage since our hasty departure for England three weeks earlier. He wondered why Mark had not challenged Aspinall's deadline, but he had not worked for the organization long enough to understand that this would have been a pointless and risky exercise. He had made his views clear to Howletts while we were away but agreed that if Mark capitulated he would go along with it. Mark had agreed, he had no choice and we were now determined to make the best of a bad decision. Geoff explained that although the basic shell of the holding cage had been completed, it contained little or no play equipment or shelter for the gorillas. But the schedule was fixed, Chris had arrived to follow instructions and it was too late to go back. There was not even time to go up and see the Lefini cage for ourselves prior to the gorillas transfer.

During our absence the staff, unsettled by what had happened to Mark, had, uncharacteristically, threatened to strike. Our first task was to call a meeting, explain exactly what the plans were and assure them that we would do our best to resolve any personal family problems which might arise over their relocation to the Lefini. Reassured that Mark was back in control, and that their worries were being taken seriously, they now approached the transfer with good-humoured excitement. In fact, the relocation would offer them financial rewards, their orphanage salaries being increased by a daily living allowance paid by the project whilst they were resident in the Lefini base camp. Albertine, Jean and Juislain were essential to the success of the operation, something they didn't need to be told. Nkodia, Paul and Catherine, caught up in the excitement of the impending move, were soon asking if they could come to the Lefini too, but they were needed at the orphanage for the other gorillas and the bonobos.

The orphanage was a hive of activity. We had only a day to prepare for the journey north.

The afternoon before the transfer Chris darted the gorillas. We crated them up in the garden ready for the move at dawn the next morning, when the town would still be quiet and we were less likely to meet with interference from the military as we left town.

The gorillas coughed aggressively at the sight of Chris's blowpipe, screaming in raw panic as the darts hit home, charging frenziedly around the cage as they searched desperately for escape routes, accusing us with bewildered eyes of betrayal. The two film crews were hidden behind the garden fence, as requested, but the gorillas were still aware of their presence and stared, white-eyed, at the faces and cameras that loomed over it.

Kola, Mbinda and Nzambi succumbed quickly to deep, oblivious sleep, but Titi, Dinga and Madingo fought the effects of the sedative, coughing and struggling for what seemed like forever before collapsing defeated. Dinga fought the hardest, screaming frantically at Chris and fighting to stay awake, stumbling like a drunk and slapping the ground with his hands in a valiant attempt at a threat display as he lay sprawled on his stomach, his legs splayed out limp behind him.

Although it might have seemed cruel to separate them into individual crates we were afraid that as they came round from the sedative they might panic and in their confusion injure one another. We pushed the crates into a circle with the steel grille windows facing one another and left them to calm down as the light faded and the effects of the anaesthetic wore off. Only Titi remained angry when he woke. He raged, hitting out with all his frightened strength against the wooden sides of the crate while the others remained silent, accepting their confinement. They finally slept and we made our way back home.

We didn't get to bed until the early hours and at three o'clock we were woken by a phone call from America for Geoff. An hour later the alarm clock went off. Meeting up with Leo, Liz and Naobi at the orphanage we offered the sleepy gorillas a drink through the steel lattice windows of their crates. They seemed surprisingly calm and for the most part thirstily consumed the drinks. Only Dinga and Madingo were reluctant to drink and we worried that they might become dehydrated on the hot journey ahead. We lifted the heavy crates onto the trucks and were soon rattling noisily out of the zoo. Nkodia waved as they disappeared from view, sad to see the gorillas go. The gorillas craned their necks, confused, to catch a last glimpse of their home for the past five years.

Jean, Juislain and Albertine sat on the flatbed with them, their familiar voices reassuring. Perched on the sides of the truck, there was a mood of excitement amongst the staff as they looked out over the rolling hills of the Plateau.

The convoy, consisting of the huge truck, our two four-wheel drive jeeps and two cars filled to bursting point with film crews and their equipment, rolled on up the North Road. Four hours later we arrived at the storage depot on the near side of the Lesio river.

A crew of forty local villagers, hired to help carry the crates over Leo's wooden walkways that traversed the swampy terrain and onto the barge pulley bridge to cross the river to the holding cage, waited in silence as they had been asked to do, to ensure as little disturbance to the gorillas as possible. They stared at the crates, fearful of the mysterious creatures inside. We again offered the gorillas a drink before the next stage of the journey. Again Dinga and Madingo refused.

As Titi's crate, the last, was finally lifted onto the wooden walkway, secured by four porters and supervised by Albertine, he let out a resounding angry bark, hitting out with his considerable strength at the flimsy sides of his crate. The porters stopped dead in their tracks as the crate shook precariously, their eyes white with fear. Albertine fiercely told them to pick it up and carry on. We hoped that Titi would remain calm as his crate was loaded onto the floating barge-bridge. If the porters panicked and released their hold, it would topple off, sink to the depths of the river and Titi would drown long before we could get down to release him.

With the last crate now safely on shore we pushed on towards the holding cage, reaching it in the early hours of the afternoon when the heat was at its worst. We stood and stared at the cage. It was worse than we had anticipated. Despite the solar netting, it still suffered from the glare of the scorching sun. The absence of interior furnishings left little refuge for these shy creatures who needed an environment that resembled as closely as possible their natural forest habitat, one which allowed cover. There were few play structures, as Geoff had warned, which meant that if tensions rose within the group the younger, weaker gorillas would be unable to escape the boisterous, assertive attentions of the stronger group members. Only one wooden, double-tiered platform measuring about three metres by four and around two metres high, had been erected in the centre of one of the two divisions of the cage. We stood and stared, the full realization of the problem sinking in.

Chapter Twenty-Nine

Kola's Group
in Trouble

When the crates were at last in the cage, Mark ran around clearing the immediate area of spectators – film crews and villagers who had stayed to gawp. Once the onlookers had shuffled away Mark and Juislain pulled the heavy bolts from the crate doors, calling the gorillas' names as they emerged, one by one, squinting in the bright sunlight and looking around anxiously at their new surroundings. Relieved to see the familiar figures of Mark and Juislain they walked close, hugging their legs, then broke off to circle the cage and investigate. The last to emerge was the youngest of the group, Mbinda, who made his way straight towards Juislain with his arms outstretched. Wrapping them round Juislain's waist, he took refuge in the physical comfort of his body, like a child.

They ceased circling and started to pick at the fruit and vegetables on the wooden platform. They remained nervous but, eventually exhausted, they huddled together as darkness fell. We went back to the base camp to eat. Juislain, also exhausted, fell asleep propped bolt upright in his chair.

Back in our tent for the night Mark found himself unable to sleep and decided to walk back to the cage alone to check on the gorillas. He found them asleep on the platform and felt a shiver of fear for them. They looked so young and vulnerable huddled together for comfort in the exposed cage on the open grasslands.

In the early hours of the morning we were woken by the persistent patter of heavy rain on the tents and stepped out into the dawn light to find the ground a predictable bog, deep puddles forming in the mud wherever we stepped. Mark rushed off to the cage to find the gorillas soaked, their lips pulled back in miserable grimaces, their eyes reproachful as they huddled dejected on the wet platform, unwilling even to step out onto the muddy floor to make their way over to greet him.

He headed back to wake Geoff. They spent the next hour sitting on the wooden observation bench outside the cage, deciding which of the most urgent improvements needed to be tackled first. The rains had also revealed a serious drainage problem. A channel needed to be dug around the cage, and the floor elevated and sloped to facilitate drainage. All this would have to be done manually to minimize any noise and stress to the animals. Overhead cover needed to be created using either large leafy branches or the timber planking that lay in piles on the other side of the river. More play structures and cover needed to be created within the cage. Releasing the gorillas from the cage was not an option at this early stage. The improvements were urgently needed, but any work with the gorillas already in the cage would further unsettle them.

Geoff and Leo's relationship had badly deteriorated by this time. Every problem that arose they blamed on one another, remaining stubbornly unwilling to be the first to solve problems, feeling that to act implied guilt. Liz had started to suffer from regular attacks of malaria, her normally resilient, cheerful nature dragged down by the tense atmosphere in the base camp as Leo stomped about moodily and Geoff remained stubbornly silent.

By the time Mark and I left to return to Brazzaville, Kola's group had already begun to display serious signs of stress. Titi, agitated and confused, strutted around the cage, barging the bars and bullying the younger gorillas whilst Kola remained preoccupied with the new and confusing situation. Madingo seemed to have lost all his confidence and put up little defence against Titi's threat displays and provocation, spiralling deeper into lethargy and depression. I had never known him to give in so easily. Mbinda and Nzambi, as the lowest ranking group members, were the least affected because they presented little threat. It was Titi, Dinga and Madingo, so close in age, their roles in the group in a constant state of flux, who would suffer from the increased tension while Kola's attention was distracted. Despite our anxieties we had to return to Brazzaville to sort out the problems that had been mounting in our absence. Paying the staff was just one of these, a hideously complicated and bureaucratic task now that we employed forty people. Naobi had coped for the past few weeks with little preparation but there was a limit to what she could achieve. We hoped Geoff and Leo, with the help of the reliable orphanage staff who had stayed on in the Lefini with Kola's group, would cope. Mark planned to return within a matter of days.

John Aspinall had announced his intention to visit the project in early January with his half-brother, James Osborne, the manager of one of his casinos. It had been planned for the BBC film crew to accompany Aspinall on his visit, but we had managed to put that circus off, insisting that more filming at this point would risk aggravating an already serious situation. This time they listened.

A couple of days later on Christmas Day Mark and I made the long drive back to the Lefini. We found Geoff in a state of deep depression. It was obvious from the state of the camp how much at odds with one another he and Leo now were. The atmosphere was tense and the gorillas had picked up on the mood of the demoralized staff. Any advice Mark tried to give was perceived as criticism or blame. Many factors had combined to create the present crisis. Impatience and film crews had certainly increased the odds of trouble in this unpredictable country. The cage badly needed improvements, torrential rain had worsened the situation and the threat of disease loomed. The gorillas' ability to fight off infection at a time when they were already under stress would be very low.

Madingo had developed diarrhoea and was still unusually withdrawn. He sat in a corner of the cage, alone apart from the odd contact with Titi as he barged past. Kola, preoccupied by his new situation, seemed incapable of reacting to quell the in-fighting and squatted, absorbed in thought. Madingo had initially appeared to respond to antibiotic treatment, but the lack of support from his bewildered group offered him little chance of overcoming his illness. I felt angry with Titi although I realized that his behaviour was prompted by fear.

Back in Brazzaville I met Aspinall and his brother at the airport. They seemed impatient to get up to the Lefini and wanted to leave Brazzaville the next day, so Leo travelled down in one of the trucks, arriving hours late as his diesel had been watered, a frequent problem now that most fuel was being imported from Kinshasa. He was forced to change cars and returned to the Lefini with Aspinall crushed in the cramped passenger seat and his brother loaded onto the flatbed alongside a mound of food supplies for both staff, visitors and gorillas. They arrived at Mah village, tired, dehydrated and irritable. Once they had settled into their cliff-top villa Leo contacted Mark by walkie-talkie to let him know of their arrival. Reluctantly leaving Madingo, Mark set off for the villa to welcome the party, irritated by the interruption from the urgent situation in the cage. He stayed chatting with them for thirty minutes, his mind preoccupied by the dying Madingo in the valley below. Muttering barely audible excuses, he left.

By the time he got back to the cage later that evening he found that Madingo had died alone, Juislain having collapsed from exhaustion in his tent. Mark sank into the mud at the base of the cage, his arms around Madingo's lifeless form, hugging his still-warm body. Sadness overwhelmed him as he sat in the mud, remembering the exuberant, playful youngster whose pranks had caused so much mirth at the orphanage and Madingo's betrayed, bewildered, tragic face in the days leading up to his death. He returned to the base camp for what remained of the night. In the early hours of the morning the heavens opened with a roar, and heavy rain poured until dawn. Every dip in the ground became a pool and Mark's feet sank deep into the sandy bog as he made his way back to the cage. Juislain arrived. On hearing the news face set rigid in an expression of speechless grief. Mark could think of nothing comforting to say, only 'sorry.'

In the cage the gorillas circled nervously, looking anxiously at Madingo's corpse. Mark and Juislain quickly removed the stiff body, observed by a worried Kola, and proceeded to bury him in sad silence, digging deep into the soft earth as the rain continued to fall.

Mark tried again to talk to Geoff. New to the project and not very familiar with the gorillas, the task before Geoff seemed overwhelming. With Madingo ill and Kola's group unsettled, work on the cage risked aggravating the situation further. The noise and presence of strangers would only increase the gorillas' stress levels. He worried that Leo's crew of local staff could not be relied on to work quietly and calmly when laying the top soil or digging the drainage ditches. He was angry with Howletts for the same reason as Mark: the decision to go ahead with the transfer had resulted in a situation he felt helpless to resolve.

On seeing the cage for himself, Aspinall agreed with Mark about the improvements needed. However, he simply could not understand why these problems had not been dealt with earlier, conveniently forgetting that we had returned at his request from England with only two days to prepare for the transfer. Mark bit his tongue. Depressed and tired he could barely muster the energy to respond politely and no longer cared about any repercussions that might result from his apparently off-hand behaviour.

Over lunch in Brazzaville a couple of days later Aspinall's brother seemed to be indicating that he felt we were at fault. He appeared to be blame Mark for his inability to get Leo and Geoff to resolve their personal animosity and work together, intimating that one or other must go. I dug my finger nails hard into the palms of my hands under the table and took a deep breath. Mark and I felt that we had done our best to carry out the programme that had been forced upon us. Following his return to England we had no further personal contact with Aspinall and attempts to reach him directly seemed to be blocked by his management.

The next day Mark took to his bed with a particularly severe attack of malaria which left him confined to the house for days on end with a recurring fever of 40°C. In the meantime Dinga, now the butt of Titi's threat displays, had started to show the same ominous signs of sickness as Madingo. His symptoms were further complicated by painful mouth ulcers, which made him reluctant to drink and aggravated the dehydration caused by his profuse diarrhoea.

With an ailing Dinga now occupying one section of the cage, and the rest of Kola's group the other, drainage work that had been started in the lull following Madingo's death could not continue. Back in Brazzaville I rushed back and forth between the house where Mark lay sick and the orphanage where Naobi was coping with more than twenty apes. Matthew Hatchwell had offered us the use of the Ndoki project's short-wave radio and so we were at least able to keep in touch with the Lefini.

The news was that Dinga was becoming progressively weaker, his dull, sunken eyes only occasionally flickering in recognition of Juislain's presence. He lay dying on a bed of leaves close to the steel-lattice wall that divided the two sections of the cage. Kola sat leaning, concerned, as close as possible to Dinga on the other side of the dividing wall. Several times Mark tried to leave his bed in Brazzaville, insisting that he must go to the Lefini, but realizing as his legs buckled under him that it was impossible. Flore tried to help by radio contact with Geoff and Liz, and Naobi travelled up to support them, but by the time she arrived Dinga had died.

We now feared for Nzambi.

Chapter Thirty

Full Circle

Geoff resigned, understandably unable to carry on after this traumatic start, leaving Mark and Naobi to split his duties in the Lefini whilst I covered the orphanage. Within several days Naobi had achieved dramatic results with the holding cage, working day and night to take advantage of the fact that there were no sick animals for whom the disturbance of the manual work might prove fatal. By the time Mark had recovered from his malarial attack enough to travel north, he was relieved to find the gorillas considerably calmer now that they were able to hide and play, diffusing their tensions in the cover of densely clad branches that lined the front wall of the cage overlooking the open grasslands. Even Titi had begun to settle, although he still displayed frequently and charged the cage walls aggressively when Leo's workers passed by. His interactions with Nzambi and Mbinda were gentler and play could be diplomatically brought to a close by the two younger gorillas by simply moving out of range behind the branches.

Dinga's death had caused great consternation back at Howletts. Although we had suffered disease outbreaks in the past, Aspinall had not reacted with this degree of concern. We still believed the gorillas would get there in the end, and we struggled to keep our heads in this crisis. We could only presume that the public scrutiny that would result from filming was in some part responsible for Aspinall's decision. Our intimate involvement in the daily lives of the gorillas made this crisis profound on a personal level. For Aspinall it was more a matter of pride and distant concern. We needed gentle support. Seeking to cast the blame for this crisis on someone was pointless. Although the deaths of Madingo and Dinga were devastating we had always known there were risks involved in a reintroduction such as this which no one had previously attempted. We thought that if Howletts imagined it would all run smoothly, they had learned nothing from the past five years' work with the gorillas. The nature of the country itself was unpredictable after all, and made any undertaking precarious. We did our best not to be unduly affected by their reaction: we hardly needed more pressure to solve the crisis. We were doing our utmost to right the situation.

Aspinall accepted Geoff's resignation and our suggestion that he be replaced by Despina Chronopoulos, a wildlife journalist who had been out to visit us on two occasions and had made it clear she would welcome a chance to work on the project. Despina was an instant success. She was fearless and apparently undaunted by the task ahead, quickly winning Titi's admiration and friendship and able to stabilize his confidence and disruptive behaviour without causing tensions with Kola.

A few weeks after her arrival, however, we started to worry again about Nzambi. Even under routine conditions back at the orphanage he had suffered from stress. He had remained small and weak as the others grew. He ran too quickly to the protective refuge of human arms and as a result never really learnt to deal with the complex social dynamics and pressures of gorilla group life. Now, lacking the buffer of Madingo and Dinga, he was more vulnerable than ever. Although Titi would play with deliberate restraint now, Nzambi felt intimidated by his sheer physical size and rebuffed his attentions, resulting in Titi losing his patience and lashing out in hurt and frustration.

As the weeks passed Nzambi lost weight and his coat grew dull. He developed painful spots in his mouth, his throat looked red and sore and he became reluctant to eat or drink. Separated from the others he spent his time with Juislain and Despina, squatting immobile and introspective for the most part, but occasionally moving over to hug them as if his life depended on it. Within days, he too died.

Chris Furley was to fly out, and it was made clear to us that to lose three out of six gorillas from this pioneer group was unacceptable. He would be followed by Peter Halliday, their head gorilla keeper, a move we considered an indication that they considered us incompetent in even basic animal management. Quite what Peter could miraculously point out that we hadn't already tried we couldn't imagine.

What was even more frustrating about this descent of visitors, and of which Howletts were possibly not aware, was that out-of-towners always needed chaperoning. By this point we could only feel resentful that this would rob us of valuable time that could be spent in the Lefini. Visitors all needed meeting at the airport, having hotels booked, transport and food arranged, as well as explanations and justifications of what we were doing and why. Our patience was at an all-time low; we needed to save the little energy we had for the gorillas alone. Mark and I had long since given up having any time or energy for one another.

Nonetheless, we tried to view Chris's impending visit philosophically, hoping that he might be able to shed some light on the deaths of Madingo, Dinga and Nzambi. But things got off to a bad start when his Swissair plane was forced to stand for two long, hot hours on the tarmac at Maya Maya airport whilst the new President Elect of the Congo, Pascal Lissouba, shook the hands of his thirty-strong coterie of advisors, exchanging pleasantries with each before climbing the steps to board his private plane, pausing briefly at the top to turn and give a regal wave.

The autopsies failed to reveal the cause of the gorillas' deaths. It was too late to send tissue samples for pathological examination back in England. Chris returned to England, leaving us none the wiser.

A few days later we decided that, as Kola's group seemed settled, it was at last time to begin exploring the surrounding forest. We thought it better not to inform Howletts in order to avoid the possible interference of imposed deadlines and more film crews. This moment was for the gorillas and ourselves alone.

The plan was that Mark, Despina and Juislain would lead the gorillas to an area of forest behind the cage that was densely clad with affromomum, a food they favoured. This patch of forest would afford plenty of potential to relax and forage whilst remaining still close to the cage. Mark and Juislain entered the cage at midday, feigning a casualness they didn't feel, and the gorillas went through their usual ritual welcome, coming over to greet them one by one. Mark then moved towards the large steel grille door and, having opened it wide, he walked slowly out. The gorillas, hesitating only for a moment, followed behind with Juislain bringing up the rear. Once out on the open grasslands Kola paused, assuming a posture of confidence he cannot have felt. Hearing Mark calling him to follow, he turned back to Titi and Mbinda, beckoning them to keep up, then moved off in pursuit of Mark as he crossed a stretch of scrub to reach their destination.

As they moved towards the forest ahead, Kola, in a poignant gesture of generosity, placed a trusting and reassuring hand on Mark's shoulder.

They crossed the narrow slatted bridge, glancing down

curiously at the stream beneath them. In time they would explore the clear, cool refreshing water and discover the succulent roots and shoots beneath its surface.

Only the gorillas' eyes betrayed the trepidation they disguised in bluff postures of confidence. They moved single file through the dense undergrowth into the heart of the forest where they stopped and spread out, curious and tempted by the thick shoots of affromomum that carpeted the forest floor to move away from the security of their human friends. Soon they were lost from view, climbing high into the densely clad canopy of trees or tunnelling into the undergrowth. Only their low pitched, contented grumbling gave them away, audible above the whispered conversation of the humans who now relaxed, smiling at one another with relief. Everything the gorillas had learnt in the orphanage forest had prepared them for this moment. They returned to join their human companions some time later, settling to rest and enjoy a relaxed siesta, human and gorilla limbs intertwined.

As the afternoon light faded, casting an orange haze over the forest, Kola raised himself to his feet, ready to start searching for a suitable nest site for the night. Mark decided it was time to return to the cage and when he stood up Kola moved gratefully behind him as he led the party back to the cage they now regarded as home.

After thirstily consuming their usual evening drink, they were soon fast asleep. Mbinda lay flat on his back with his legs propped up against Kola's belly, Titi nestled into Kola's neck, his arms and legs splayed out, his pendulous belly distended with the food he had gorged in the forest. Mark, Despina and Juislain made their way back to the base camp for the night. Glancing back at the sleeping trio they looked at each other and smiled in mutual recognition of the day's triumph.

After hearing Mark's ecstatic account of the day over the

radio, I confidently informed Aspinall that this long-awaited event in the gorillas' lives had gone even better than we could have hoped, and assured him that things now seemed to be taking a turn for the better. Mark stayed in the Lefini for the rest of the week to ensure that the gorillas' progress continued as it had begun, before returning to Brazzaville to await the imminent arrival of Peter Halliday.

Peter was to spend two days at the orphanage and two days in the Lefini. He arrived with a video camera lent by the BBC, who had requested him to make a video diary of his trip for inclusion in their documentary, which was now seriously off-course. Film crews and filming seemed to us to bring out the worst in people – ourselves included – whilst the gorillas adapted to life in the forest, more follies of human behaviour were to unfold.

Peter carried a notebook everywhere, scribbling furiously in it in every spare moment. As his visit progressed we realized that, oddly, at no stage was Mark asked to appear before the camera. In fact, Peter seemed to switch it off the moment Mark appeared on the scene. Eventually Peter confided to Despina that he was acting under direct orders from Howletts that Mark was not, under any circumstances, to appear on film in the same frame as the gorillas.

Despina, of course, relayed this enlightening information immediately to Mark, who decided he needed to read the contents of Peter's mysterious notebook. Opening it up, Mark told me over the radio that evening he had read – amongst general observations about Brazzaville, the sweat and the filth of Central Africa – that we, Mark and Helen, were megalomaniacs who had deliberately understaffed the project to increase their power. Further, Mark's interpretation of what he read was that Peter seemed to believe that Naobi, with her past links to the Bonobo Protection Fund, harboured a scheme to steal the bonobos from the Foundation, presumably with Mark's connivance, and set up a rival project of her own in Zaire. It all felt very depressing. Relations between Peter and Mark became even more strained.

About a week after Peter's departure both Mark and Despina developed dengue fever, a mosquito-borne arbovirus endemic throughout sub-Saharan Africa. They were both covered in an angry rash and their joints ached. The unpleasant disease, called 'breakbone fever' for a good reason, left them exhausted and demoralized. We remembered the mysterious spots we had seen in both Dinga and Nzambi's mouths before they died and wondered whether they had died of dengue fever. Although the spots had been plainly visible against the pink mucous membrane of their mouths, they would have been invisible elsewhere, obscured by their dark skin and the thick hair which covered their bodies. At the time it was with a sense of poetic justice that we greeted the news that Peter had contracted the same disease and was now hospitalized back in England. A simultaneous outbreak of another more serious haemorrhagic fever, the deadly Ebola virus, across the river in Kikwit, a small town just outside Kinshasa, must have struck fear into the hearts of Peter's doctors back in Kent.

News of the outbreak of Ebola virus dominated local radio and television in Brazzaville. If it spread to Kinshasa the consequences would be even more serious. The Zairois military had quarantined Kikwit but, predictably, cash changed hands in return for escape from the doomed town. The orphanage staff were well aware of the threat the deadly virus would present if it crossed the river into Brazzaville, and of the rumours that it was carried by primates, but they never let it affect their work. After two months the epidemic burned itself out, and we all breathed a sigh of relief.

Chapter Thirty-One

The Ndoki Forest

John Aspinall's next visit seemed as ill-timed as the previous one. Inadvertently he arrived during the outbreak of dengue fever – this time accompanied by his wife, Lady Sally. Covered in a rash and running a high fever, Mark insisted on dragging himself out of bed on the morning of their arrival, determined to welcome them to Brazzaville, knowing that his failure to do so would be interpreted as a deliberate snub. We sincerely hoped to repair the damage done to our working relations with Aspinall over the past few months. He seemed pleased with the rapid progress Kola's group were making in the Lefini Forests, but despite efforts on both sides it seemed that whatever damage had been done could not be undone. Nor did we want to risk a repetition of the past few months. We believed our advice and management of the gorillas had been overruled at a critical point, and we felt little confidence that we would be able to continue our work without further confrontation. We were tired and beginning to feel that it might be better to leave, now that the gorillas were well on their way. Already there was talk of further filming in the Lefini.

We left Brazzaville to spend a week with Kola's group and reflect on our future while Despina took a well-earned break in Brazzaville.

The night of our arrival she was packing up to leave early the following morning. Gathered around the wooden table, our faces illuminated in ghostly pallor by the white light of the gas lamp, a busy cluster of moths and mosquitoes darting and dancing in the glow, we chatted late into the night about plans for Kola's group as they familiarized themselves with their new territory. Despina was aware of the friction between ourselves and Howletts, but assured us that should we leave the project, she would remain for as long as she could to help Kola's group adjust to their new life in the wild.

The following day we decided to take the gorillas to a new part of the forest, curious to see how they would react to unfamiliar, swampy terrain. Crossing the grassland and leaving his now familiar haunt behind, Kola moved ahead of us, his relaxed, swaying stride exuding an easy confidence. Mbinda and Titi followed close behind. Their luxuriant coats of glossy hair gleamed brilliantly in the bright light, the sun reflected at changing angles from their muscular broad backs as they swayed in a lazy side-to-side motion through the long, straight shards of grass. They were now finding 90 per cent of their food in the forest and had grown enormously. Titi and Mbinda broke into high-spirited play, tumbling together, crashing through the long grass and then hurrying to catch up as we neared the border of the forest.

Seeing Kola disappear into the shadows of the cool forest, Titi stretched up on two legs to grab a hasty handful of orange berries on the forest border, stuffed them into his mouth and thundered after him. We struggled along behind through the knee-high brown swamp, our feet becoming entangled in the grasping tendrils of roots below water level. Kola seemed entirely at ease, tunnelling through the thick undergrowth and overhanging lianas as thick as rope.

After some time he stopped and stood still in the reddy-brown water. Using his hands to push and pull as if kneading the water, he sifted the earth beneath, every now and then pulling up a succulent root or stem and crushing it whole into his mouth, barely distracted from the task of searching for more. Titi watched and copied while Mbinda pressed his face close to Kola's, nibbling the shoots that escaped from the corners of his mouth.

The forest floor was like a constantly moving, soggy sponge, sucking our feet into the murky obscurity of the tea-coloured water. Even the small patches of apparently stable land were like floating islands. Kola showed no hesitation in leading the group up to the dense canopy above where they crammed their mouths with vegetation, eventually spreading out, grumbling with pleasure. We waited, crouched on the boggy ground, until, at the end of the afternoon, they made their descent and joined us to sit propped against the sprawling thick buttress roots of an immense tree.

Ready now to hand over responsibility, Kola eagerly followed Mark as he made tracks to leave the forest. On reaching the familiar grasslands he overtook and strutted ahead, sure of the route back. The cage was soon in view, fronds of emerald green now enveloping the vast manmade structure that had stood so stark and uninviting some months earlier. Proud of his achievement and needing to release the repressed tension he had felt at times during the afternoon, Kola raised himself upright and, pursing his lips into a tight circle, hands poised over his chest, he exhaled a rapid hooting-panting sound as he beat his chest in a steady rhythm, 'pok-a-pok-a-pok'. His display climaxed with one last resounding 'pok' as he dropped forward on his hands with a thud and slapped the ground in a final gesture of triumph and supremacy. His exuberant message carried in the still air through the forest that had, many years ago, been familiar with this sound.

A couple of days later the gorillas came across a clear-water stream. It was a particularly hot day and Kola ventured hesitantly into the shallowest part of the stream. After a few minutes spent paddling in the cool water he started slapping his hands gently on the surface, soon thumping more forcefully and squeezing his eyes tightly shut as drops of water splashed up and into his face. Titi and Mbinda were more cautious and waited on the bank, watching intently. As Mark stepped into the stream and waded out to the waist-high water in the centre, Kola watched, intrigued, before carefully negotiating his way across a log that straddled the stream. Stopping once he was level with Mark, he stretched out a long arm, daring Mark to pull him in but still tightly clasping the log with his feet, his other hand clutching a robust overhanging vine. He pushed hard against Mark's chest, hoping to topple him, but pulled his hand away just before Mark could grasp hold of it to pull him in. At the sound of Kola's low-pitched giggles, curiosity overcame Titi and he ventured out onto the log behind Kola, shoving with all his might to push him into the water. The two hefty gorillas then started to battle for supremacy of the narrow log, wobbling precariously as they pushed, shoved and giggled before Titi gave in and retreated to the safety of the bank. Eventually tired of the game with Mark, Kola moved off and Titi came out to replace him, watching, shocked and curious, as Mark lowered his head into the water and disappeared.

As he re-emerged, Mark cupped his hands, filling them with water, and lifted them towards Titi, offering him a drink. Titi slurped up the cool water and shook himself as Mark splashed the remaining drops over his head. He then retired to the bank to reflect. Some time later all three gorillas were immersed up to their waists in the water, as if they had never known anything different.

By the end of the week we felt sure that, although the gorillas would still need humans to ensure the protection of their habitat, it would not be long before their ties with us would no longer be a necessity, purely a pleasure that they could choose to exploit on their own terms. We hoped that perhaps in the future we would return to the Lefini to find Kola's offspring roaming the forest, a new generation of wild gorillas whose lives would have been untouched by the hand of man.

We returned to Brazzaville in silence, unable to believe that we might never see Kola's group again. We had decided to resign. We felt unable to carry on, doubtful that we could achieve more under such strained relations with Howletts. We now faced the painful reality that we would soon be leaving the Congo with little prospect of returning.

As we had not had time, over the past six years, to travel within the country, we decided to take Mike Fay up on his offer of a trip to the Ndoki forest in northern Congo. This experience was to prove pivotal to my understanding of our experiences with the gorillas over the past six years.

The airport official who took our tickets was old and blind. He stared blankly at the two scraps of paper that guaranteed us seats on the little Fokker 134 bound for Ouesso, some 800 kilometres north of Brazzaville, the last town before the miles upon miles of primary rainforest, the Ndoki, that sprawls to the northern border of the Congo, spilling over into the Central African Republic and Cameroon. Handing the tickets back to us with a cursory nod, he waved us on and up the narrow steps to the interior of the plane. Behind us, a child screamed in seeming terror as her mother dragged her on board, her cries subsiding to whimpering sobs as we rose steeply from the tarmac.

About an hour later we sat waiting on the small patch of tarmac that was Ouesso airport, alongside piles of bushmeat ready for loading onto the plane for sale in Brazzaville. Ouesso, a sleepy town on the Sangha river, had once been an important trading post for companies extracting timber, rubber and ivory from the forests. Now it was a decaying legacy of the colonial rule that had ended some thirty years before. After a brief interrogation by the local police, we were allowed to continue our journey north by river.

As we climbed into the pirogue it rocked in the murky tea-coloured water, stirring up the red earth and sending ripples across to the opposite bank. As the motor whirred we pushed upstream, our Bantu boatman, knowing the eddies and currents like the back of his hand, smiling serenely as he sat and guided the boat, occasionally waving to a passing acquaintance. The Sangha, one of the many tributaries that flow into the Congo river, was once the main trade route for the north, servicing the small villages dotted along its banks.

As we pushed deeper into the interior the stillness of the river was broken only by islands of floating vegetation that erupted from the surface and thrust skywards, weeping fronds draping into the water on all sides. Branches torn from trees at the river's edge floated past us downstream. There was no gentle transition at the river's edge, only a sudden, solid wall of rich green, matted vegetation from which moisture dripped silently onto the surface of the water. Beyond these walls lay the mysterious, murky underworld of the forest.

I remembered Joseph Conrad's description of this river from *Heart of Darkness*: '. . . you lost your way on that river as you would in a desert . . . till you thought yourself bewitched and cut off forever from everything you had known once – somewhere far way in another existence perhaps.' I felt as if I had travelled back in time, to a world with no apparent sign of man, a parallel world existing alongside the modern one.

Eight hours later, when black night had wiped out the

relentless sun and the river came alive with sinister, shadowy shapes, we arrived at the project base camp, about half a mile upstream from the small village of Bomassa.

It was cold now, sitting in the boat close to the water. Clouds of frenzied insects, attracted by the heat of our bodies, hovered round us as we clambered up the steep bank. The rocking motion of the boat continued now as an internal rhythm, despite the fact that my feet were on firm ground. I turned back to face the river. The moon glowed luminous in the dark sky, casting a silvery film on the silent water.

That night I lay awake, listening to the unworldly sounds of the forest. The harsh scream of a tree hyrax punctuated the monotonous hum of nocturnal insect life. The distant, reverberating thud of a gorilla chest-beat reminded me that we had an early start ahead us. We were to travel deeper into the forest in the hope of our first sighting of wild gorillas.

The following morning we climbed into the project land-cruiser and followed an old logging road that cut a swathe through the forest. We were soon on another pirogue, this time gliding silently through the cool, murky waters of the Ndoki river as it tunnelled its way through the dense undergrowth. Our pygmy boatmen sat at either end of the dug-out, beads of sweat glistening on their muscular backs. Occasionally, with a movement as natural as breathing, they swatted at the tse tse flies that pursued us.

About an hour later we emerged from the oppressive darkness into a clearing. Sunlight reflected from the water and long fronds of thick swamp grass lined our route. The light was blinding and I looked up at the giant trees now visible on either side. We finally banked and continued on foot. The forest was alive with the hum of insect and bird life. We moved deeper into its core, alert to the mysterious rustlings and trembling vibrations of animal life moving across the soft, yielding layer of leaf-mould that carpeted the forest. Indistinguishable, shadowy forms moved ahead of us, melting further into the depths.

At Mbeli bai, a natural clearing, we sat to rest and wait, hoping that the gorillas would visit the clearing to feed on the succulent, swamp-growing vegetation. The plaintive cry of a fishing eagle that swooped down, dipping into the reedy water, carried in the thick air.

We continued to wait. A gentle rippling of water alerted us to the presence of a Congo clawless otter moving gracefully beneath the surface. The sunlight caught his smooth head as he half emerged from the water before resuming his dance, twisting and turning as if in sheer delight at the discovery of his own agility.

The rustle of undergrowth and the sound of crunching branches signalled the arrival of gorillas. As we held our breath, a silver back emerged into full view. The silvery pelt of hair on his back shimmered in the sun, almost white. He stopped, raised his head to sniff the air, and turned to look at us. A brief moment of kindred recognition was dramatically broken as he slapped the ground defiantly, giving one short, resounding bark that carried throughout the open space of the bai. Satisfied we were no threat, he turned and beckoned his waiting family to follow. They moved cautiously at first, then gathered speed to catch up with their leader; females with infants on their backs, adolescents barging one another in their excitement, older, more serious black backs self-consciously strutting stiff-legged at the rear.

The silver back sat down, waist deep in the water, and started to pull up the reeds, stripping them and cramming them into his mouth, his powerful jaws crushing them effortlessly to a pulp. The females sat feeding close by, keeping watchful eyes on their youngsters. An adolescent male pestered his mother, jumping on her back as she took time to relax after a tiring morning of foraging in the dense forest interior. She humoured him briefly before losing patience and signalling her irritation with a gentle swipe of one arm. He moved off to find a more enthusiastic playmate. I was reminded of Albertine rebuffing the boisterous attentions of Kola's group. They were no different from our gorillas back at the orphanage.

As I watched, transfixed, I felt I finally understood the suffering of our gorillas on their arrival at the orphanage, so recently wrenched from their peaceful existence in the forest. I knew now for certain that we had been right to struggle on, despite the tragedies along the way, in order that they could once again regain their natural world.

As the fading sun cast an orange glow over the bai, the gorillas ambled off, melting back into the forest as they sensed the onset of darkness, in search of sites in which to nest for the night. Shortly after, we too left, heading back to camp before all the light was swiftly obliterated by the descending tropical night.

We returned to Brazzaville the next day, from this world that had remained unchanged since the origins of man.

Chapter Thirty-Two

July 1995:
Journey's End

Back in dusty, dirty Brazzaville, life at the orphanage continued as usual, as if nothing had changed or would change. I now viewed the trials and tribulations of the gorillas with a new sense of optimism, knowing that they were just stepping stones along a path that would lead them to a wild future alongside Kola's group. The transition that had proved so painful for Kola's group would be eased for other gorillas who would arrive in the Lefini to an already established, calm routine and other familiar gorillas who had already paved the path ahead.

As it was now clear that our negotiations with Howletts had reached an impasse we gathered the staff together and explained, as best we could, the absurd situation. They were incredulous and angry, not only because they realized that we would not have reached this conclusion unless we felt we had no choice, but also because they felt personally threatened, afraid that along with Mark and me would go the recognition and understanding of their hard work and their dedication to the gorillas over the past six years.

Our departure was set for 20 July. The staff busied themselves organizing a leaving party for us in the bar neighbouring the zoo. With a sense of disbelief, we silently packed our belongings into crates the morning before our departure, unable to voice our feelings for fear of breaking down. Juislain came to the house, bringing gifts for us to take back to England. He too maintained a stony silence, caught between anger and sadness, sitting in the armchair with his head in his hands, tears trickling silently down his cheeks.

Soon after he had left, Albertine knocked at the door to present us with a blanket she had crocheted herself. We tried to hide our distress behind casual conversation. She left for the orphanage where the gorillas' routine carried on as usual.

At about three in the afternoon we all gathered in the bar. The girls were dressed in their Sunday best, their matching dresses and headbands brilliantly coloured fuchsia, yellow, green and blue, a mosaic of dazzling colour against the background of their dark skins. They had all prepared local dishes and busied themselves in one corner whilst the men sat drinking beer. The wooden tables were soon piled high with enormous quantities of chicken, fish, manioc and sweet potato. We sat down to eat.

The Mah village chief had travelled down from the Lefini for the event and made an ostentatious entrance to the bar, dwarfed by several of his numerous sons. He waited to be welcomed and then proceeded to one of the tables where the staff, although disgruntled that he had turned up unannounced and without additional food, passed several plates to his hungry coterie and watched with barely disguised disgust as they were greedily consumed.

As the afternoon wore on the initial atmosphere of cheerful camaraderie started to crumble. With a dramatic flourish, Jean suddenly raised himself to his feet and leaned over the wooden table, his head bowed. Exhaling a deep groan, and fuelled by a large quantity of beer, he sobbed convulsively. Drawn into the drama, Paul, Albertine and Catherine gathered around him, linking their arms in a circle and murmuring reassuring noises as they led him away from the table. His loud sobs set off a chain reaction from the rest of the staff who then all started wailing and moaning in competition with one another in the sort of theatrical display normally reserved for funeral wakes.

Unable to cope any longer, Mark and I left the hysteria to walk through the zoo to the orphanage, our departure unremarked by the staff who remained caught up in their own dramatic grief. As we neared the exit the old Chief of Mah silently appeared before us and grasped Mark's hand.

'We'll always remember it was you,' he said, 'five years ago, who appeared in our village with only your rucksack and talked of your hopes of bringing gorillas back to the Lefini one day.'

Back at the orphanage we entered Sid's cage for the last time. The gorillas approached, following their usual routine and hoping for a good-natured wrestle. But, as they neared, they sensed our mood. We played half-heartedly and hugged for the last time, unable to explain to them the significance of this final embrace and the fact that we would not appear the following morning as we had done nearly every day of their lives since their arrival at the orphanage six years earlier.

As I held Max tightly, a painful lump rose in my throat and tears started to trickle silently down my hot cheeks. He touched my face, dipping his finger in the salty wetness and licking it with curious concern. I could not look at Mark. The gorillas' gentle, compelling eyes searched ours penetratingly, puzzled and worried by this unexplained outburst of tenderness and emotion. As we left the cage they stared after us, bewildered. Max was quiet, unable even to give his usual goodnight whooping call as we walked away and out of their lives.

Morning inevitably came and, numbed by sadness and disbelief, we went through the motions of checking in at Maya Maya airport and boarded the plane. Soon Brazzaville and the orphanage were shrinking below us, fading like a dream. As we flew north over the rolling forest-clad hills of the Lefini, we peered out of the small window to catch a last glimpse of the deep green canopy of trees beneath which Kola's group roamed. Our journey had come to an end, but the gorillas' journey would continue.

Epilogue

Although it was a cold, wintry morning in Wales, I could sense my feet moving methodically beneath me as I followed the wooden walkways across the Lesio river. Inhaling the familiar, musty smell of the damp forest, eventually I emerged onto the open grassland beyond, and walked on towards the Lefini base camp.

Where the camp had once been lay a pile of shattered, rotten planking. There was no sign of human habitation, and I stood on the abandoned site feeling like an intruder. I remembered our first days there when, full of nervous excitement, we prepared to take Kola's group into the forest.

I walked on, into the forest. Even there a sense of fear pervaded as I broke the quiet solitude with the soft thud of my footsteps on the springy leaf-mould, branches crackling beneath my feet. Animals, although hidden from sight, sensed my coming and moved swiftly out of my path, scuttling deeper into the shadowy undergrowth. I wondered whether the gorillas were watching quietly nearby to see who their human intruder might be. Sunlight, filtering through the green canopy above, made dappled patterns of light and shade. I sat down, remembering. The forest continued to hum with its persistent rhythm.

Some time later my thoughts were interrupted by the rustle of branches nearby. Raising my head, my eyes came to rest on the familiar contours of a gorilla. They *were* there! Recognizing me now, they all emerged behind Kola, one by one, grumbling with pleasure as they ambled towards me. I was soon buried by a mass of hairy, loving limbs as they sat on and round me, long arms winding round my neck. The familiar, musky smell of male gorillas was overwhelming . . .

Waking from this vivid dream, I felt the dampness of tears on my cheeks. We still had no idea what had become of Kola's group. Since the outbreak of a brutal civil war in the Congo in June 1997, news had been patchy. We did know that the younger gorillas and the bonobos had been evacuated from the orphanage to the relative safety of Aliette Jamart's sanctuary outside Pointe Noire, along with some of the project staff.

We had feared the worst for Kola's group, who had recently been joined in the Lefini by Sid, Rupert and Djembo. But my dream was to closely mirror reality. Communications a few days later confirmed that the Lefini gorillas are alive and well, following a sighting. Having lived alone in the forest for months on end, they have proved their ability to adapt and survive in the wild, probably the only reintroduced apes in history to have survived a civil war without human assistance. Mayoko is now pregnant with the first orphanage baby; maybe one day Mark and I will return to the Lefini to find Djembo likewise carrying a baby on her back, with Kola, the proud father, strutting by her side.

The first year back in England I was numb and could feel nothing but sadness, disbelief and loss. We move to Aberystwyth so that Mark could pursue post-graduate studies at the University of Wales, and I worked in the intensive care unit of the local general hospital. I carried with me intangible, incommunicable feelings as I went through the motions of daily life. My past was alienating me from the present, and I struggled to make sense of it. It was Conrad's *Heart of Darkness* which seemed to sum up my feelings – sentiments which if I hadn't read I would have thought were uniquely my own.

No, they did not bury me, though there is a period of time which I remember mistily, with a shuddering wonder, like a passage through some inconceivable world that had no hope in it and no desire . . . the sight of people . . . trespassed upon my thoughts. They were intruders whose knowledge of life was to me an irritating presence, because I felt so sure that they could not possibly know the things I knew . . . I daresay I was not very well at the time.

But now, in my relief that the gorillas are alive, I can confront my memories with a clearer conscience and greater acceptance. I am able to picture the gorillas clearly, reassured that we were right to press on, pushing ourselves – and them at times – to the limits.

It's a question I'm often asked, whether I feel our work was worthwhile. How can I possibly say no? And I'm sure Albertine, Jean, Catherine, Juislain and Nkodia would say the same. The gorillas have enriched and influenced their lives as much as they have ours, and we can only trust we have offered them some enduring hope in return.

Index